"Disturbing, brilliant, hilarious—it's as if Proust had written *Jesus' Son*."

—Ben Lerner

"Raw, fresh, and relevant, *White Out* transcends the recent rash of addiction memoirs to meditate upon addiction as a disease of memory. Like an avalanche in a haunted Candy Land, this book is an onslaught of connections between past and present, between a blizzard of writing and the blank world of terminal addiction."

—Nancy D. Campbell, PhD, author of *Discovering Addiction: The Science and Politics of Substance Abuse Research*

"A terrific memoir."

—Clancy Martin, *Chronicle of Higher Education*

"A cautionary tale full of black, self-deprecating humor . . . Hip, bleak and funny."

—Michael Heaton, *Plain Dealer*

WHITE OUT

WHITE OUT

THE SECRET LIFE OF HEROIN

MICHAEL W. CLUNE

WITH A NEW PREFACE BY THE AUTHOR

McNally Editions

New York

McNally Editions
52 Prince St., New York 10012

Printed in China
Originally published by Hazelden Press, 2013.
First McNally Editions paperback, 2023

ISBN: 978-1-946022-60-8
E-book: 978-1-946022-61-5

Editor's note
This memoir is based on the author's actual experiences.
Certain people's names and identifying details have been changed
to protect their identity. Some conversations and descriptions
of events have been compressed or imaginatively
recreated and are not intended as exact replications.
The lyrics in chapter 2 are from "Bling Bling," by B.G.
featuring the Hot Boys, Cash Money Records, 1999. The lyrics in
chapter 7 are from "Shimmy Shimmy Ya," by Ol' Dirty Bastard,
Elektra Records, 1995.

Design by Jonathan Lippincott

1   3   5   7   9   10   8   6   4   2

CONTENTS

ACKNOWLEDGMENTS

I'd like to thank Jon Sternfeld, Rebecca Traynor, Aaron Kunin, Colleen, Barbara, and Michael T. Clune, Sid Farrar, Stan Apps, and Jimmy Kinnon.

"Evidence suggests that addiction represents a pathological usurpation of the neural mechanisms of memory."

—STEVEN E. HYMAN,
American Journal of Psychiatry 162:8,
August 2005

"To study the self is to forget the self."

—DOGEN (1200–1253)

PREFACE

I was watching a basketball game on TV the other night, and I saw an ad that said, "Beat the Stigma," talking about addiction. I imagined someone around my age seeing that ad and comparing it to the original public service ads about addiction, Nancy Regan's "Just Say No" campaign from the '80s. And I imagined this person nodding their head, thinking, *We've come so far.* TV used to tell addicts not to take drugs. Now TV tells people not to look down on addicts.

The right people really have gotten control of the TV. Look at us. From the benighted prohibition and criminalization of the Reagan era to our current progressive, scientific understanding that addiction is a disease. That addicts just need treatment. That they didn't do anything wrong. That it's the stigma. The stigma is the problem.

I sat there watching the ad, imagining this person like me in every respect but one, watching and nodding and feeling good, and I felt bad. I felt bad about the negative things I was thinking about this imaginary person, who might be you.

No, I thought, *stop it.* They're great, you're great, and it would be great if the stigma was really the problem. Or even a problem. It would be great if an important problem with addiction was the attitudes of *other people.* It would be great if addiction really was a disease like diabetes, easily and successfully treatable with modern methods, and if it was just the stigma that kept people from seeking treatment, that kept people dying in the dark.

But the stigma isn't the problem. Social attitudes aren't the problem. Never in my life—whether during my ten years as an actively using addict or during my twenty-plus years living clean and sober—never once have I suffered from anyone's negative attitude about addiction. I've been arrested, robbed, beaten by cops, beaten by dealers, beaten by junkies, shot at, overdosed, seen friends overdose, seen friends die, and never once was anyone's bad attitude about addicts or addiction the problem.

The problem was drugs. And drugs are still the problem. I think people know this. I think the people on the TV know this. I think they know if you have a real problem, a problem that can't be solved, then you give the people an easier problem, a problem that can be solved. We can stop the stigma. We can decriminalize. Compared to the drug problem, these are easy problems. These are things we know how to do.

A hundred thousand people died from overdoses last year. That's about three times the number that died in car accidents. And it doesn't include the people who died in car accidents because they were high on drugs. Addiction gets worse every year. The stigma gets less. We're winning the stigma battle. Stop putting addicts in jail? OK, we'll just die out of jail. Five addicts will die during the time it takes you to read this preface. If you're a fast reader. If you skim.

Drugs are the problem. They're still the problem. I've been clean for over twenty years. Let me give you an example of the kind of problem addiction is, the *scale* of the thing. In April 2019 I went to the dentist. I had a mild ache in a molar. He said the whole tooth was totally rotted all the way through, that they couldn't do anything more with it. It was hopeless. The tooth was a total piece of shit and would have to be extracted.

He gave me the number of a dental surgeon and I called and made an appointment. I talked to my dad, who'd had many teeth extracted, and he told me it was no big deal. When I got to the dental surgeon's office I told him that I'm a recovering addict, and that I wanted to avoid opiate painkillers. He looked in my mouth and when he got out he said you're going to need opiate painkillers.

Then he shot me up with Novocain and he went in there with a wrench and I realized that dentists have soft, delicate hands and seem like doctors, like intellectuals, but when you really need dental care, you go to a dental surgeon and their main qualification is brute physical strength.

This guy had arms the size of my legs and white hair, and he put the pliers on me and *wrenched* and *wrenched* and *wrenched,* and despite the Novocain, the pain was like a hundred Hitlers gnawing on my nerves, gnawing them right down to the roots, and then just sinking Nazi teeth up to the hilt in my brain. There was blood everywhere. I was making horrible sounds out of my throat, and the dental surgeon was saying just hold on for one more second, saying it through gritted teeth, and I was writhing in my chair with tears pouring out of my eyes.

Then it was over and he was wiping the pliers on his white coat and I thought, *I never knew something like this could happen in America*, and he said, "I'm going to write you a prescription for Percocet."

There was a nurse there who said maybe that's not such a good idea, this patient is a recovering addict, but the dental surgeon just ignored her and wrote the prescription and gave it to me.

I drove off. The Novocain was still strong, and once the actual brutal wrenching had stopped, I didn't feel too bad. They'd given me a pamphlet about the dangers of dry socket. It said not to eat solid food. I thought, *Well maybe I'll get the prescription filled but I won't use it.*

It was surreal standing there at the CVS waiting for Percocet. I'd been clean for seventeen years, three months, and twenty-two days. No alcohol, no marijuana, no cocaine, no heroin, no Percocets, no Oxys, no Vicodin, no Ecstasy, no amphetamines. Nothing.

I took the bottle directly home and gave it to my wife. The amber bottle glowed in the sun. I put the Protocol into action.

The Protocol is what recovering addicts are supposed to do in a situation like this.

> Give the medication to a friend or family member.
> Tell them to hide it and not to tell you where.
> Even if you ask.
> Take the medication only if you really, really need it.
> You will probably lie to yourself about how much you
>   need it.
> Do you really need it?
> No.
> No.
> OK, but
> Take the medication exactly as prescribed.
> Stop taking it while you are still uncomfortable.
> Then tell the family member to flush it down the toilet.

I was in my office on the second floor of my house writing an email when the Novocain started to wear off. It wouldn't be crazy to refer to my house as a "mansion," I reflected just before the Novocain wore off. Things have gone pretty well for me since I got clean, I reflected before the Novocain wore off, looking around my spacious office. This place sure is a long way from the bare, metal shelf beds at the Cook County jail on 26th and California. Or even from the relatively plush suburban jails. To say nothing of the Baltimore jails. At least the Cook County jail didn't smell like piss.

Then the Novocain wore off. I called my dad and said, "*What the hell*?" He chuckled. "I didn't want to scare you," he said. "You mean you knew it was going to be like this?" I was holding my face when I said it. My voice was a little muffled. I was maybe crying a little. "Yeah," he said. I went down and told Lauren and she left the room and went to wherever she'd hidden the bottle and came back and gave me a pill.

I went and sat in front of my computer and played *Slay the Spire*. I felt the Percocet come on. I remember my dentist, the regular one, the one with the soft hands, saying once when I had a root canal that he didn't prescribe opiates because he'd read somewhere that they didn't remove the pain. They just made it so the pain didn't matter.

That dentist understood nothing. It's like saying there's no point in flying to Florida to escape the winter, because it's still winter in the place you left. It's like saying there's no point in cutting off this gangrenous limb, because the limb will still have gangrene after you cut it off.

When the Percocet wore off, I thought, *OK, I just needed a breather, I can deal with the pain by myself now. It's not like it's going to kill me.* So I didn't take any more Percocet the rest of that day, or that night when I couldn't sleep because of the pain, or the day after. I ate my meals through a straw. I picked pieces of bone out of my gum.

"Is that normal?" Lauren asked, watching me hold up a sliver of bone from my gum.

I developed a kind of stoop. The pain wasn't in my back. It wasn't in my limbs, but I walked around stooped over. Unceasing pain makes you stoop. It makes you tired. You can feel yourself getting older. Those seconds and minutes you used to skip over, now you have to go all the way through them.

It's a scientific fact that there's no way to know exactly how long a single second is. It's not like an inch. You can't lay a second next to another second and see if it's the same size. The truth is that seconds might be all kinds of different sizes. Ordinarily this is an abstract, philosophical kind of truth about the difference between time and space, but when you experience extended chronic pain, this truth loses its abstract quality and you understand that all seconds are not the same size and that there are long seconds, and there are longer seconds, and there are Very Long Seconds.

The next morning I asked Lauren for another pill. The bottle said to take one every four to six hours. I waited the full six hours before asking her for the next one. It wasn't like I looked idly at the clock and thought, *Wow, it's been six hours already, time for my next dose.* No. I was getting up from my chair at five hours and fifty-eight minutes. I was asking her at five hours and fifty-nine minutes. I had calculated that it took her approximately forty-five seconds to leave the room and come back with the pill. I gave her fifteen seconds extra. If she took sixteen seconds extra, it wouldn't have been OK. I would have said something.

And it was as if all this time, inside my skull, a calloused old scabbed-over eyelid was slowly rising. There's an eyeball inside my skull, and when it opens, my other eyes, my outside eyes, the eyes on my face, grow dim. This eyeball in my skull is made to see just one thing. It has only ever seen one thing, and now the ancient long-closed lid was slowly rising, and then it was up, and the eyeball was looking at the thing it was made to look at, and the thing was still there inside me, and the thing was the first time I ever did heroin.

That night, sitting next to Lauren watching a TV show while on Percocet, I felt no connection to her. It was as if all the nearly invisible connections, all the little threads that connect our nerves, our memories, our feelings, to the people around us, all those fine filaments of perception that had slowly grown back over years of recovery—it was as if they'd all snapped, and I was floating in outer space. Sitting there on the couch next to her floating in space. In high orbit. Orbiting the eyeball inside my skull.

The next day, I stopped taking the Percocet. I was still uncomfortable. I was still in pain. It was no longer quite as bad, though, and as I was sitting there around four hours after the last dose, I thought, *I have to stop this now.*

I called my wife and I watched as she dumped the rest of the pills into the toilet and flushed it.

OK. Breathe. I'd followed the Protocol; I was still clean. Still recovering.

But the whiteness, the whiteness I write about in the book you're about to read, the whiteness of the first time I did heroin, the whiteness of the memory disease, that whiteness, after so many years, when it filled the eyeball in the center of my skull . . . there was a second when my vision dimmed.

And it was like all the sound goes out of a crowded room. And you can hear yourself breathing. And you think, *Things aren't what they seem*. Houses, marriages, children, careers, can vanish.

The whiteness is real. It's under those other things. Those other things are made of it—and look! Their outlines are starting to blur. They're starting to turn white . . .

For the next couple months, I went to more NA meetings than usual. The eyelid in my skull closed up again. It had only been open for a couple dozen hours, after all.

Call it the Pain Medication Paradox. That's one aspect of the problem of addiction, a problem that has nothing to do with a stigma, nothing to do with anyone's attitude. And maybe you'll say, well then, if it's such a problem then just don't take pain medication. Paradox solved.

Sure. How about you get a molar extracted, an extraction with "complications," as the surgeon later described it when I went back, an "unusually difficult" extraction, how about you go through one of those and then *you* don't get pain medication?

Pain is horrible. It's inhumane. Literally dehumanizing. I was walking around like an ape on the second day. And opiates are still the only thing that works. We haven't invented anything else that works. Should addicts be denied pain medication? Forced to writhe on the floor in pain for the crime of being born an addict? Is that progressive? Is that modern? Is that humane?

OK, you say, so give the addicts pain medication if and when they really need it. Follow the Protocol, just like you did. You're OK now, right? You just celebrated your twentieth year in recovery.

Yes, but what if things had been a little bit different for me? What if—on one of the innumerable occasions when someone offered me a drink—at a wedding reception, a Christmas party, an airplane ride, a dinner, a literary reading, a basketball game—what if on just *one* of those occasions, I'd reflected, hey, I never really had a problem with *alcohol*. My problem was *heroin*, not *alcohol*, and I've had a long day, a hard day, a stressful day. Surely I can control my use of *alcohol*, after twenty years, come on! Just one drink, just one little drink . . .

Or what if after being clean ten or fifteen years, I just decided to stop going to NA meetings? My wife has never seen me on dope. My daughter. My colleagues, my friends—none of them have ever seen me on dope. Why not stop going to meetings so much? There's so much to do, life's busy. It would be so easy to stop . . .

Or what if I got depressed? What if I just got depressed—depressed about the political situation, the climate, the state of literature, the state of the arts, the fact of death, the distance of my youth, hurtling away from me at lightning speed? I can barely see it anymore, a green blur in the distance. What if I finally just got really bummed out about the nature of time? And, like normal people when they get depressed, I stopped doing some things for a while. Took a little break. Stopped meditating, stopped exercising, stopped keeping my daily recovery journal, stopped reading recovery literature, stopped talking to recovering addicts . . .

What if I'd fallen prey to any of the innumerable things that cause recovering addicts to drift away from recovery? What if I hadn't gone to a meeting in one or two or six or twenty months before walking into that dental surgeon's office? What would have happened?

I can tell you what would have happened. It happened to a friend of mine. Call him George. He'd been clean for over ten years, stopped going to meetings. Things were going good for him. He didn't need to go to meetings anymore. A year or two later he had some kind of medical procedure and took Percocet, and when the Percocet ran out, he found some dope and now he's dead. Like the five addicts who will die as you read this, if you're reading fast.

Let's go further and imagine that I'd never really gotten into going to meetings at all. If that mysterious thing that I write about in the book you're about to read had never happened to me, and I'd never really given up trying to get high. Like Cash in the book. Or Funboy. Or millions of other addicts who are exposed to recovery but for whom, for whatever reason, that mysterious, maybe even mystical thing, never happens, and they never grasp that the only way out of addiction is also out of yourself.

A thousand little things, a thousand considerations of the most rational, the most progressive, the most reasonable kind can prevent a person from taking that step out of themselves, out of everything they know and are, out of the skull with the single interior eyeball, out of their mind. And if you don't go out of that mind, you die.

As long as there's a really effective way to stop pain, there will be addicts, and as long as there are addicts, many of them will die. That's the kind of problem addiction is. And the Pain Medication Paradox is only one aspect of it. There are many others.

Don't get me wrong. I'm not against the "Beat the Stigma" campaign. I wouldn't be opposed to a new "Just Say No" campaign either. I'm for suboxone treatment centers, halfway houses, twelve-step meetings, decriminalization, recriminalization, all of it. I'm not against doing anything or everything that helps. But don't fool yourself. Addiction is a public problem. But it doesn't have a public solution.

It has only private solutions. Unobjective solutions, nonscientific solutions. Solutions that speak in the first person.

Here's mine.

Michael Clune
Cleveland Heights, 2023

WHITE OUT

ONE

MEMORY DISEASE

My past is infected. I have a memory disease. It grips me through what I remember. For example, seven years ago in Baltimore, Cat wakes me up to kiss me on her way to work. I'm about to fall back asleep when I remember about Dominic. I remember how fun he can be. I sit up in bed and think about it.

It is mid-June which in Baltimore is not a fresh thing. Mid-June is already midsummer. Veins filled with heavy blue. Humid, ninety degrees. I sit in bed thinking and the things I should do like renew my driver's license or protest my parking tickets are like chewing on broken glass. Then I remember I can go to Dominic's. I just think casually about going over there and maybe hanging out. I don't wait to have a shower.

I pull up at Dominic's, get out of the car, and someone is already yelling at me.

"Dom don't need you coming around here." It's Dominic's brother. He stares at me.

"Is Dominic here today?" The time for polite questions seems already to have passed, but I say it anyway. I say it in the ingratiating high-pitched voice I use these days when I'm forced to speak to people. Dom's brother spits, barely turning his head.

"Dominic's gone, he don't live here anymore, get the fuck up out of here."

The brother looks like a deflated version of Dominic, white all around the pupils, wearing a tool belt and work boots. He doesn't drink or do drugs. Doing drugs makes your pupils swell in your iris. Not doing drugs shrinks the whole package, and you can see crazy white all the way around. When I was six I read in a book that Tarzan could recognize crazy people by the white that goes all the way around the iris.

"Have you happened to see Henry around today?"

"Man listen to me, Dominic don't need you around, fuck Henry I don't know where that one-armed freak is, if I see your monkey ass here again I'ma call the cops."

As soon as he says "monkey" the door opens and Dominic himself shuffles out.

"Hey Mike come on in. Me and Henry was just trynna think about that other thing for you." Dom is an enormous bear of a man, thick shaggy black hair, mumbly lips, big eyebrows. His whole face is camouflage for his coded speech. His eyes always on the ground, one expression. He is beyond shame.

Dom's brother walks through the door and angrily starts hammering a light-fixture bracket into a wall. Dom and I follow. There is absolutely no furniture or wallpaper or pipes or carpet or tile anywhere to be seen in the room. Light's coming through a single window with a sheet stapled over it. There must be forty staples in it. The brother's work. I see Dominic has a syringe sticking out of his neck. I just like to be around him. Things happen around him. He's like an open door things walk into and out of. Some of the things stay for a while.

Syringes, for instance. He has a bearlike bulk but he never eats. He's a gathering of things. When that magnet inside him finally stopped spinning and all the things dropped to the pavement for the cops to pick up there was maybe ninety human pounds of him left for the ambulance, according to Henry, who was there, according to Henry.

In that bare front room at Dominic's there is a trembling joy in the air. The thick sun of June gets trapped, pools, and grows cloudy. Proto-organisms form in the cloud of wood-color, heat, and sheet-light. I'm full of angels who fasten their lips and wings and hands to Dominic's body, until he looks like a beach a thick flock of seagulls has landed on. By the time we get to the kitchen he doesn't even look human.

The human form is not one I'm too committed to anyway. As Henry said once, I have a vein that starts in Baltimore and ends in Philadelphia. And here's Henry. One arm. The missing arm is like an anchor dropped in the ocean of what he should look like and doesn't. It keeps him anchored. He has a high-pitched granny's voice.

"Hey Mike we was just trynna think about that other thing for you." Dom sits heavily down in a chair, his neck goes out like a Slinky and his head is just way back.

"It's good to see you Henry. Man is it hot out today!"

This is the part I think I need to remember. Or I need to forget. It's kind of hard to put together. Addiction is a memory disease. I was there at Dominic's. I remembered one hour ago, sitting up in bed and thinking about renewing my driver's license. I remembered six months ago, writing notes to myself in scary big letters and taping them all over the apartment so when I woke up I would see them. "No dope today!"

I also remembered talking to one of the teenage prostitutes who sometimes slept on mattresses on Dom's floor. She said that Henry once told her he lost his arm by getting high and falling asleep on it in an awkward position. He slept for three days, and when he woke up it was dead. They had to cut it off. The story deeply affected both of us. Everyone knows how your arm can fall asleep in an awkward position. Everyone knows sleep is the cousin of death.

So it came right down to it.

"Mike, we was trynna think about that other thing for you," Henry said solemnly. I'd been asking them to see if they could get me some OxyContins. I wasn't ready to ask them for the white thing. I waited.

"And, between us, you know Dom is gonna keep trying, you know he don't wanna let you down." We both looked affectionately at Dom passed out in the chair. He was going to keep trying. He would *always* keep trying. He was probably trying now, in his way.

"But between us there's no way you're going to get it. It'll never happen. First, because there's this lawyer who comes through and buys all we can get the first of every month. How much? Dollar a milligram." That figure brooked no argument. I lit a cigarette and bowed slightly to the phantom lawyer.

"Second, the pharmacy's numbers computer . . ." I tuned out. The genius of Dom and Henry's paranoia was in the details, but I didn't have the energy that day.

"So Mike, we can't get you into any of those Oxys." I tuned back in. "But you might want to think. You might want to see about the white tops. 'Cause we can get those. We can get plenty of them. They're cheap. And they're good. Matter of fact." He closed his eyes. I saw a half-empty white-topped vial on the corner of the table. "They're pretty good."

Henry said it twice. In this kind of situation language is superfluous. Pure waste, a luxury. We both knew I couldn't give a damn about those Oxys. White tops. Wishes begin in white. Jesus is white. Madonna is white. The queen is white. The moon is white. The white tops are white. A picture starts out as a white space. A white space is a picture of the future. The future poses, the camera snaps, the picture is pure white. Dominic's white teeth in his gaping red snoring mouth, like a kind of teasing promise: inside it's all white. Cut Dominic in two and you'll find white inside. I bet when they cut off Henry's arm it was pure white in the middle.

In Baltimore that summer the best heroin was sold in little glass vials with white stoppers. White tops. The color of the stopper was like a brand. If it was good, its reputation would spread. ("Where's Dom?" "Dom's dead." "What was he doing?" "White tops." "Who's got 'em?" "Fathead." "Where's Fathead?") Eventually dealers with inferior product would start using the good color, and then the people with the hot dope would have to change to red or blue stoppers. It was a cycle. I'd been off the stuff for almost six months, but as soon as I saw that empty white top, I got a funny, destiny feeling.

You might think the whiteness of the white tops isn't that important. After all, over the past few years I'd bought red tops, blue tops, black tops, and even yellow tops. Of course, the drug itself is often white, but it can also be brown, and the white is really just an effect of the cut. But the first stuff I ever did was in a vial with a white top, and its whiteness showed me dope's magic secret.

The secret is that the power of dope comes from the first time you do it. It's a deep memory disease. People know the first time is important, but mostly they're confused about why. Some think addiction is nostalgia for the first mind-blowing time. They think the addict's problem is wanting something that happened a long time ago to come back. That's not it at all. The addict's problem is that something that happened a long time ago never goes away. To me, the white tops are still as new and as fresh as the first time. It still is the first time in the white of the white tops. There's a deep rip in my memory.

Dope never gets old for addicts. It never looks old. It never looks like something I've seen before. It always looks like nothing I've ever seen. I kind of stare. I'm kind of shocked.

"White tops, Henry? Really?" It's always the first time I've heard of it, the first time I've seen it, every day, forever. Take a look at your shoe. Your television. Your car. Your girlfriend. Now compare that sight with the first sight.

You see? When you first get a new car you notice everything about it. The color is so beautiful, so shiny, so deep, so intense. After a few weeks you hardly see it. After a few months, there's a sense in which you don't see it at all.

That doesn't happen with dope. Dope never gets old. It never gets familiar. It's always new. It's a deep memory disease. This disease is much stranger and simpler than nostalgia. With nostalgia, you see a thing. The thing triggers a memory of a good time. Then you start to want that good time to come back. That's complex. It's a multistage process.

Now watch what happens to the addict. I'm sitting there at Dom's, minding my business. Henry's kind of talking, I'm kind of listening. Then I see a white-topped vial. Wow. I stare at it. It's the first time I've ever seen it. I know I've seen it ten thousand times before. I know it only leads to bad things. I know I've had it and touched it and used it and shaken the last particles of white from the thin deep bottom one thousand times. But there it is. And it's the first time I've ever seen it. The first time I encountered dope isn't somewhere else, it isn't in the past. *It's right over there.* It's on the table.

Something that's always new, that's immune to habit, that never gets old. That's something worth having. Because habit is what destroys the world. Take a new car and put it in an air-controlled garage. Go look at it every day. After one year all that will remain of the car is a vague outline. Trees, stop signs, people, and books grow old crumble and disappear inside our habits. The reason old people don't mind dying is because by the time you reach eighty, the world has basically disappeared.

And then you discover a little piece of the world that's immune to habit. There's a little rip in my brain when I look at a white-topped vial. The rip goes deep, right down to the bone, to the very first time. People love whatever's new. Humans love the first time. The first time is life. Life is always fading. The work of art is to make things new. The work of advertising is to make things new. The work of religion, the work of science, the work of philosophy, the work of medicine, the work of car mechanics. Their tricks all work, a little bit, for a little while, then they get old. The addict, alone among humans, is given something that is always new.

It's not the feeling of doing the drug that stays new. The drug high starts to suck pretty quickly. Pretty soon it sucks so bad you quit. Never again. Then you see a white top. Or even imagine you're seeing one. And it's the first time you've ever seen it. Addiction is a memory disease. Memory keeps things in the past. Dope white is a memory disruption agent. The powder in the vial is a distribution technology. It carries the white down the tiny neural tunnels where the body manufactures time. Dope white turns up in my earliest memories. I remember Mom's white teeth. My future whites out.

I'm cured now. Ten years. How? How did I escape my white mind and body? How did I exit the white pollution of the past and the future, the white mind where every thought and feeling is a long or short road to the white tops? I'm outside. I'm free. But how? Can you run from yourself? Try it. It's impossible. But I did it. I ran out of myself. How? Once you get a glimpse of something that never gets old you'll never be able to live like the others. I don't want to give too much away. There's a flaw in my memory. Luckily there's also a flaw in time.

Dom wakes up. He pulls himself together in a literal way. His eyes kind of go back into their sockets. He is a big hearty man. The syringe is still in his neck. It makes him look kind of military, like he's a soldier from the future. Henry, with his missing arm, looks kind of military too.

"I'm going to get the white tops, Mike," Dom says. Henry stands up. "Get the walkie-talkies, Henry." Henry goes over to an open black gym bag, takes out one walkie-talkie, takes out another, then takes out a gun.

"When I'm halfway there," Dom says, "I'm going to say OK through the walkie-talkie. When I get there, I'm going to say OK. When I get the stuff. When I get halfway back. Mike, if more than five minutes go by between when you hear from me, give Henry the gun, open the door for him, and get out of his way."

"Yes Dom." I say it in the deferential high-pitched voice I used to reserve for cops or teachers. Now I use it with everyone. "I want you to be careful Dom. I really care about you." I pause. "I don't know if I ever told you this, but I really like you. I want you to take care of yourself. When you come back, we should talk about getting you some help."

Language is a total luxury in a white out. A full sentence is like a Rolex. I'm still straight, but already feeling really luxurious. I feel like blowing my nose with twenties. "I'll even drive you to get help, if you want."

"OK." Dom says through the walkie-talkie. "OK." "OK." "OK."

·

The ancient Mongols believed the soul lives in the head. So when he captured his most hated enemies, Genghis Khan would have their eyes ears nose and mouth sewn shut before they were decapitated, so their soul could not escape the death of the body. My memory would probably seep out through my neck in a white fog.

It was three months later. I knocked on Dom's door. Rain was pouring from heavy brown clouds. He opened, looked furtively around, then stood aside as I went in. He was holding his gun. "I got troubles, Mike." I nodded.

"Fathead says Dom fucked up the package." Henry squittered. Dom squittered. A rope of spit hung from his lip. "But it sure was nice Henry," he said.

"They say if you was to lay out a man's veins all in a straight line they'd go from Baltimore to Philly," said Henry. "And old Henry'd be one of them old-time railroad workers, driving a spike in every three feet."

"And I've been working on the railroad too," said Dom. "All the live-long day."

I gave Dom eighty dollars in folded tens and twenties. That's what it took, day in and day out, just to keep that white light shining. And if it ever dimmed the devils came out. Now the white light was so dim they were sticking their little paws and claws for whole seconds inside me, like children testing the water at the beach. The day before I'd bitten down too hard on a forkful of potatoes and taken a big chip out of my front tooth. I guess I'd thought the potatoes would be harder. I didn't used to make that kind of mistake.

Dom took the money and Henry opened the closet door. He moved a coat from over a hole in the floor, and pulled a bundle out of the hole. Then he pulled five little white-top vials out of the bundle and tossed them to me. I got shy with desire. Ran to the bathroom. When I got out of the bathroom the dimming white light was bright again inside me and the devils were burning to death in it.

When I got out of the bathroom Fathead was standing in the hall between Dom and Henry with a big hand over each of their shoulders.

"Hey there Mike!" he said brightly. He moved his hand to Henry's neck and gave it a little squeeze.

"Ow, Fathead!" Henry honked.

"I said hey there Mike." I kind of stood there.

"Hey Fathead."

"Why don't we go back into the kitchen where we can all sit down? You still have chairs back there, right Dom?" He gave Dom's neck a friendly squeeze. Dom didn't make a sound.

We all trooped back to the kitchen and sat down. Dom's eyes were a little bloodshot, and his skin was even whiter than usual. Next to him, the off-white aluminum refrigerator in the corner had a healthy human glow. I hadn't noticed it before. It looked kind of friendly. Like it wanted to tell me something.

"Let me tell you how to get that permanent white, son," I imagined it saying. "Just slip your head in here and have them boys shut the door real hard on your neck."

"That's a real nice refrigerator, Dom," I said.

"Thanks, Mike," Dom mumbled. His big black-and-blood eyes opened on me like dogs' mouths.

"Maybe tomorrow," Fathead said, "you should see if you can sell that refrigerator, Dom. Maybe you could get two hundred dollars for it. Then, if you found twenty other refrigerators and sold them for two hundred each, you could pay me what you owe."

Fathead was a powerfully built white man about forty-five years old. The previous winter he'd been released from prison after serving eleven years. He'd made some good contacts in prison, and when he got out he started dealing. He'd bunked with Dom in prison for a couple years. Dom had gotten out first, but they stayed in touch, and Fathead began fronting him packages the past spring. Fathead had a huge habit, which he'd had since his twenties.

He'd kept it going straight through his prison years. His pride was that he'd never once gone through withdrawal in the whole eleven years. This was a unique, almost impossible achievement. Even the street dealers from the nearby projects who had only contempt for addicts had respect for Fathead. He was also some kind of religious freak, which I think they also respected. I did too, kind of.

Now he prepared to shoot up in front of us. Almost lazily, demonstrating that this was pure fun, that the white fire was always burning strong in him and never went out.

"Men," he said, emptying a large vial into a spoon, "there are two forces in this world. What are they, Dom?"

"God and the creature," Dom whispered through papery lips.

"God and the creature," Fathead repeated. He closed his eyes. "And the creature, the creature must be induced."

He lifted a lighter under the already blackened spoon. Then he paused. Kind of chuckled. His face took on a kind of grand-fatherly softness.

"When you've got a little dog, and you want him to come in for the night, and you put a little dish of water at the back door, and he comes in, what is that?"

"Inducing the creature," said Dom.

"How about when you don't want the dog pissing all over the kitchen, and he does it, and you give him a little pinch?" He put down the lighter and circled Henry's one arm with his hand. Henry flinched, but Fathead, after letting his hand rest around Henry's arm for a couple seconds, just picked up the lighter again.

"Inducing the creature," Dom whispered.

"I had a lot of time to think when I was locked up," Fathead continued, drawing the fluid into the syringe through a cotton ball. Microscopic white grains swam through that fluid, some-times two of them would meet, and a second of time would spark out. I wondered what drugs did to you.

"I had a lot of time to think and read, and I'm a lot older now. And maybe I'm not an intellectual." I was a graduate stu-dent at Johns Hopkins, and when Fathead had found this out he took to calling me an intellectual.

"And I hate intellectuals. Vanity. Listen to me." He held the syringe before all of us. I could never have afforded a shot like that. It should have been in a museum. "Inducing the creature," he said softly. He felt expertly along his neck till he found the pulsing vein. There was a black tattoo of a cross running down his neck and the vein pulsed along the cross. He slid in the needle and pressed down on the syringe.

His eyes closed for maybe ten seconds. Henry shifted uncomfortably. Fathead's blue eyes shot open.

"The creature is induced to crawl. Induced to walk. Induced to beg. To soil itself or not to soil itself. The sin is not the inducement. That's what those old Christians in the joint never understood."

Dom nodded dully. Dom could probably have burned out a century with what was moving inside him at that moment. A stolen century. Stolen from Fathead.

"The sin is not the inducement," Fathead continued. "That He may raise up the Lord casts down. Even unto the pit. This shit we think we're doing here." He laughed. "Another eye burns in our eye, another hand reaches through our hand. This," he held up his thick, needle-scarred hand, "this is a glove." He gazed thickly on it. "An abode for any spirit of the air. Every unrighteous and unclean spirit."

He must have learned to talk that way in prison. Maybe in solitary. He didn't really seem to be addressing us. When he talked like that you kind of saw a different side of talking. As if talking wasn't meant for talking to people.

"And that's what God is," Fathead said. "When the creature is induced to crawl out of the creature. I've seen it myself. The whatever leaving his eyes, 'dying.' Crawling into the invisible world. A thousand spirits curled up in a spoon. You should see the spirit leaving a man's face; you can feel the room get thicker. I've done it myself. I'll do it again."

"Tuesday," Dom said weakly.

"Fuck Tuesday," Fathead said. "The first time I give you something nice you fuck it up."

"It just got tooken, Fathead," Henry gabbled. "It got tooken, it all got tooken, that's all, like we said, maybe that pimp, maybe those hoes, maybe some customers."

Fathead's response was obscure.

"You're a little, little monkey, Henry," he said.

Then he balled up his right hand into a fist and brought it down, hard, on Henry's open hand. Henry only had one hand, so the effect was kind of intense. Henry yelped and stuttered but Fathead kept his fist planted on Henry's open hand like a railroad spike.

"And those fucking whores you've got staying around here, Dom? I saw their little pimp come by the other day when I was leaving. Are they like sixteen? You know what the time on a charge like that is? What, does he give you like a hundred a week to let the whores crash here? He's scum. Driving a little Honda? Thinks he's a pimp?" Fathead drove a new black Mercedes S500. His eyes and face were solid zombie surface. I wasn't getting anything from him for free. I needed to get out of there. I got up.

"Where do you think you're going?" He'd never spoken to me like that. I thought he understood. There was a sheet stapled to the window. Fathead's gun lay on the table next to his empty syringe. I thought he understood. I wasn't serious. Well, maybe I was serious. But I wasn't serious.

"I gotta go teach, Fathead, it's almost one and I gotta teach at one-thirty." Moving slow, he half-stood up out of his seat and threw his fist into my face. I stumbled back against the wall. I didn't feel anything but there was blood on my hands when they came away.

"You're high, you've been doing dope here, it's my dope, I haven't been paid for it, you've been stealing from me." Fathead spoke the truth. No hand raised against him would prosper.

"Now, if you want to leave, you can tell me where this piece of shit," he jerked a thumb at Dom, "has stashed the dope. 'Cause I know it's here."

This was a Bible situation. If I stuck by Dom's half-assed story that the dope had been stolen I risked getting caught up in his iniquity. Or I could rat Dom and Henry out right in front of them. An eye for an eye.

"It's in the closet in a hole in the floor under a coat," I said. Henry started honking and gabbling. Dom stared down.

"I wish I was dead," he said. He didn't say it to anyone in particular.

"Well maybe we can see about that, Dom." Fathead stood up. "You can go, Mike. You're a real friend. A real creature. Here," he tossed me a vial.

"Wow!" I said. "Thanks a lot, Fathead! You're awesome!"

Henry was whimpering at the table. I don't know what he was whimpering for. Fathead didn't kill either of them, not that day or that week. Dom would live for another four whole months, and I heard it was just an overdose that killed him. Natural cause. And Henry would have been the first to agree that if Fathead had shot him dead on the spot, he'd be doing him a real big favor. "Wow! Thanks a lot, Fathead! You're awesome!" You could say what you liked about Henry, but he was no idiot. He had a good head on his shoulders. He knew he needed a hole in it. He'd tell you.

But maybe I was being callous. Maybe Henry was whimpering because the white light was starting to dim in him, and with Fathead about to take all their dope and pistol whip them both, he wouldn't be able to score for hours, maybe not all day. Maybe he felt the squittering devils already dipping their fingers into his spine, the rats sniffing at his phantom arm. Henry told me once that when he went through withdrawal he felt it like rats chewing on his missing arm. He was probably lying. But he had every right to sniffle and whimper. No dope was a whimpering problem. A crying problem.

Plus Henry was superstitious like Fathead. He thought nothing changed when you died. When you were dead you didn't stop needing white tops. You just stopped being able to get them.

But I had one, and now I had to go. Part of being a graduate student is being a teaching assistant and teaching a section of one of the big lecture courses. I couldn't afford to miss another class. People might think I was irresponsible. I was worried. But I had a vial.

As I drove I thought lazily about turning my car into the oncoming traffic. Bang! Lights out. I wasn't superstitious. I thought it was all over when it was all over. Bang! I thought this about every six seconds. Bang! I didn't even really notice it. Just background noise. Just inside talk. And I had a vial. I looked in the rearview mirror. My lip was swollen, there was blood on my teeth, and I was getting a black eye. I smiled. I had a vial. I peered at it. Maybe twelve solid hours of white time. Plus the four still left in me. It gave me confidence. Bang!

Three minutes. I parked illegally and ran into the building, clutching my book and notes. Nancy saw me, blanched, "Mike what happened to you?" "Later," I mouthed. I hated her. I passed Todd; he looked stunned. "Later," I mouthed. I hated him. I had a vial. Standing outside my classroom, I took a deep breath. I hated Jason. I hated Mandy. I hated Cash. I hated Dave. I hated Eva. I hated Mom. I hated Charlie. I hated Jenny. I hated Chip. I hated Funboy. I hated Andy. I hated Steve. I hated Ashley. I hated Cat. I rubbed the vial in my pocket while I recited this little prayer. I felt better. I opened the door and went in. The room of whispering students fell silent.

"Are you OK?" one shocked girl asked as I opened my book and arranged my notes. There was a little blood on my notes. I didn't know the girl's name. I didn't know any of their names, but I got by with pointing. I looked out at the class. One kid had a smirk starting, but the rest looked anywhere from shocked to scared. Pussies. What did they have to be scared of?

"Your teacher is a hero," I announced. I waited for a second. "I was showing my friend from out of town—a woman—around Baltimore when a black man ran up to her and grabbed her purse. I grabbed it back and he hit me several times in the face. He also hit my friend. This made me very angry. I hit him back, he fell to the ground, then I stood with my foot on his neck until the police came. I told him if he moved I'd push my foot down."

The evidence of violent struggle was all over my face and my shirt. Most of them had probably never seen a black eye before. They'd all seen the impoverished black people of the city. The class of white and Asian kids smiled and clapped.

"You *are* a hero," one girl said.

"I had my foot right on his neck," I said. I was a great person. I was glad Fathead had punched me. I would let him punch me every day for a vial like that. Every minute. I was glad I was a hero. I was glad I hated everyone. I was glad I had a vial.

Two in the morning. My eyes were open staring at the ceiling. Dry shocked eyes. Cat slept beside me. The hero story wouldn't work on her. I told her I'd walked into a door. She didn't believe it. I didn't care. I'd gone to bed at eleven, as I did every night, and I'd do my best to sleep until eleven the next day. Cut down on awake time. Cut down on dope consumption. Cut down on expenses. Cut down on problems.

But it was only 2:00 a.m. and I was wide awake.

Almost every night, I would awake in terror. Covered in sweat. 2:00 a.m. The clear spot in the center of the white wheel. The eye of the rotating white storm. I saw everything clearly at 2:00 a.m. Tomorrow I'd wake up and do the tiny bit left in the vial. This would give me maybe two hours of white time in which to get eighty dollars and cop more. Yesterday I'd done the same. There had to be some mistake. The day after tomorrow I'd do the same.

If I took any longer than two hours to score in the morning the devils would dig their claws into my spine. It would definitely take longer than two hours. This could not be right. This was my fourth relapse. Tomorrow the police might stop me again. I might overdose again. I was going to have to steal every dime Cat had. For starters.

Sometimes, when I woke at 2:00 a.m., I'd get up and write a note to myself in big bold letters and leave it where I'd see it first thing in the morning. "No Dope!" "Don't do it!" "Call rehab!" "My life matters!"

But I didn't write anything that night. Yes, I saw everything clearly. But this wasn't the one moment of clarity that changed everything. In white time nothing happens only once. Everything that happens, happens every day, happens again and again, has always happened, will always happen.

TWO

THE CASTLE

The phone woke me up. I turned over and lifted my head a few inches off the bed, looking around. A little pile of white dope lay on my dresser. The tiny white wheels of tricycles spun inside the white grains. One of Cat's socks on the floor. Tick, tock. The phone rang. I was like a map of Iraq. A curious, impersonal hate knotted and unknotted itself in me. I giggled when I thought how all this might be affecting someone else. Me, you. We're all connected. The phone rang.

I picked up the phone. I was connected to Henry. His unreal peeled voice. I said his name and he answered me Henry style.

"I can't get anywhere and I can't go anywhere," he said. It'd been a few weeks since the Fathead episode, and I'd kind of stayed away.

"Why the fuck—" I whispered.

"I got to get a ride." It sounded like he was crying. No not crying. Honking. The mournful honking of one-arm Henry. Henry was his own thing. Like birds. I imagined hundreds of him, honking sadly.

"I got to get a ride," he said, practically.

"Uh."

There was something wrong with the dope on my dresser. I'd copped it in Druid Hill two days before. It worked, but it made me sick. I'd been lying on my bed, alternately using and puking for two days. Lose-lose situation. Sick from the bad dope, or sick from no dope. Right now I was in between. The nausea was receding and the withdrawals were starting. I looked at the little pile of white dope on my dresser with love and hate.

"Can you pay me?" I asked.

"Sure, I'll help you out, Mike, just swing on over to Dom's and scoop me up."

I got up unsteadily on my loose, bloodless dope legs and went on out and over. If I could get some dope that didn't have poison in it that would be good. And if I couldn't I would still have the bad dope. And that would be good.

No one was at Dom's when I got there. I looked up at the sky. It was October. I looked uncertainly into the clear sky, my eyes widening and narrowing. Like standing too close or too far from someone's face. There were a couple kids sitting on the curb smoking cigarettes.

"Hey, you waiting on Dom and them?" one of the kids asked me.

"Uh, yeah," I said.

"They be back soon." The kids smirked at each other. They were maybe fourteen. I looked down at my dirty jeans.

"You kids like Cash Money Records?"

"Hell yeah we like Cash Money," one kid said.

"I like them too," I said.

Cash Money was the hottest rap label that fall. Juvenile, B.G., the Hot Boys. They invented the term *bling-bling*. That term has been misunderstood. For the Cash Money Hot Boys, money was a way of disappearing, not a way of showing off. They sang about money that blinds. "Tell me what kinda / Nigga got diamonds that'll bling-blind ya?"

Cash Money sang about imaginary gun-diamonds, diamonds that shut everyone's eyes. Imagine walking onto the street with money so strong it blinded motherfuckers. The people staggered around with burnt-out eyes and I walked free in the shining world. It was invisibility music, better than tinted windows.

"Hell yeah, we like Cash Money," one kid said suspiciously. "But we ain't wanna buy no stolen CDs." I had about thirty or forty stolen CDs and a stolen electric guitar in my trunk. I casually popped it open and pulled out a new Cash Money hit, *Tha Block Is Hot.* I tossed it to the kid.

"I said I ain't wanna buy no CD!" he said and caught it. He balanced the disk case flat on his palm. The rappers' faces on the cover disappeared in the sun.

"I'm giving it to you," I said, closing the trunk. "I'm an A&R rep for the label. I travel around to find out what's hot on the streets. Then I go back to Cash Money and they read my reports, and modify their raps accordingly." They stared at me.

"Look, I write reports on the real street feeling. Cash Money changes their raps based on what my reports say. So when you see me talking to Dom, or Henry, or you, it's not for fun. I'm using this shitty little car so I don't draw attention." I was telling that shitty little story to disappear a little. Big lies like that made me feel a little more see-through.

"You met B.G.?" the kid asked suspiciously.

"Sure I met him. He has a platinum syringe, with little diamonds on it." I was going to say he had a working gun carved out of a single enormous diamond but I stopped myself. But then I said this.

"You kids know what grenades are?"

"Duh."

"You know the difference between a live grenade and a dead one?"

"Yeah."

"Well one time I went up with B.G. in his helicopter, and we flew around New Orleans, all high, just tossing live grenades out the goddamn windows."

Just then Henry and Dom shuffled around the corner. Every event in this book is true. It happened. Here comes Dom and Henry rolling around the goddamn corner.

And if you had been up in a helicopter that minute, you could have gotten all three of us with one grenade. Sitting ducks.

I'll be your little spy. I'll set them up, you knock 'em down.

•

"You can tell the difference between a live grenade and a dead grenade by the sound," Henry said. "You shake it, and if you hear a little tinkle, it's dead and you gotta get a new one."

"That's lightbulbs, Henry," Dom said. "I said that's fucking lightbulbs you are talking about, not grenades."

We were sitting in an upstairs room at Dom's. It had been stripped down to the bone. A few of the drop-ceiling tiles were missing. They'd been stripping copper piping to sell. Dom was wearing his brother's tool belt, a black wife-beater, camouflage shorts, dead white legs, big red flip-flops, and a Band-aid on his neck. Junkie chic, fall 2000.

"Whaddaya mean lightbulbs! I was in the Army!" Henry honked, "I was in Vietnam! Whatdaya think happened to my arm?"

"You were not in Vietnam," Dom said.

"And no one knows what happened to your arm," I finished.

"No one knows what happened to anything," Henry said mysteriously. Henry had located some good dope. Dom paid, I'd driven. All sickness was forgotten. And now we were shooting some unbelievably potent coke.

"Little devils," Dom whispered. He was looking down into a palm full of red-top vials. He had a needle sticking out of his arm. Staring straight ahead mouth open like someone had pressed pause.

"I got sticker shock," he said suddenly. He picked the needle out of his arm and stuck it quick in and out again. "I got sticker shock." We laughed slowly. Like people trying to breathe underwater.

The daylight came in through the window. Two happy little 7UP cans sat on the floor with us.

"The girls downstairs are still sleeping," Henry said. They still had the prostitutes in there. Even after Fathead's friendly warning. "Lazy girls," he added.

"Get out of bed and get ahead," I said.

"Get out of bed and give head and give me the bread," Dom said. We laughed slow.

Then I remembered what I saw when I was little on a television show called *The Electric Company*. They had electron microscopes that showed the surface of a human eyelash. It was like the moon. Enormous flat worms crawled slowly across it. There were no colors there. The no-color of total realism.

"I think this coke is helping my vision," I said. I was staring at the colorless wall across the room. "X-ray vision. I can see every little groove and hollow."

"Every nook and cranny," Dom said.

"That's not X-ray vision," said Henry. "If it was X-ray you could see behind the wall. X-ray vision cuts through things. Like a buzz saw. What you've got is infrared vision."

"But I don't see any red."

"*Infra*red," Henry said, "Infra means smaller than. Smaller than red. Red is like the outside of the house. Then you open the door and go inside the house. That's infrared."

"Little infrared living room and kitchen," I said. "Little infrared cups and saucers."

"Every nook and cranny," Dom said. Infrared. Smaller than red.

"I'm infrared-blooded," I mentioned. I thought of a colorless sun. The world below color. The real world.

Meanwhile an ant was stepping very carefully across the dirty wood floor. One leg, then the other, then the other, then the other. When he put one of his straight legs down into a little crevice between the floorboards, I saw a tiny puff of dust rise up. My breath caught in my throat.

"What do you think about those hot teenage hookers you got downstairs?" Henry said to change the subject.

"This is what I think," Dom said. He unzipped his fly and took out his big flaccid white penis. We laughed fast and slow. There was a sore on it.

"The only thing I hate worse than girls is fags," Henry said mysteriously. "It's time to go, though."

Henry didn't have a watch. In fact his whole left arm was missing. He kept his time down deep in his veins, and he was right. It was time to go.

It was always time to go at Dom's. We had just stopped starting to sit down, and now it was already time to start standing up. We were always on the move. It might not have looked like it. Dom's mouth hung open and his eyes were closed and his penis was flopping loose out his pants. But deep down he was moving. He was on top of things. There was never a single second to spare, never an instant to relax.

This fact might surprise a casual visitor. At any given moment, the house was full of people with their eyes closed and their mouths open. On chairs, under chairs, on the floor, on the toilet.

But after a while you realized everyone was moving. Just very, very slowly. They were starting to get up or starting to get down. There was never a moment of real rest. That's why everyone was so bone tired. Everyone was always moving. It just didn't always look that way. From the perspective of a rabbit, a turtle looks like it's sitting still. Take some of these joyriders. Lawyers coming through the door to buy some Oxys. Looking at their watches, on the way to some meeting.

Those lawyers came in looking for quick-stop service and what they found looked like a motionless swamp. Like Mississippi or Mexico. You pull up at the gas station and there's one old lady asleep in a chair under a shitty third-world tree. You go inside and the cashier is asleep on his folded arms. A ten-year-old boy is dozing on the step. An ant is crawling across his lips. A slow-crawling ant.

These lawyer types are impatient, always in a hurry. They paid top dollar for the damn pills and they expected service. They opened the door and Dom was on the floor. As their eyes adjusted to the no-light they could see he was slowly moving, like spilled oil.

"Um, Dom, I really must get going. I called ahead. Please if you could just, maybe, hurry. Let me help you with that, I can get that for you."

"Let me just get my . . . my . . ."

"Your keys, Dom, they're right here on the floor. Here they are, take them." They were always finishing his sentences for him.

". . . my gun." Because the turtle wins the race. The turtle wins in the end. The rabbit moves fast, but he only moves for eight or ten hours a day. But the turtle is always moving. Plus the dope-body makes new kinds of time. Secret hours inside the hours. Dom's green, leather neck. His deep-sea metabolism. Always moving.

That day, it took us two hours or so to come in, to get down and get the drugs in, and then to get up and go out on another run. If you filmed all that, and then played it back fast, you'd see. Like they do on the Discovery Channel when they show you the seasons changing on the savanna. All the endless gray and green matter you think of as still, is actually always moving. Even the trees. Even the mountains.

You'd see us move like that, slowly sitting down and slowly standing back up. But I bet you'd never see us sitting completely still. What the hell is there to sit still for? You think these drugs are free?

We moved slow on purpose. One time Dom lit a firecracker under dozing Henry's chair and Henry fell off so quick he blurred. Fast was no problem for us. We moved slow for conservation.

To conserve the precious drops of dope inside us we moved slowly. Like you move a full glass of water slowly so you don't spill it. Moving fast spills the dope, it speeds up the metabolism. The idiot heart chews up those twenty-dollar vials faster and faster. Maybe there was a little bit of brain damage too.

I never thought of myself as slow. In fact, all I thought about was getting some rest, just a little time to rest.

OK, I guess I could tell I wasn't exactly Speedy Gonzalez. Sometimes the same view of floor or wall would lodge in my brain like a shard of glass. Then I knew I hadn't moved in a while. Maybe hadn't even blinked.

And sometimes I gently hit the car in front of me as I was slowly starting to hit the brake. Sometimes the car behind me would honk as I was slowly starting to hit the gas. Sometimes I would think it was May when it was July.

One time I woke up, and the little punching bag in the back of my throat was all swollen up. I mean it was huge. It took up almost the whole throat hole. The tiny bugs in the air had to go past it single file. I don't even know what that little punching bag is called.

"What're you doing back there?"

It was itchy as hell. I scratched it gently with the tip of a syringe.

And who knows what caused that. Air bugs maybe. Something you never even noticed suddenly swells up. Swells up into your day. Squeezes out the fun.

Later that day I met one of the people who wanted to kill people I knew. I'd heard about these people.

"You seen Dom, man." The young dealer's cap was pulled down low, the brim pointed straight at my knees. He said it again. It didn't really sound like a question.

"No," I said, surprised. "I just need a white top and a nickel of coke."

"Yeah, well," he said, nodding at a runner across the street who came running up with the dope, "nigger owes, doesn't pay, gets got."

That sounded simple. And I knew Dom owed and didn't pay. Witness Fathead. But I thought that maybe now Dom was just a little too low to get got. A little too deep. Deep down.

For example, I went fishing once when I was a kid. I put a hook and a weight on the end of a long line and it sank down out of sight. There was a little plastic disk attached to my fishing line. The disk floated on the surface of the water, to let you know the place where the line dropped down.

Dom's face and head reminded me of that disk bobbing on the water. His visible body was just a marker, marking the place where he went down. I'd seen three hundred dollars of dope go into that body in one sitting. Go in and go down. How can you stop it? Who or what is it?

"Nigger needs to get got."

I mentally wished the teenage dealer good luck. I didn't think he knew what he was dealing with. Dom shot overdoses in his neck. He woke up crawling. Crawling for more. I didn't think Dom could be stopped. He was something uncanny. Raw habit.

But then I wondered how easy it would be to stop me. How easy would it be for me to stop?

I'd gotten in the bad habit of scribbling down "Quit Dope" notes when I woke up freaked out in the middle of the night. When I woke up suddenly like that, I kind of surprised my life. I saw it as it was when it thought no one was looking at it. Looking up at my life from that angle way down deep in the night, I saw what was wrong. I knew I wouldn't remember the secret in the morning. I'd be back in it. I'd be it.

Lying awake in the middle of the night I knew the answer, and I knew I wouldn't remember it. Those deep-night panics were moments outside of memory. Unconnected. The hyper-clear night thoughts didn't stick around. They evaporated at the first breath. Writing was invented for the thoughts you can't remember. Writing is an aid to memory. So I'd scribble down "Quit Dope" notes and "My Life Matters" notes and leave them in obvious places around my apartment.

Every morning I'd wake up and throw the notes out without reading them. Then I'd drive, steal, score, and pass out.

I knew how to write. Reading was the problem. It is easier to write than it is to read. In the middle of the night I started to wonder how to get myself to read the damn notes. I began to experiment with different colored ink, super-big letters, super-small letters. But by then developments had rendered this night-time project obsolete. By spring, daytime things had got me thinking about quitting in the daytime.

First, there was the billboard, right on Charles Street near the train station. It had a picture of a stethoscope floating in a sunny sky. At the top it had a doctor's name and phone number in big block letters. And below that, in even bigger letters, it read:

HEROIN DETOX

ONE DAY

SAFE PAINLESS MEDICAL PROCEDURE

$1000

That billboard rose right in the middle of the main street in downtown Baltimore for maybe a year. I saw it every day. So I started to figure there were some people who wanted to get off heroin.

I know it sounds odd, but back then that came as kind of a surprise to me. I'd quit before, of course. But it was always a practical, short-term thing. No money. Habit too big. Gotta back off it awhile so I can get high on ten dollars again. That kind of thing. But really quit? Quit for good? I wasn't used to thinking of heroin as something you wanted not to do. At least not in the daytime. It took me a little while to figure it out. It was a process of deduction. If there's a billboard advertising a way to get off dope, there must be a desire to get off dope. Where there's smoke, there's fire. And if it costs a thousand dollars to get off the shit, people have got to want to get off it real bad.

A thousand dollars. We're talking about junkies. A thousand dollars is fifty twenty-dollar white tops. So the presence of that billboard implied that there were some junkies—probably rich ones, but still—who were willing to trade fifty white tops for no dope.

That didn't make too much sense to me. People said the doctor had a way of taking you off it with no withdrawal. It still didn't make much sense, but it was something to think about.

Plus I'd been kind of seeing my ex-girlfriend Eva again. She was living in New York with the guitarist for some band. She'd tell him she was visiting her parents and drive down to visit me. We got extra high and tried to have sex for hours. I'd tell her how great it would be if she'd just move in with me. Cat was a drag. Eva understood. In late May she came down for the last time.

On a humid Sunday afternoon we drove fast to cop. Then we drove slow through the dusk after fixing. Down Route

40 through the east side of town. Deep Baltimore. It was my favorite Sunday drive. We stopped at a red light. On the left-hand side there was a glass-enclosed building. It looked like a car showroom, with the raised floor and full-length windows designed to display the new vehicles. But instead of new cars, the building sold new wheelchairs.

Some were motorized. Some had red leather. One had thick armrests like a couch and an extra-high back. It turned slowly on a mirrored dais. On the sidewalk in front of the building, an old man leaned on his cane and stared at the beautiful wheelchairs. The setting sun lit up the chrome spokes.

The light turned green. But we couldn't go because an old woman was slowly caning her way across the intersection. When she was about halfway through, the light turned red again. A car behind us beeped. I looked in the rearview mirror. It was a very old man in a Buick. I could see his angry lips moving in my mirror.

"I got a new name for old people," I said. "You want to know what I call them?"

"What?" Eva said.

"Faggots," I said. I was joking around.

We drove a little more.

"I can't take this," she said.

"Take what?" I said. "I was just joking around calling the oldsters faggots. I don't have any kind of problem with real gay people. In fact, one time I did something kind of gay myself."

She began to cry softly.

"It was an accident," I said. "I was drunk."

"It's not that," she said, wiping her eyes and looking out the window.

"Then what?"

"You want me to move in with you. But everything with you is so . . . makeshift."

For some reason that word seemed particularly damning. It was the worst thing she could have said to me. I didn't say anything for a while.

"Yeah, I know it's makeshift," I said finally. "But this is a special party time. Not makeshift, more like fun. A special occasion. Not makeshift. Don't leap to conclusions. Don't assume life together would always be makeshift or something. If you move down here, the regular days will be . . . organized."

I imagined us holding hands in my bare apartment, with the sickening smells of home food coming in from the kitchen. I imagined me slowly putting on my shoes to go to some kind of job. I shivered. She did too. She went back to her guitarist boyfriend. That was something else to think about.

Plus if you owe and you don't pay, you get got.

Well, that didn't really apply to me. I always paid. I paid with bouncing checks and stolen credit cards and stolen cartons of cigarettes and stolen amps and emergency wires from every relative I had. One afternoon I even walked down the corridor of my own apartment building, knocking on doors and asking for twenty dollars.

"My wallet was stolen." How could I not pay you back? "Look at me," my face said, "I'm your very own neighbor. I live right across the hall."

I never ever paid anyone back anything. There were some awkward elevator rides with the neighbors. But money was basically free. I pawned my TV, for example. I still had a couch. There were even some quarters that had fallen under the cushions. So it was hard for me to see money as a really pressing reason to quit.

Still, I started to think vaguely that maybe this couldn't last. Even in the daytime I thought it. Not when I was going to get high, of course. But once I got high and had a couple hours before I had to start looking for money again. It-can't-last thoughts started to stick around.

"This can't last forever," I told my friend Todd one day. He was the last person from my graduate department still talking to me. He was a junkie too.

"What the hell do you mean this can't last forever?" he said. His little eyes jumped in and out of his simple, junkie, bare-bones face.

"I just mean that nothing lasts forever," I said. "Even the president can't go anywhere he wants. He has to tell his security guards for instance."

"I'm almost free," Todd said. "Eight days ago I did half a vial. Seven days ago I did a quarter vial. Six days ago I did one-eighth. I did one-eighth for three days in a row. Then I did a quarter vial by accident. Yesterday I did one-sixteenth. Same today." He paused and looked at me with unconcealed hatred.

"*I'm* almost done! *I'm* almost out! So fuck off!" He sat there gasping at me. A few days later I heard from Henry that Todd had been buying two white tops pretty much every day.

Still, Todd's little outburst stuck with me.

"He doesn't even have to think about it," I said to myself. "He just totally wants to quit." I found this to be a challenging idea. Todd just absolutely wants to quit? With no doubts? I could hardly believe it.

Not that I thought he was insane for wanting to quit. Not insane, exactly. In fact, when I thought about it, I could think of all kinds of reasons to quit. Some of them were even obvious. Cops, for instance. A cop had stopped me a few days before, and I'd pushed my vials into the air-conditioning vents. He tore the car apart and didn't find shit. Cops can be stupid as hell.

But there were some other, vaguer reasons. Little things I'd noticed about myself lately. Little disturbing symptoms. A certain heaviness to moving and breathing, for example. The spooky feeling I got looking into the mirror. I started finding odd notes I'd written in the middle of the night. And there was a certain uncanny quietness to sounds. Even loud sounds. A certain . . . Never mind. I was basically fine. What the hell was Todd talking about? I called him up.

"Hey, Todd."

"What do *you* want?" He sounded like he had a cold.

"Um, I was just wondering about what you said the other day. I know about all the bad stuff that can happen, and it can't last forever, et cetera. But is it true that you really want to quit? Really? I mean right now?"

He hung up. I decided that you can never really know what goes on in another person's head. I needed a second opinion.

"Hey, Henry," I said.

"Whaddaya want?" he said. We were at Dom's. Henry was sitting cross-legged on the floor. He was literally counting pennies.

"I'm busy trynna count these goddamn pennies," Henry said.

"Henry, have you ever tried to quit?"

"Hell yeah," he said without looking up. He lifted the pennies one by one from the pile on his right side and dropped them on the pile on his left side. With his one arm, he looked like a crane. A makeshift crane.

"So?" I said.

"So what?" He looked up at me, annoyed.

"So how was it? How was quitting?"

"How the hell does it look?" he grunted and resumed craning the pennies from the right pile to the left.

"It was impossible," he said. "I've tried, of course. Dozens of times. Give my right arm, like they say. Already gave my left. Didn't work. Hee hee."

"What do you mean, you can't quit?" I said over Henry's junkie giggle. "You can't quit? You want to quit and you *still* can't?"

"It's impossible, Mike," he said, straightening up and looking me right in the eye. "After the last time, I promised myself. I'll never try it again. Quitting chews you up and spits you out, and you are still hooked. It's impossible to quit. Just forget it. Waste of time to even try."

I sat shocked and sweating, right there in the middle of a forty-dollar high. I looked at Henry's one-armed torso. It spoke to me.

"You must change your life," it said.

"Impossible for a junkie to quit," he said.

I didn't have a thousand dollars. So I couldn't go to the billboard doctor. But my friend Tony K. told me about another place. A certain Dr. Hayes ran a clinic on Maryland Avenue, near the hospital. Tony said they gave you some kind of special medicine that cut the withdrawals in half.

The clinic was called the Center for Addiction Medicine. When I called them, they explained I had to pay one hundred and fifty dollars up front, cash, for the treatment. The rest, they'd bill to me. I happened to have two hundred dollars left from an insurance check I'd gotten to fix my car. I'd run it into a light pole a while back. Too slow on the turn, too slow on the brake. I resolved to go to the clinic and get clean.

The next day, when I woke up, I threw out the "No Dope Today!" sign on my dresser and went and spent twenty on a final white top.

"You're bad," I said as I poured those last magic grains out of the vial.

"You little devil," I told the dope as it went away into me. It was gone. I drove over to the clinic. There were four or five people in the ratty waiting room when I got there.

"Oooh, ooooh, ooooh." A young black woman rocked back and forth moaning on the threadbare couch. A white guy with a red face and a yellow happy-face T-shirt was talking to the receptionist.

"I. Need. My. Medicine," he was saying. I shut my eyes and listened to the dope whispering sweetly away inside me.

After twenty minutes or so they called me back. A tired-looking nurse asked me some questions and filled in my answers on a chart.

"How many dollars, on average, would you estimate you spend on heroin per day?"

"Two hundred," I lied. It was more like eighty, unless I got lucky. But I figured if I said it was more they'd give me more medicine.

"I will now take your payment of one hundred and fifty dollars," she said. She actually held out her hand. I was surprised. In regular doctor's offices, it's a clerk who takes the money. I had a couple sneaky ideas about what to say to avoid paying. But the nurse looked tired. She didn't look like she was in the mood for sneaky. Plus she had the secret kick-dope medicine right there. I wanted to quit. I was still a little high, and I still remembered. I gave her the money.

Later I realized the reason they made you pay in cash was to discourage people from coming back so many times.

"The medicine we use here is called buprenorphine. It is an opiate agonist. This means that it has both opiate properties—which will help to reduce your withdrawal symptoms—and opiate blocker properties—which will make it hard for you to get high while you are taking it."

"Yeah, well, I'm not planning to get high. That's why I'm here." Duh.

"The program lasts for ten days," she continued. "We will give you the buprenorphine for three days. That's the maximum allowed by law. It won't take away all of your withdrawals, but it will help. We will administer it here, so you need to come here every day to get it. Patients typically like to arrive as soon as we open, which is 8:30 a.m. We will also give you other, nonopiate medications. A high-blood-pressure medication, a muscle relaxant, an antidiarrhea medicine, and Tylenol."

She handed me a small baggie with the Tylenol and the other worthless pills. She then gave me a small, square, green lozenge and told me to put it under my tongue and let it dissolve. I looked at it doubtfully. I put it under my tongue.

By the time I got to my apartment I wasn't feeling so hot. It was about six in the evening now. The windows were open. Soft evening light lit the floorboards; soft summer air ballooned in the thin curtains. They looked so cheap to me, so poor. I felt a sudden twinge of sadness.

Here we go, I thought.

On my coffee table I had two big bottles of water, a bottle of Gatorade, and a little pile of Tylenol and antidiarrhea pills. I hadn't gone more than twelve hours without dope in over nine months.

I looked at my watch. It had now been eight hours. The electric tension in my legs, the pinpricks of sweat coming out all over my skin, the twist in my guts: I recognized the eight-hour symptoms. I even kind of liked them. In the mornings I'd relish these symptoms, sometimes even putting off my first hit for six or seven minutes. I'd savor the eight-hour burn. It made that first morning hit all the sweeter. Four minutes, five minutes. Bam! That morning dope was like rain in the desert.

But now the pain was different. It wasn't the pain that comes before a hit. I'd quit. Dopeless. I had the morning pain without the morning hit. That future hit was missing, and the pain was naked without it. I looked at my watch. It had now been eight hours and four minutes since my last, my final hit.

I lay down on my makeshift bed. I pressed my naked burning foot to the cold plaster wall. I got up, swallowed all the pills on the table and lay back down.

Sounds of laughing voices rose from the street below my window. The breeze moved in the thin curtains. The curtains wrinkled with sadness. The sunlight went away on the sounds of the voices, on the bare wood floor of my apartment, on the sad, wrinkled curtains.

Sometime after dark I moved into a new level of withdrawal.

Now I realized that the eight-hour burn was just an inkling. A premonition. I didn't want to know anything about this.

I shoved myself up against unconsciousness, trying desperately to get in. Sleep. Dreamless, motionless, senseless. It was like the cold plaster wall. I could feel the good absence of feeling on it. I pressed my burning limbs against it. But it was closed. A wall, not a door. I pressed up against it, awake at fourteen hours.

Fifteen hours.

Ever since I was little, I've told myself stories to fall asleep. A little cushion of fantasy between waking and sleeping. I lie down and start imagining some pleasant scene. Like I'm on a sailboat in the Caribbean with my friends. Or no, I'm a pirate. Walking on the deck with my sword. I start walking slowly, with big pirate steps. The black metal cannon barrels gleam in the moonlight.

Then I notice a fine green parrot has landed on the deck. Its beak has opened. Then I don't know what else. Then I wake up.

That first night of kicking, I imagined I was living in a castle. A blizzard was raging outside. I'd been trudging though the blizzard, carrying my sword and shield, fleeing the enemy. I knocked on the massive oak door of the castle. I heard the slow sound of the bar being raised and the door swinging open. The friendly warmth rushed out, strong friendly hands pulled me, fainting, inside.

"You must be exhausted," said a tall, handsome man in chain mail. "Well, everything is going to be fine. We have everything you need in this castle. The walls are strong; the enemy will never get in. And we have enough supplies to last for years in here." I nodded and tried to smile.

They showed me to a room high in the walls. A big fire roared in the fireplace. A clean, white bed deep with cushions lay piled in the corner. I stood for several minutes gazing at it. I repeated the contents of this room in the castle over and over to myself. I was shivering terribly.

"They also have hundreds of soldiers to protect me," I told myself.

The red light of my electric clock bled through the thin walls of the castle. 3:22. I reached down to get the bottle of Gatorade on the floor. My abdomen was segmented like an insect's and the Gatorade was hot like insecticide.

"They have hundreds of soldiers to protect me in this castle. The blizzard rages outside. It is warm and safe and deep inside the castle. I'll fall asleep now." But the shivering cold came through the thick castle walls. They had to move me deeper inside the castle, where I'd be warm.

They had to move me again. Deep in the castle's heart, to a windowless room, with an ancient glowing furnace and a fire burning in the fireplace. They'd never heard of drugs. I heard hundreds of soldiers rushing in the corridors.

"They're going to their battle stations," I told myself. I stared at the red digits on the clock. I turned over and over in the bed. My vibrating legs made red electricity. 4:51.

"They're going to their battle stations." I invented the name of the enemy. The history of the country. The names of the people in the castle army. "Henry Abelove, Lieutenant." I counted their weapons. Lieutenant Abelove led me on a tour of their supplies and armaments.

"Here we have the lumber room, where all the lumber for the fires is stored. As you can see, we have enough to last two full years of siege. We will always have enough fuel for warm fires here in this strong, safe castle."

He showed me the vast hall where they stored the weapons. He told me about the theater the duke had ordered constructed high in the upper keep. He told me the names of the books in the libraries. 5:30. The castle had everything that was needed, all right. I spent hours telling myself about all the good things in the castle. Listing them, counting them.

But something was missing. Despite the plentiful stores of food, everyone in the castle looked starved and crazy. Despite the vast fires, the huge furnaces, the halls piled high with entire felled forests, I could not stop shivering.

"There is no sleep in this castle," Lieutenant Abelove said sadly.

"But," I said, "I thought that one first enters the castle, and then passes through into sleep." He shook his head.

"This entire structure is built along the wall of sleep, but at no point does it penetrate it." I tried to follow his words.

"Can't we use some of these weapons, some of this fuel to break through?" He shook his head sadly. I tried to stop thinking about the castle.

"Now I'm on a pirate ship," I told myself.

I tossed and turned on my bed in a windowless room deep in the heart of the castle. The sleepless armies rushed through the halls on their way to battle stations. They had never heard of dope. They had never seen white-topped vials of dope. Except in the distance, through the castle's tiny windows.

The white blizzard raged outside, but the strong white sleep couldn't get in. Sleeplessness was an invincible fortress. It had enough fuel, enough food, enough weapons to withstand two years of siege.

"Sleep can go everywhere but here," I said, sleepless.

The red numbers of the clock read 7:40. I stood up in pain and slowly drew back the curtains. Red sun erased the red numbers. I struggled into my clothes. The fabric felt like sandpaper. My shirt was soaked with cold sweat by the time I reached my car.

I drove straight out of the castle. I reached the Edmondson Avenue dope spot ten minutes later and gave the runner my last sweat-soaked twenty. The white sun rose at 8:05.

THREE

THE FUTURE LASTS FOREVER

Writing is an aid to memory. It helps me to remember what I never experienced. Through this writing, I remember sitting in my car on Edmondson Avenue. The sweat-soaked twenty clenched in the bones of my hand. The ghetto street scene clenched in the bones of my face. Watching for the runner. Shaking.

That moment never existed. I wasn't there.

Well, I was there, kind of. It's hard to explain. If you've ever looked out at the sea on a clear day you know there is a line where the sea and sky meet. That line doesn't really exist. It's an optical illusion. I was there in the car on Edmondson Avenue the way that imaginary line is there between the sea and the sky.

I hung there suspended between the first time I did dope and the next time. Between the original eternal white bliss of my first time, and the next eternal white hit. I was the imaginary line that kept those two halves from meeting. Those two heavens. The pressure of all that white bliss above and below, and I was between and thin and imaginary.

Hurry, runner. One white top, please. I'll do it right here in the car. The way the horizon looks in a thick white fog. I wanted to be there in that car on Edmondson Avenue the way the horizon isn't there in a white blizzard.

But once that dope hit me I only felt thicker. A thicker barrier between that first-time dope and the next dope that would bring it all back again.

After fixing I watched myself getting fatter there in the car. I wasn't a line anymore. I was growing thicker and realer by the second as the dope ticked through my heart. Growing arms, legs, eyes, swollen fingers, dirty jeans. I could see my hand in front of my face. There was no white blizzard. I could see the potato chip bags on the floor of my car. The withdrawal was gone, but that was it.

So I was there in my car on Edmondson Avenue after all. I only wanted not to be. I looked at my big hands. I noticed the potato chip bags on the floor of the car. 8:06 in the morning. Eight hours until the eight-hour burn. Twelve hours to the castle. I feel lucky to be writing this now. Writing is a way of not being somewhere. And there's nowhere I'd rather not be than there.

Writing is an aid to memory. Writing is an AIDS for memory. OK. I drove from Edmondson Avenue right to the Center for Addiction Medicine. It still hadn't opened by the time I parked and walked up. There was a line of addicts waiting by the entrance.

"Hey, man." I turned around. A guy around my age in baggy shorts, wearing a gold chain.

"Oh. Hey." I vaguely recognized him.

"Kicking sucks, huh," he said.

A cigarette dangled loosely from his thin lips. His pupils were the size of ant heads. He was obviously high.

"Hey." Another junkie shuffled up to us. He nodded politely to me. "Kicking surely does suck."

He was high too. He was actually grinning. The first guy started to open his mouth. Then he closed it. Then he smiled. I began to smile a little, despite myself.

The clinic doors opened at eight-thirty and the already-tired-looking nurses started to shepherd in the line of eighteen or twenty sad, grinning, kicking, high, desperate, happy junkies.

"Have you used any drugs since you were last here?" The nurse studiously avoided my eyes, looking down at her clipboard.

"No," I said. She looked up and fastened her eyes on the wall above my head.

"You know," she said. "We also offer a medication called ReVia. This drug completely prevents you from getting high for twenty-four hours. As long as you take it every day, you can't relapse. Some people find it helpful. Once you've been off narcotics for forty-eight hours, we can start giving it to you. Taking it any earlier, however, will dramatically increase your withdrawal symptoms."

"Well," I said. "It's only been about twenty-four hours for me. But the withdrawal symptoms really aren't so bad. I guess that medicine you're giving me really works!"

She nodded tiredly. She gave me the little green lozenge of buprenorphine. I cleverly pretended to put in my mouth, and pocketed it. *This stuff really works,* I thought. *I better hold on to it until I really need it.*

The guy with the gold chain was outside waiting for me.

"Hey, can I get a lift, man?"

"Sure," I said.

Now I was really quitting. I knew what to expect. I was prepared. I could use some like-minded company. Some reinforcement. He settled heavily in the passenger seat and we sped off.

"Where you going?" I asked.

"Westside," he said. We drove for a few seconds.

"Man, I can't wait to get off this shit," I said.

"Tell me about it," he said. He fiddled with the car cigarette lighter.

"It's ruining my life," I said.

"I've lost my girl, my job, and my car," he said.

"It's the devil," I said.

I looked quickly over at him, then looked at the road.

I rubbed my right knee a little bit. He was rubbing the side of his left leg. For a split second, our fingers gently touched. I drew my hand quickly back. Then I slowly put it back.

"I am so glad I finally decided to quit," he said.

"Is it hot in this car or something?" I said.

He rolled down his window. Then he rolled it back up. We drove for a few seconds in silence. I looked quickly over at him and caught him looking at me. He quickly turned away. I felt myself blushing.

"Where did you say you lived?" I asked.

"I, uh," he swallowed. "I don't really want to go home right now."

I swallowed.

"I don't really want to go home either," I said softly, carefully, not meeting his eyes.

"So what do you want to do?"

"So what do you want to do?"

We said it together. We laughed shyly. I rubbed my knee. He rubbed his shoulder.

"It's not so healthy to stop all at once," he said.

"It's a strain on the heart," I said.

"And the liver," he said.

"And the brain," I said. We were pulling up to Pulaski, a great drive-through dope spot on the Westside.

"I don't have any money," he said.

"I don't either," I said. The stout baggy-shorts dealer walked up to my open window. He recognized me. I was a good customer.

"How many, yo?"

"Two," I said. The dealer walked away. The guy next to me poked me in the shoulder.

"Man, I said I don't have any."

"Shut the fuck up," I hissed.

The dealer came back. I had two single dollar bills in my palm. The dealer watched me close, looking puzzled. He reached slowly through the window with the dope in his fist. I looked normal. He looked me quick in the face and then jerked his hand back. I grabbed his fist, which slid out of my grip as his other fist hit the side of my head.

"Go man!" the guy beside me yelled. People were scrambling on the street. Coming out of bushes and from behind parked cars.

"Motherfucker!" the dealer screamed.

"Motherfucker!" screamed a tall kid within a red bandanna.

"Motherfucker!" screamed a fat, bald, middle-aged man.

"Motherfucker!" screamed the guy beside me. I sped off. Rolling up the window with one hand, holding my bloody nose with the other. Fifteen or twenty Pulaski folks scrambled in the rearview. The car zigzagged fifty feet up the block and ran up the curb onto the sidewalk.

"Motherfucker!" I yelled. I hit reverse and the car's undercarriage screamed and sparked on the concrete.

A ten-year-old kid was the first to arrive. He hit the rear passenger window with a golf club and the glass cracked. The original dealer ran up fast and started pulling quick up and down, up and down on my locked door handle. Another guy ran over to my partner's door and started doing the same. I saw a couple more ten-year-olds running up, laughing. One was dragging what looked like a dumbbell.

"Get those bitches!" someone yelled. I gunned the motor and the car revved and screeched.

"Oh God, they're shooting!" the guy beside me yelled. "They're shooting at us!"

The car scraped off the curb and I hit the gas, screeched around the corner onto Route 40, and started flashing past the stop signs and traffic lights. After maybe a minute I slowed down.

"They weren't shooting," I told the guy next to me. "You know how much heat that would bring? Shooting two white guys?"

"Fuck you, man. That was one of my spots. Now I can't never go back."

"You're quitting, remember? Plus, you can totally go back there. We didn't get away with any dope, did we? We're still good customers."

"And I ain't no bitch," he sniffled. I looked in the mirror. My nose was bleeding a little but otherwise I looked all right.

"I ain't no bitch," he muttered. He hit the dashboard. Hard.

"Ow!" he said.

"We need some money and I don't mean maybe," I mentioned.

It was one of those bright, clear Baltimore summer days that make the whole concept of "nice weather" meaningless and irrelevant. The cocksucker next to me needed me for a ride, if he was ever going to score, so I let him worry about the money. My job was to drive. I drove aimlessly while he mumbled and muttered. Whenever I saw a truck or a bus, I thought about crossing the double yellow lines and catching it head-on. A disappearance rush.

"OK," he said finally. I really don't remember that guy's name. But now I could see he was both chubby and an addict, which usually doesn't go together. His gold chain was both thin and fake, which also doesn't usually go together. Everyone in this world is unique, my mother used to say.

"Head back to Fells Point and go down Eastern. My grandpa lives up there. He should have gotten his check yesterday." He paused. "Unless Mom's already snatched it up," he added darkly.

That sounded sordid. But (a) I had made a promise to myself to quit dope, (b) it was bad for your heart to quit too abruptly, (c) my rear window was all smashed in, and (d) if I was ever going to get moving with quitting, I needed to get high right now. Right this very second.

There was a wheelchair on the lawn of the shitty concrete building where Grandpa lived. Fatty pushed it over to an open window, and used it to climb in. About three minutes later the front door opened and Fatty appeared waving happily.

"Come on in!" he said.

I put the car in park and walked in, ready for anything. Inside it was dark and urinous. Fatty motioned to a faded couch. I sat down gingerly. I noticed one end of the couch was piled with porn magazines. There were empty McDonald's bags all over the floor. Grandpa eyed me suspiciously.

"Now Grandpa, this is the man I was telling you about," Fatty yelled at the old man. "He's here to collect the fee so I can go back to electrical school in the fall."

They both looked at me. I wiped my nose, which had started bleeding again.

"Um, yes." I said. "Your grandson is an unusually, um, promising electrician. We are all very excited to have him. But I do need to collect that fee today. Otherwise, he may have to go to jail."

"What?" the old man said.

"You gotta talk louder," Fatty told me, looking annoyed, "can't you see he's practically deaf?" He picked up a pencil and rapidly wrote something on the back of an old lotto ticket. I leaned over to read it.

$80

SCHOOL FEE

FOR ELECTRICAL SCHOOL

The old man looked stupidly at the ticket for maybe a minute.

"I promised your mom. I won't give you any more," he said finally.

Fatty put his mouth practically to the oldster's ear and yelled out:

"I NEED THAT SCHOOL MONEY RIGHT THIS MINUTE, GRANDPA!"

There's no need to give all the details on this one. It's not very uplifting. Suffice it to say we finally got sixty dollars out of the old man. Plus a handful of Percocet I snatched out of his medicine cabinet while Fatty was helping him into his wheelchair. Fatty had to promise we'd give the old guy a lift to the store when we got done taking care of the school fees. We left him sitting there forlornly on the lawn in his wheelchair.

His wheelchair did look real nice, though. It was brand new, practically. It had the red leather armrests. I bet he wouldn't feel too bad if he did have to wheel himself to the store. Not in that thing. Its chrome spokes sparkled in my rearview. Sly old dog. I bet he wouldn't feel too bad at all.

"He's a smart old guy," Fatty said.

"Nice 'chair," I said.

"Heart of gold," Fatty said.

We drove right back to Pulaski to cop. Fatty was nervous, but it was just like I said. I gave them two twenties and they gave me two white tops. No one had any hard feelings about earlier.

"So what happened last time?" asked the dealer casually, leaning on my window waiting for a ten-year-old to run up with the dope.

"I miscounted," I said. He nodded. Just a mix-up, happens all the time on Pulaski.

The next morning I asked for the ReVia.

"Quitting is going great," I told the nurse. "In fact, it's a lot easier than I thought it would be. But I'd just feel better if I was on ReVia. Relapse-proof, like you said."

"Well, OK," the nurse said slowly. She checked my chart. "It has been over forty-eight hours, so you should be OK." She looked up at the wall above my head. "Are you absolutely sure you have not had any dope in the past forty-eight hours? This could be painful if you're not. You're sure you are clean?"

I made a yes-type noise.

"All right, then. We'll start you out with a very small dose. Over the next few days we'll increase it, and then you can start taking the pills every morning."

She took out a dropper and a bottle, and put a single drop of the clear liquid on my tongue. I swallowed savagely. *Good,* I thought. *Bring it. Kick that shit out of me.*

I walked quickly to my car. Halfway there the ReVia hit me. When the drop touched my tongue, it seeped into my blood. When it hit my blood, it sped to my heart. My heart shot it into my brain.

Once inside my brain, tiny ReVia molecules began covering up all my dope receptors. Putting chemical gags in the open dope holes. I'm not an expert on the science. I went from high to full-blown twelve-hour withdrawal in a few minutes. Picture someone cutting trenches three inches wide and two inches deep all up and down your legs and back. And then pouring gasoline in the cuts. And then setting you on fire.

OK, I'm exaggerating. Junkies are famous for shamelessly exaggerating the pain of kicking. The sad truth is that the physical symptoms of withdrawal really aren't so terrible. If you've ever had a bad case of the flu, you basically know what the physical symptoms are like.

Doesn't seem to live up to the fuss, huh? In war, people get shot and travel for weeks through the jungle. They get gangrene and saw off their own feet and keep going. In the business world, people go to work with a bad cold. They sit hunched over their keyboards typing up reports with one hand while blowing their nose with the other. They don't even write about it. They tough it out in silence. They make their co-workers sick with their germs. That's their reward.

But soldiers with wounds and businesspeople with colds are bad comparisons. Because when the dope leaves the junkie it takes everything he has with it. The purely physical symptoms of withdrawal are unpleasant, but they don't come close to explaining the relapse rate. Just try to put yourself in my shoes. You do the last of your dope and barricade yourself in your shitty apartment, saying "Never again!" About ten hours later your sense of who you are goes. A couple hours later your sense of where you are breaks down. Then your sense of why the hell you're kicking disappears. Plus you feel like you've got the flu.

With no motive, no direction, and no name, in the no-time of deep withdrawal, the junkie's brain is totally exposed to memory. To the memory disease.

When my vision cut out, imaginary dope vials posed under the light of paradise. When I opened my eyes, the impossible white spiral bliss was hovering two inches above my empty face.

In my peripheral vision, I sensed the scenery and ambience of my first time. I bit down hard on the inside of my cheek.

I managed to drive back from the clinic and stagger into my building. Little white-top vials full of white powder shyly opalesced from the white walls of the lobby. I made it up to my apartment and collapsed writhing on the couch. Cat's and Eva's smiles twisted back and forth over the walls.

When you've got the flu, your brain releases endorphins to dull the pain and put you to sleep. Kicking, your bare nerves twist in the dry sockets. I corkscrewed into the hard cushions of my couch. Loneliness turned inside the pain and desire. I started to tell myself a story to try to go to sleep.

Some time later, I noticed there was a phone in my room in the castle. I slowly picked it up and dialed Eva's number.

It rang three times.

"Hello," she said.

Her real voice was too much. I sobbed through my clenched teeth.

"Is that you, Mike?"

"Y-y-yes."

"Oh my God. Oh my God. Darling."

White dope shone in the folds of her rich voice, in the shallows of her vowels.

Ten days later I was back at the Center for Addiction Medicine. They made you wait ten days between detoxes. Like the $150, the policy was designed to encourage the junkies to take detox seriously. I had the cash, though. I'd bought some expensive vitamins from Rite Aid with stolen checks. L-Carnitine 500 MG, $48.99. Three bottles. Vitamins are the best for buying with bad checks. They're portable. They have relatively high cash value. Plus, and perhaps most importantly, they have a vague aura of healthy living. Vitamins don't light up a store manager's junkie radar the way cartons of cigarettes do.

You could always steal the vitamins and then try to return them. But that was a real hassle. Those Baltimore Rite Aid managers weren't stupid. It was much better to buy the vitamins with a bad check and then return them with the receipt for cash. No questions asked. I always felt good walking into a Rite Aid with a couple bottles of L-Carnitine and nice fat receipt.

"Do you have a receipt, sir?" The clerk looked skeptically from the vitamins to me.

A look of fake panic crossed my face. I pretended to look frantically through my empty wallet. The clerk smiled coldly. Then I smiled back, and slowly took the receipt out of my shirt pocket.

"I think you'll find everything is in order," I said smugly.

A receipt was my passport to pleasure. Or to freedom, in this case. The Center for Addiction Medicine was a devil for that $150. They didn't take any shorts.

"The program lasts for ten days," the nurse said. "We will give you buprenorphine for three days. That's the maximum allowed by law. It won't take away all of your withdrawals, but it will help. We will administer it here, so you need to come here every day to get it."

She droned on. I nodded like a maniac, listening too closely to the scripted words. I was serious. I went home and spent a long night in the castle. Lieutenant Abelove introduced me to all sixty members of the castle guard. Personally. By name. I memorized their names. In the morning I struggled into my clothes and drove slowly and erratically over to the Center. I got the buprenorphine and drove back home. I was making it. And after my experience with the ReVia, I realized that the bup (as they called it) really did take the worst edge off.

This isn't so bad, I thought. The breeze wrinkled in my sad curtains. *Just like the flu,* I thought. The sun crept across the floor. The phone rang.

"Hello?"

"Hey, Mike. Bet you didn't expect to hear from me."

It was Funboy. A junkie friend I hadn't seen in maybe two weeks. I had a vague feeling I was supposed to be mad at him. But I couldn't remember why.

"Oh. Hey. Look, Funboy. I can't do anything. I'm kicking."

"That's awesome, Mike. Yeah! Right on."

"I gotta get going."

"Sure, sure."

There was a few seconds of silence. I didn't hang up.

"So I kinda gotta get going," I said again.

"Sure, sure. You know . . ." Funboy trailed off.

"Know what?" I asked quickly.

"Sometimes . . . No, never mind. That's awesome, Mike!"

"What were you going to say?" I asked.

"Well, sometimes you gotta step it down."

"Step it down?"

"I'm just saying."

"What?"

There were ten seconds of silence. I couldn't wait to hear what Funboy was going to say next. He took his time.

"They got twenty-fives down at Druid Hill," he said finally.

My jaw dropped.

"Twenty-fives?"

"That's right. Big quarter-gram vials for twenty-five dollars. Man, that's all I been spending! Twenty-five dollars a day. Just one of them things. Per day. You know how I used to have a forty-dollar-a-day habit? Well, one of them shits does it. Man. Just one of them damn shits. I even wake up and I even got a little bit left."

"Damn, they got twenty-fives?"

That changed everything. They usually sold dope in twenty- or forty-dollar vials. Ten-dollar scramble on the Eastside. But twenty-fives? What did that even look like?

"What do they even look like, Funboy?"

"Oh man. Fat white tops that big full to the top with little rocks of raw. Them rocks are packed in white powder. That powder has little brown streaks of pure raw in it," he said dreamily.

"How big are the vials, Funboy?" I asked.

"That big," Funboy said again into the phone.

I sighed. He was an idiot. I realized I would have to take a look at one for myself.

Looking in the phone book, I found another detox clinic, on the far north side of town. I took I-83 and got off at Northern Parkway. The clinic had a long driveway. And trees. They were serious.

"We offer buprenorphine detox only once in each patient's lifetime," the nurse said sternly. "You can only have this treatment once at this clinic, so it is necessary that you are completely committed to freeing yourself from your addiction."

I gave her a check for $150. She gave it back to me. I gave her the cash, in tens and fives and singles. At this clinic, they injected the buprenorphine. I liked it better that way.

That night I tried to drive myself into sleep by telling myself stories about my bright dopeless future. But by 4:00 a.m. I was talking to Henry Abelove. The next morning I accidentally got on 83 going the wrong way. I got off and then remembered that I couldn't get on 83 going north at this exit. So I had to drive five blocks up and one over to catch the next northbound ramp. Or was it six blocks up? Or three over? Then I unexpectedly ran into a charming little dope spot down in Patterson Park.

Convinced I couldn't get clean in Baltimore, I headed across country to the Chicago suburbs and kicked in my father's basement. I told everyone I had the flu. It worked. The key was that I didn't know where to score in the suburbs and I didn't try to. Plus I got arrested for driving with a suspended license and when they let me out of jail my car had been towed and I didn't have any money to get it out. So I couldn't even try to score.

Well, I did try to score. Lamely. Half-dead from kicking, I crept around Waukegan in my stepmother's car, leaning out the window and asking people at bus stops where to cop. But all I ever got was crack. I wanted to believe it was dope really bad, but it was crack.

"Hey what you got, man?"

"Crack rock, tens and twenties."

"How about some heroin?"

"We ain't got it man."

"Come on, I really need it."

The dealer looked at me. He saw I wouldn't take no for an answer.

"OK, here you go."

I gratefully gave him the money and he gave me the crack. Smoking crack while kicking is a really terrible idea. But in the Chicago suburbs I was unable to score any heroin that wasn't also crack. But, given that it was the North Shore of Chicago, I deserved some credit for even getting the crack. After about five days the withdrawals started to subside. My father gave me money to get my car back. My appetite came back. I started to smile again.

I spent the next six weeks in Chicago, recovering. My life, which had been so chaotic, settled into a comfortable pattern. At noon I would get out of bed. I would walk from the house to my car, which was parked on the side of the street. I would drink whiskey in my parked car and read Taco Bell wrappers while eating Taco Bell and drinking whiskey. A couple hours later, I'd drive the fifteen miles over to my friend Cash's apartment to smoke pot, take ephedrine, and play a video game called Star Wars Racer. I'd spend about five hours there. Then I'd drive back, taking the long, slow roads because my vision would start cutting out by then.

But let me tell you a little bit about Star Wars Racer. In the game, you control a futuristic racing machine. It looks kind of like a car. It works exactly like a car. You race around a futuristic video-racing course. The goal of the game is to out-race your opponent. My opponent was Cash.

"There you go, Mike! There you go," Cash said encouragingly. "Your hand-eye coordination is starting to come back. Your will to succeed is coming back. You're hungry again. It's the old Mike again!"

He beat me every single time. It was a kind of lesson. At the end of August I drove back to Baltimore. I got the sheaf of bills out of my mailbox in the lobby of my apartment building, and went up the elevator. It was early September and grad school was about to start back up. I was done with coursework, but would be teaching a composition class to earn the stipend that was supporting me while I was supposedly working on my dissertation.

"I'm going to really get going on my dissertation now," I said. "I've conquered dope, I'm strong and healthy, my future is bright."

I put the bills on my table and started responsibly to shuffle through them. Then I saw a little white powder out of the corner of my eye on the tabletop. In two seconds I'd rolled up a five-dollar bill and snorted it up. It tasted like dirt or dust. I sneezed. I had tears in my eyes. I ran out the door to cop some real dope.

A year later I was with Cat in Boston. We were visiting a friend of hers. I'd been off dope for two months. Cat didn't even remember that I'd ever used hard drugs. Or at least she didn't mention it.

I was tired after our long drive from Baltimore to Boston. I threw our bags on the bed of the guest room and went to the bathroom. I opened the medicine cabinet. Inside was a half-full bottle of Percocet. I took five instantly. I started to sweat with panic and desire.

"What's wrong, honey?" Cat said.

Her lovely long blonde hair set off her perfect tan skirt and long tan legs and high tan leather heels. It made my nose itch. It made my arms horny for needles.

"Nothing. I'm just a little tired. You guys go on out without me."

I took a cab to the local Greyhound station. I ended up copping from some skinheads.

Johns Hopkins at Bayview on the east side of town offered a detox program for heroin addicts. They shot me up with bup and gave me Tylenol in a baggie, just like the other places. But they had a more hands-on approach, a more psychological and scientific orientation.

"So what made you decide to get clean?" the nurse asked me. I was kind of surprised. This wasn't in the script.

"I just realized that heroin addiction was interfering with my future plans," I said cautiously. She nodded. I went on enthusiastically.

"You have to have something to believe in to quit," I told her. "You can't just quit for nothing." She nodded encouragingly.

"And I believe I have a bright future. It's like now my future will be my high."

I had just recently come up with this, after failing at the Center for Addiction Medicine again. Now, hearing myself tell it to someone else, I began to feel confident.

"Has any recent event caused you to want to quit?"

"Event? No." I paused. "I'm quitting because I've decided it is the rational thing to do." I smiled.

"Well," she said, "people often seek treatment due to some traumatic event. Did anything bad happen recently?"

"No," I said. "I'm more concerned with what hasn't happened recently. Being clean, for instance," I joked.

"Think," she pressed me. "Are you sure nothing bad has happened? Something that really might motivate you? Trouble with the law? Eviction? You discovered you have AIDS?"

What the hell was up with this lady?

"No, absolutely nothing bad has happened to me," I said firmly. "I have decided to quit because of my future. My bright future motivates me."

She smiled sadly and gave me my shot.

I lasted three days that time. It happened on the afternoon of the third day. I was going up the elevator to my apartment when I suddenly remembered what white tops look like. The doors opened at my floor. I quickly pressed the "close door" button with one finger and the button for the ground floor with the other. I tried not to think about what I was doing.

"Hurry, hurry, hurry, hurry," I said.

The doors closed. The elevator started to descend. Between the third and second floors the elevator clanged to a stop. I was the only one on it. It was the middle of an October weekday.

Most of the other residents would be at work, in the library, or in class. I was stuck.

This is a sign, I thought. *This is obviously a sign. The world is telling me that I have a choice. That I can make it. I can make it without dope. Remember my future.*

I banged on the elevator door. I pressed the emergency call button.

"Hello?" a heavily accented voice answered through the staticky elevator speaker.

"Ah, yes, I'm stuck up here in the elevator, between the third and second floors, I think. Could you come get me now?"

"You want to make order?"

"What? No. I'm . . . look, I'm stuck on this elevator!"

"Say more slowly please again," the voice said.

I suddenly recognized the voice. I broke into a cold sweat. It was the proprietor of the shitty Chinese restaurant on the ground floor of my building. Somehow the call box line was connected to his restaurant.

"Um, look I think there may be a mis—"

The line went dead. I began to wonder if the world was telling me to get high. I pressed the call button again.

"Hello?"

"Um, look. I know this seems weird, but I really am stuck in the elevator in this building. 3400 North Charles. Two-and-a-half floors above you. If you could just call the management company right away and—"

"If you no want order Chinese food no call Chinese restaurant!"

The line went dead. I slumped against the elevator wall. I closed my eyes and imagined a white top's cold head and beautiful glass throat. It was singing a little song. I jabbed the call button frantically.

"Do not hang up! This is not a joke. This is a serious emergency. There is a pregnant woman here in this elevator and—"

The line went dead. I remembered how fresh dope sometimes smells like new paint. My nose watered.

"What about my bright future?" I asked myself.

"The future lasts forever," I answered.

I banged fast and slow on the metal elevator door.

Twenty minutes later someone heard me banging and called the apartment people. They let me out and I ran down to my car and sped off to Pulaski Street.

The next day I wrote a threatening letter to the management accusing them of "false imprisonment." Plus I told them about how the elevator call box was connected to the Chinese restaurant. That was a serious conflict of interest.

In the letter they wrote back, they were careful not to admit any wrongdoing. The specter of their legal liability did not, however, entirely escape them. They offered me three months of free rent. That came in handy. Three months lasts a long time when you're a junkie. But the future lasts forever.

FOUR

HELLO, STRIPE

Where did the white tops get in? There are white doors and windows all through my life, but I remember a couple early ones.

For a long time, I would go to bed early. In summer, my bedtime came when it was still light out. There was a tree outside my window. Once it had two main branches. But by the time my memory starts it was Henry-shaped, its missing branch, lost in a storm, anchored it in the ocean of time before memory.

"Time for bed, Michael; give your father a hug."

"Yes, Dad."

With the lights out it was still light in my room. Sometimes my parents would be sitting out in the yard and their laughter would come in through the half-open window. A fan would be on, slowly mixing sleep into the heavy light. I'd fall asleep with one sticky eye on the tree. All those summer evenings, and eventually the one-armed tree got caught in me. Twelve years later, I recognized Henry the first time I saw him. Memory is like that.

My first word was *clock*. It's an unusual first word, spoken with unusual clarity, and my mother reports being startled, thinking someone else was in the room. My best friend was Dan Rest. I met him the week we arrived from Ireland. His last name is one of those deceptively simple German words, like *thing,* that obviously mean something else. Clock. Dan was completely American. I still had a strong Irish accent, and came equipped with all kinds of outlandish Irish things. Like a red leather satchel my mother gave me to take to first grade. Everyone else had backpacks made of some thin light material. I wanted a backpack like that. I quickly became an expert in these American things. I carefully studied backpacks, lunch boxes with cartoon characters on the outside, shiny Capri Sun juice pouches, Big Wheels, G.I. Joe action figures.

I knew the soft plastic hand strap of the lunch boxes better than the machine that made them, and could distinguish it from the slightly harder plastic of the cartoon thermos top, and the still harder plastic of the thermos body. I soon grew so proficient I could make these things out of my body. At night, lying in bed, my body was a factory for Big Wheels and blue nylon backpacks.

I had to make them, since my parents didn't have very much money at this time, and my mother was determined to exhaust the stock of Irish things before buying anything new. Of course, most of the things I made were invisible and didn't do me any good at school. But some did. My version of the movie *Gremlins* for example. *Gremlins* was the hottest movie at school, in the parks, on the block for a whole season. Some parents, including my own, wouldn't let their children see it, so those that did had a certain special grandeur.

I soon realized I had to see *Gremlins,* but since I couldn't see the one in the theater, I had to make it myself. I got a workable script from Dan, whose enlightened parents had taken him to it. It went like this: A father gets an unusual pet for his son, a Mogwai, a kind of small cute white furry animal. His delighted son names it "Gizmo." The old Chinese man the father purchases it from tells him not to get it wet and not to feed it after midnight. When the kid gets it wet, Gizmo multiplies. When the new Mogwais get food after midnight, they turn into terrifying monsters: gremlins. The worst gremlin is Stripe. He attacks people with a chainsaw. He drives a car. He throws lots of Mogwais into a big swimming pool.

I made the film that night before I fell asleep, and I was ready during recess at school the next day. The way this worked is that the kids who had seen the new cool movie would stand in the center of a semicircle of other kids, and trade reminiscences about it.

"Do you remember when Stripe gets that chainsaw? That was awesome!"

"What about when that tractor crashes through the window in the living room? Awesome!"

I stepped into the circle. "How about the part where he spills that glass of water on Gizmo?"

They looked at me. "*You* saw *Gremlins*?" I replayed the scene in my mind. The water blots out Gizmo's dog shape, leaving the thick body dough curling on the floor. Little stalks shoot up. Some thicken into dog shapes. Some turn into trees. One becomes a book. "Sure. He spills water on Gizmo and then there are all these other Mogwais. It's awesome!"

My conviction and intensity were not faked, and they saw and believed. I'd lain awake all the last night playing the movie in my mind. Standing in that circle, I saw every scene in color. My movie had grown far beyond the bounds of Dan's skimpy script, but I kept those rich scenes secret. The scene in my movie showing how Stripe actually gets the chainsaw remained secret. Other things about Stripe remained secret. The special secret of Stripe's birth remained secret.

You see, to me, this movie was more than just a way of increasing my status with my little friends. I really wanted to see *Gremlins,* but my parents wouldn't let me see the one in the theaters, so I had to make my own. In order for my *Gremlins* to be real, I needed that circle of kids. I didn't need the movie to be cool with them. I needed them in order to see the movie. That circle of kids was the projector that played the film I'd made. Focused by that semicircle, the watery images I'd made up in bed the previous night took on vivid colors, became real.

The others' presence was what allowed me to see something I couldn't see in any other way. Not just Stripe holding the chainsaw, but Stripe the master of water, Stripe born inside his enemies, born *of* his enemies. My *Gremlins* was real. In this movie made in my body and projected on that school recess semicircle, everyone and me dissolved. I didn't do it just to make friends. No one just wants that. People want something real from people. We want some thing. Relations between people are a means to an end, like ladders and cranes and movie projectors. People get together to bring new things into the world.

Another incident illustrates this principle. (Or is it an illness?) This was even earlier, touching that region of deep memory where my way of walking, the way I tie my shoes originates. There was a children's game called Candy Land and everyone had it, even me. Candy Land was beautiful. It was a board game, like Monopoly, and you moved your little piece around the board based on the cards you drew. I think it was one of those games without winners or losers, like life.

The board was a triumph of Art: It showed inherently beautiful things in a realistic way. Gumdrop mountains, a molasses swamp, candy canes a thousand feet tall. Like all great artworks, it was also a map, a map that showed new things in the little town we lived in. One afternoon on the swings I announced that Candy Land was a real place six blocks away from my house.

I continued to announce it to anyone who would listen.

"I know where Candy Land is. It's about six blocks away from here." Almost nothing lasts for a week in childhood. Wait a week, and if it's still there, it's real. The majority of the things that actually lasted tended to be dull things like chairs and people, so a certain disillusion, a certain suspicion of joy, already had a hold on even the youngest children of my block.

"Candy Land isn't real," my little sister, Jenny, said doubtfully.

But after a week I was still saying, "I know where Candy Land is." We were gathered by the Henry tree in my backyard, about eight of us, all little, except two monstrous eight-year-olds lurking in the background.

"Candy Land isn't real," Dan said doubtfully. The two older kids laughed, but they waited to hear what I'd say next.

"Yes it is, it's six blocks away from here."

"How do you know?" Marc asked.

"Because I heard the mailman talking about it. He didn't know I was there. He was talking to my mom. 'I have to go deliver my mail to Candy Land now, Mrs. Clune, so I can't talk to you anymore.' I was hiding. Then I came out and he gave me a Tootsie Pop."

This story, so weighted with real things, such as the mailman's known habit of distributing Tootsie Pops to children, was practically impossible for anyone to deny. Would saying my story wasn't true involve saying that it wasn't true that the mailman gave out Tootsie Pops? But we had all tasted those Tootsie Pops. We loved Tootsie Pops!

"Then how do you get there?" Dan asked. This was the great turning point. It was at moments like this I realized the magic fact that the inside of my body is bigger than the outside. My heart expanded. I could see the sun, blinding white on the candy canes.

"I told you and told you. It's six blocks away. I'm going to go there tomorrow after breakfast. I'm going to go on my tricycle. Jenny, you can bring the wagon."

"Can I bring my soccer ball?"

"Yes."

"Me too," Dan said. I nodded.

"Everyone can come, if you aren't scared."

But it *was* something to be scared of, since none of us were allowed beyond the block we lived on. Marc and Eric lived just one block away, and they required special permission to visit my house. When it was time for them to leave, my mother had to go with them and watch them cross the dangerous intersection of Kedzie and Michigan. There was so much traffic at that intersection there was a traffic light. If you stood out there, you didn't have to wait too many minutes before a car or even a bus drove through.

So the idea of us traveling six blocks on our own was just as difficult to believe as the idea of Candy Land. Marc and Eric, made acutely sensitive by their neurotic mother of the dangers of getting run over when crossing just *one* street, looked frankly stunned. The other kids shifted uncomfortably. The idea that we could cross six blocks on our own was turning out to be much more difficult to believe than the existence of Candy Land itself. In fact, it was impossible for anyone but Jenny to believe it. One of the eight-year-olds snorted. "You kids can't go six blocks!"

Perhaps originally I had put Candy Land at such a vast distance because if no one could go there, no one could prove it wasn't real. But now I wanted to go to Candy Land so badly that no obstacle would stop me. I paused. I thought. Yes.

"Candy Land is really only two blocks away."

Everyone looked at me. Marc and Eric suddenly smiled. Elizabeth, Dan, and the other Dan started smiling. "Yesssss!" Dan hissed, pumping his fist. Neal dropped the stick he was holding. Jenny began clapping insanely, then pushed my tricycle over. Ronald Reagan got shot, and my mother would be still crying about it when we went in for dinner a couple hours later. We were going to Candy Land.

"Everyone meet in front of my house tomorrow after breakfast." It would be almost impossible to wait.

"You have to *remember*," Elizabeth whispered to the other Dan, poking a sharp stick deep into his side. In doing this, she showed an uncanny wisdom regarding memory. You can't just expect to remember something, no matter how important it seems at the time. You have to make a place for it in your body. Elizabeth made a place for Candy Land in Dan's body with her stick, and tomorrow he would be waiting outside my house before anyone else showed up.

In the manic hours before dinner we gave ourselves over to discussing what Candy Land was like. I had no special authority in these discussions. I was just another participant, just as eagerly curious as the rest, advancing my tentative ideas, accepting the criticism of others, and offering my own. Discussion centered on five topics. (1) The size of Candy Land. (2) The Gumdrop Mountains. (3) Time in Candy Land. (4) Ability to take candy back from Candy Land. (5) Relation of Star Wars to

Candy Land. No consensus was reached on any of these topics, though almost unbearably exciting possibilities were opened, especially in the discussion of #5.

The older kids were active and eager participants. No one knew exactly what the imminent discovery of Candy Land meant, but it was clear that formerly decisive differences in age could have no significance in this new world. We dispersed at dinner. My mother was red-eyed and explained to us how horrible it was that anyone could shoot the president. They showed the sequence on television. Secret Service leaping around and waving Uzis and shoving Reagan into a car. It was amazingly confusing, but I got the sense that people wore suits to conceal guns. I don't know how I slept that night.

I don't know who I was. I was maybe five. I was rather different, and much larger, than I appeared. I'm past thirty now. Maybe today it's not so intense, but it's not as if this identity-problem thing stops in childhood, as if it's a "condition," like being small. I know people sometimes talk about this trouble with the self as if there is more than one person inside the "I." As if "I" is like a little town or community. Or they say the "I" is made up of a bunch of different things that are not "I's," and it has cracks in it, like a geode. Some even say there is no "I." Some say God lives in the "I." Or God is the only "I" and we are always "you." Some say we die and are reborn ten thousand times every second. Or that the "I" is like a swinging door between different rooms. Or like two helicopter blades spinning so fast they look like one. Or a prison. Or anything you can make a sentence say it is. Or a devil. Or a kind of dog.

I think it's lots of these and more. For example, I'm writing this. I'm drinking some water. I do this and that. Now I'm happy and now I'm sad. But where exactly do the different states of me stop and start? I've never been able to find a seam or a stitch anywhere. Not even between the states most impossible to fit together. Not even the cure for the memory disease. From a distance, to other people, the cure looks like a real break, a real difference between a bad, sick me and a good, cured me. But when I look closer, as I'm looking now, where exactly is the difference? The difference spreads out until it's hard to see.

Whoever I was, and however I slept, I couldn't eat my breakfast. Jenny did.

"We're going to Candy Land today, Mom." I glared at her. White all around each iris.

"That's nice, Jenny. You kids have to remember to take all your stuff inside when you come in. It rained last night and your dad found one of Jenny's dolls ruined on the sidewalk today when he left for work."

Jenny began to cry, was comforted, ate some of my untouched breakfast, clapped her hands. Out of control. I had to go to the bathroom. Breakfast plates cleared, dressed and ready. Mom let us outside. The other Dan was waiting on the sidewalk. He looked like he had to go to the bathroom.

"Are we . . .," he said weakly.

"Candy Land," I said. I felt like I was going to throw up.

We didn't have to wait long. I couldn't have waited. Dan Rest came on his Big Wheel. Neel came on foot. Elizabeth came on foot. Marc and Eric crossed the street under the eyes of their bathrobed mother, then ran up to us. One of the eight-year-olds, to his lasting shame, showed up. He rode up on a large bike without training wheels, looking down, not meeting anyone's eyes.

With me in the lead, we set off down the block. Candy Land, as I'd specified the night before, was two blocks down. At the big white apartment building on the corner of the next block, which we could see distantly from my house, we would turn right, and when we turned that corner, we would see Candy Land.

I wasn't lying. I was more like a kind of oracle. I was as hopeful, submissive, and suspicious of the god or thing that spoke through me as any of my companions. A sincere seeker. In retrospect, I'm sure that eight-year-old had actually turned that corner before, but there he was. And he was so old he was already listening to rock music. He even said he had a Billy Idol poster in his room.

The white apartment building grew larger as our little caravan biked, skipped, and jogged forward. I stared wonderingly at the bright façade, impressed by the mystic quality of the white bricks set in one face of a building whose other face turned toward Candy Land.

There was some laughter and talking, chiefly from Jenny and Eric, while we were still on our block, but after we had crossed the deserted street to the next block, everyone was silent. This was new pavement. Unfamiliar squares of lawn, strange mailboxes, strange flowers. Six, almost seven steps between sidewalk cracks here, unusual, inexplicable. It was five on our block.

"This is a really old block," Marc said in a hushed, astonished voice.

There was no more thinking or wondering, only steps and pushed pedals and breathing. The white building loomed, impossibly solid, built in 3000 B.C. I saw there were four cracks until the corner. Three. Two.

"OK everyone, wait up." That was Dan, with his admirable American practicality. We waited until Jenny and Eric caught up with us. I looked at Elizabeth. Her mouth was open. Marc was smiling, his face lit by the sun coming off the white apartment building. His small white teeth.

"OK." We moved forward. The apartment building came to a sharp edge, then stopped. I kept my eyes firmly on the ground, two inches before my feet. I heard nothing but my heart. The sidewalk turned at a right angle and I turned with it. I looked up.

There was a vast white space. Clocks and guns and tricycles were falling slowly somewhere in the whiteness. Rising forever, falling forever. There was a fish wearing a kind of silver belt. It swam closer and I saw its tail was a thumb. It was a human hand. The big hand of the watch pointed at the two.

"Whoa," I said.

"Yeah," Chip said.

"Wow," said Eva. "What time is it?"

"Two." We all started laughing. The first time you do white tops, the dope feels kind of good as it leaves your body. A kind of tickling, like moving an arm that has fallen asleep.

FIVE

EVERYTHING IS GREEN

That was in July of 1997. My diseased memory is like a mummi-fied baby. Whiteness wrapped in whiteness. Like Candy Land, a memory might look dusty with colors, but as I unwind it, it grows white. The first time I did dope is the mummy's white heart, pumping whiteness. Chip, Eva, and I did it together. We had been inseparable since January. A love triangle. A triangle is a magic shape. A pyramid is a kind of triangle. The ancient Egyptians recognized the sacredness of the space spread open by the triangle's three points.

In a relationship between two people, there are only two points. The relationship is a straight line between two points. A straight line takes up no space. It is abstract. Spacelessness is the key feature of an intense relationship between two people. The clichés of love relationships between two people (I disappear into you, nothing else exists for me when you enter the room) express this spacelessness.

Lovers see each other's bodies as doors or windows to some-where else. Individually, they are still in the world, but their relationship is not. The odd concept of "soul" probably comes from this odd experience of love between two people: I am here but not here. This can be wonderful and uncanny, like nitrous oxide.

In a love triangle, there are no souls or empty spaces, no disappearing. The space stretched between the three points is full, tense, electric. Eva lounges on the couch, turns her wonderful smile on me. I smile back. Chip, pretending to do a crossword puzzle, watches us. As he watches the look pass between her and me, he thickens and charges it. His gaze puts the moment between Eva and me into three dimensions. He keeps it from disappearing. The space between the three people in a love triangle is the most solid space on earth. A body doesn't cast a shadow there.

It was in this bright space that the white tops first showed up for me. They didn't show up right away. It took about six months, and it began that January.

January 1997 should have been the start of my final semester in college, but I'd been suspended for the first half of my junior year for disciplinary reasons, so I would have to come back the following fall. January in Oberlin, Ohio, is glacial. If you live in an expensive house, or even in a clean one, it has a certain icy blue grandeur. But if you live in "the filthiest house in America," it feels like someone spit on you, and you couldn't or wouldn't wipe it off. It feels like you wet your pants and sat in them. There's something sordid about that kind of cold. The smell of stale cigarettes and sour beer. You can see your breath in the living room.

Always a little numb. Like being poorly anesthetized for an operation. Six of us rented rooms in that house, and if you include boy- and girlfriends there were ten to twelve people living there. It was a big old white house on a pleasant corner lot about five blocks from campus. I think a room went for about $180/month, and it included heat, which the devil landlord kept on the low end. The paint was peeling and it had a caved-in look from the outside. Maybe that was an optical illusion from knowing what the inside was like. Really, it didn't look too bad from the outside.

"The filthiest house in America" wasn't our idea. We called it "Big Five," an obscure student name the house had had for years, and which was said to derive from an old Prince Buster ska song. But in early January our neighbors sent in photos of our living room to the *Jenny Jones Show,* which was soliciting participants for a show on the nation's dirtiest houses and the scumbags who live in them. When the Jenny Jones people got the pictures they sent a camera crew out. They filmed us sitting and talking in the ankle-high pile of empty pizza boxes, cigarette butts, broken glass, used condoms, records, squirt guns, and stiff paintbrushes. They filmed the vintage dentist's chair, the velvet Elvises, the mannequins. They filmed the beer sludge in the bathroom and the gouge on the wall where a thrown TV had landed. Then they flew three of the pretty girls that lived with us out to Chicago to tape the show.

Ann got picked to go. She was Sparky's girlfriend. I felt I should have gone instead of her. But she was prettier than me. They wanted the contrast, I guess. One angry woman in the audience called Ann a tramp. Ann looked proud. She was trying to appear educated and superior to such bourgeois name-calling. But on TV she came off as looking proud to be called a tramp.

Part of the Jenny Jones deal was that they did a complete makeover of the ground floor of the house. ServiceMaster came out with masks and work gloves and cleared the place out. Then came the painters and carpet guys and fake plant people and furniture delivery guys. When it was all done, it looked like a doctor's waiting room. I waited to get high in it.

The whole makeover cost Jenny Jones over twenty thousand dollars. At the end of the semester we would become embroiled in a dispute with our landlord over ownership of the new furniture and Scott and Christian would end up setting it all on fire and throwing it off the roof. We were all middle-class kids, training ourselves for our inevitable drop out of the middle class once we graduated. I remember Christian, drunk at 10:00 a.m., dressed in his white painter's suit standing nervously next to one of the Jenny Jones painters, looking as if he were auditioning for a working-class job. How about no job? Class feeling is deeper than an ocean.

But that's in the future, after graduation (the future lasts forever). At the end of that January, I sat gingerly at the edge of one of the new couches. I thumbed through a magazine. I took tiny nibbling bites from a slice of bread I held in one hand. I took large swigs from a bottle of Mylanta. I took smaller swigs from a bottle of Pepto-Bismol. Alix sat down across from me. "How's your ulcer, Mike?" She probably didn't mean it to sound callous, but it did. And actually she probably did mean it to sound callous. She was my ex-girlfriend, who now, through a series of strange reversals, was living in Big Five. I was still technically involved with a Korean violinist who actually had a Stradivarius. I even held it and drew the weightless bow across the strings. It was worth millions of dollars. The chairman of Mitsubishi or someone like that had bought it for her.

"It sucks, Alix. I can't drink. And if I can't drink, I can't get drunk." I was eager to talk about it. I felt she was obligated to listen since she'd been there the night the ulcer had erupted. We'd been drinking in a Chinese restaurant when the dull pain that had been throbbing in my stomach for weeks suddenly disappeared. It was gone, then there was a sudden *twist*. I don't know how else to describe it. I'm kind of partial to this sensation because it is one of the few feelings in my memory the whiteness has never touched.

They say you can't remember pain. This *twist* sensation wasn't painful, and it wasn't exactly pleasurable. It was a high, sweet sensation. At that upper register of sensation the distinction between pain and pleasure falls away. You can remember something like that. The center of me shifted and twisted, and when it was over there was no center anymore. I ran to the bathroom and just made it. I limped home to bed and threw up for the next few hours.

I lay alone in the cold, sordid darkness with my belly full of glass. The sound of drunken laughter came up through the floorboards. There was warmth in it, summer warmth. I'd never felt so lonely. I kept thinking, *I can't drink anymore.* No center. I'd been standing on wet cardboard and pouring whiskey on it. Now I'd fallen through. I hadn't been to the doctor yet, but the message of that divine twist in my stomach was pretty clear: No more drinking for a long time. And without drinking to dissolve the walls and locks and bars of me, I couldn't relax around people. And if I couldn't relax around people, there would be no Candy Land, no *Gremlins,* no magic, no escaping, no dissolving. Transformations suspended. A secret, ancient loneliness with no language. Alix's blonde laughter wheeled high above the wall.

Many hours later, Alix crept up the stairs and opened my door. I was still awake. She leaned close to me, vodka fumes rising from her half-open mouth.

"Are you feeling better?"

"Kind of," I lied.

"We're having so much fun. Come down and have a drink?"

"I can't." She stumbled a little and stood up, looking around at the dark nothing on all sides of the half-open door.

"It's *boring* up here!" she tittered drunkenly and walked out, leaving the door open.

So the rest of January and all of February and March I wasn't relaxed at the bars or laughing at the parties. I was waiting on the couch in the Jenny Jones waiting room at Big Five. The doctor said it would probably be three months of the strong medicine he gave me before the ulcer would be healed. After a while the daze of loneliness lifted a bit and I noticed there were a couple of others who spent a lot of time on the couch. It was in the middle of a movie that I noticed. A zombie movie.

"So tell me what I've missed," Chip said, sitting back down on the couch and opening his sketch pad.

"Well, he accidentally left the door open when he went back up to his hiding place and now . . ." I gestured at the screen. The zombies were slowly eating him. They moved through his flesh like they were wading through water. Their stone eyes were just more zombie surface. Perfect. Their clothes were eaten out. The flesh that showed through was whiter than bone.

"Is he the last one left alive, then?"

"Yes."

"Good." Chip passed me his sketchbook. It was a poster design to advertise the party Big Five was throwing that weekend. In the center was a pair of dice. IMAGINE THE

POSSIBILI-TITTIES was printed in large block letters at the top.

"Nice." I said. We threw these parties periodically to raise money, trading on the house's vague reputation for licentiousness to charge hundreds of freshmen five dollars each to stand on the crowded porch in the freezing cold holding an empty cup and asking where the beer was.

"What are you going to do while the party is going on?" he asked.

"I don't know."

"Why don't we go bowling?"

Chip was a master of mildly pleasant activities. Confidence-building measures. Card games, crossword puzzles, bowling. To me this was immensely attractive. The movie was over. I was sitting on the couch tearing a piece of paper into smaller and smaller pieces. The pieces got too small. I started flicking my cigarette lighter. I reached down to the floor, picked up a filthy cigarette butt, and began pulling it apart. Chip looked up.

"Why don't we play a game of chess, Mike?"

I nodded gratefully. People like Chip founded civilization.

"Your move, Mike."

"Why don't we listen to a little Pixies?"

"Why don't I just put on some tea?" No intense, bright flashes. Just a steady, accumulating process. After college, when he moved back to New York, he even attracted a sort of salon of interesting and artistic people, who flocked to the pleasant, open atmosphere that rose from his constant, mild, unobtrusive activity. In the old days, as I gather from novels I've read, a woman would have done this kind of thing. And if the figure of Woman has a human face in my memory, her face is not my mother's. It's Chip's. The little knickknacks and curiosities he'd collect. Little witty turns of speech. Regular habits. He had OCD.

He also had the feminine power of bringing something new into the world. And the feminine power of making a place for it, where it would stay and grow. He made cradles for it, knitted sweaters for it. When I discovered a new kick, it might wipe out a day or a weekend. For Chip, it would become the new crossword puzzle. It would be there every day.

"Your move." Is it worth describing people who just disappear? But they don't, not really. They go into memory. Into the memory disease. Not quite people anymore. Today, for example, as I write this, it's lovely June. The light reminds me of something . . . a cloud opening, and a blue memory snake coils out. There are faces moving in its sides. "Your move." Eva walked in, kissed Chip on the forehead, and slumped down in the chair.

"Charlie's driving me crazy! He made us rehearse the scene like six times in a row, all the way through. And he'd just *be* there, crouched down, *staring* at us!"

"Charlie is crazy," Chip said cleanly, moving a rook.

"I should have been there," I said. "I'm the co-director." Eva laughed and turned to Chip.

"Mike came during the last rehearsal. All he did was tell everyone they had to make their voices sound *stranger.* He made us say our lines over and over again really quickly until the words stopped making sense. Then he'd tell us to stretch out the vowels crazily. Even to add extra sounds. Here's what my first line sounded like." She demonstrated. It was incomprehensible.

"It's supposed to be a surreal play," I said defensively. "And the writing isn't really very good so we have to express the surreal through other means."

"But it sounds like gobbledygook! No one will be able to understand a single word!"

"Well Charlie likes it," I countered.

"Yeah, that's the terrible thing, Chip. That was like the only idea of Mike's that Charlie liked. I mean, it's the worst idea ever, *guaranteed* to make the play totally unwatchable. And Charlie loves it! He's all *intense* about it. He'll walk up behind you, 'Now break that word down. Break it down!' It's so creepy."

We laughed. The play was going to be a complete disaster. We'd just gotten another two grand from the college for costumes. The production was like an octopus. It had nearly every one of our friends in its tentacles. Todd was doing electronic music. Dan was doing silkscreen posters. Liz and Scott were designing sets. Emily was helping with costumes. At least thirty others were involved at various levels. Gary and Lisa were even driving a van into Cleveland twice a week on play business. Charlie rushed back and forth without sleep, without shaving, like octopus blood. He kept the octopus going, until it collapsed on May 15 in the amphitheater, sagging and pumping blood under the glare of one hundred and twenty tiki torches, fifteen floodlights, and maybe a hundred drunken spectators.

Eva looked at me slyly.

"How are things with your girl?"

"Bad," I said. "The ulcer makes it so I can't drink."

"So?"

"So I don't know how to do it. I haven't had sober sex since I was like," I paused and thought, "eight. And that was with my uncle. So I didn't have much to do." Chip laughed.

Eva looked shocked. Fake shocked. Her mouth opened. Eva's fake shocked look was the center of sexiness. It was a hole in sexiness and everything slid down toward it. It would be under me in two months, her open-mouth shocked look, red cheeks, heavy breaths. My life was sliding down toward it.

She started to laugh, and her sexy punctured look smoothed out with a ripple. Like a baby swallowing. Now it was blonde hair, warm blue eyes, fine Dutch cheekbones. Only a little tremble in the smile showed that her face unhinged and opened around thick jets of ecstasy. That her eyes shot disappearance beams. Not that I knew for sure. Not yet.

Chip looked up and saw me looking at her, and her looking at me. The line between us thickened, opened out, and grew solid. A place in the world. The living room of Big Five, March 1997. The day had been warm and it was foggy out. Eva went into the kitchen and returned with a beer. I felt a phantom twist and a pang of loneliness. But Chip didn't drink and he was showing me how to do it. He had acid reflux. Plus I don't think he even liked drinking.

"Your turn," Chip watched the chessboard. Zombies moved slowly through the rain outside. I studied the board, lighting a cigarette. Chip flipped through a magazine.

"Class feeling is deeper than an ocean. Who said that, Mike?"

"Chairman Mao," I said, studying the board. Eva flipped through the channels, found *Gremlins,* and sat watching it as she sipped her beer. Out of the corner of my eye I saw Stripe spray-paint a white circle on the wall of the closet they'd trapped him in, and disappear into it. Eva laughed.

"Man, you're taking *forever,*" Chip muttered.

"Just chill out." I leaned in to move, then sat back. I was happy, I realized. Maybe happier than I'd ever been.

People get together to bring new things into the world. And after a couple triangular months, something new was starting to show. Just in time, too, because the triangle was starting to collapse, two points were starting to slide together. Eva standing behind Chip's back, mouthing "I love you" to me and laughing. I was laughing. Chip was laughing. If she kept that up, space itself would start collapsing. There isn't very much space between two people in love. "Two is the loneliest number." Other things were starting to collapse. The octopus play. The fragile respect enforced by the doctor's waiting-room furniture.

"How about this?" Christian dropped a bucket full of bricks through the Jenny Jones coffee table. As soon as everyone saw it everyone knew it was just what we needed: a nice hole to put garbage in. Spring was sliding in. Spring was sliding thousands of needles into whatever was solid, fast, or frozen. Ice, the color gray, sleep: All died the death of a thousand needles. Voices didn't carry the way they carried across the smooth frozen spaces of winter. They sank into the mud. Or the husks melted off and released thousands of whispers: "OK just for a second or two but I hear Chip coming . . ."

The beach was under the sidewalk. Peace and heat rose through the holes appearing everywhere. The spring revolution.

Eva had given me a light green military-style jacket and I wore it everywhere. There was a photo in a book I had. It showed a man with a peasant hat and a jacket kind of like the one I had walking along a sidewalk. He had a folder under his arm and a man and a woman on either side of him. They were obviously all good friends. The caption read: "Josef Stalin walking to a meeting of the Central Committee, May 1922."

That was the time! When he could still just walk down the street, unafraid, unparanoid, to a meeting of the Central Committee. It became a little mantra for me: "I'm walking to a meeting of the Central Committee." The casualness, the soft green light of revolutionary power. I was smoking a lot of pot. Wherever I was, I was also somewhere else. The picture of Stalin gave me a sort of symbol for this magic feeling: There he was, just a man walking down the street, but he was also something else! I didn't know what else I was. That's what made smoking pot a soft revolution. A spring revolution.

If it was a surprise to see Stalin just walking down the street, it was also a surprise to see me. A surprise to me. The spring, the end of ulcer pain, future love, love of the future, and pot conspired to blur me out. Moving through the weeks like a Slinky, spread out over April May and June like a pack of cards spread out on a table. Talking with Charlie at the rehearsal, eating lunch with Emily on the grass, sitting in Professor Morris's Islamic Mystical Poetry class: Put a knife through any one and it would go through all three. I was never completely in one place. Except when I was with Chip and Eva. Then the Slinky folded up, the cards returned to the pack, my body didn't cast a shadow.

A couple other people, using enough force, could still nail me to a single instant.

"Hey, Mike." It was Charlie. He was wearing a sky-blue suit that must have been made in the seventies. Perfectly pressed, perfectly preserved. "Hey, Mike."

"What's up, man?"

"Do you remember the people who lived behind my dorm sophomore year?"

"Yeah."

"What do you think of them?"

"They remind me of garbage," I said. I laughed.

Something in Charlie's face stopped me.

"Be serious, Mike. This is very serious. In fact," his face lost all elasticity, "this is really very serious." As a child, you learn very early to identify a wide range of facial expressions. These are so various, and express so many degrees of feeling, that they appear to exhaust all the possible movements of the human face. But they do not, and I know they don't, because I was looking at Charlie, and he wasn't wearing one of those expressions. He wasn't wearing one of those expressions I'd ever seen before.

"Do you," he half-whispered, "do you remember those *fucking* people?" I shook my head.

"What people, Charlie?" I was sitting in a lawn chair smoking on Big Five's spacious lawn. Charlie was about three feet away, crouched on his haunches facing me. He lobstered slowly up, still crouching, one thigh at a time, until he was a foot away from me. This didn't look easy. He was a big guy, six foot two, maybe 230 pounds. In addition to his many other creative talents, he was a modern dancer. It had given him thighs of steel.

"I really don't know," I said. I paused. I was about to say, "I really don't know what the hell you're talking about," but I thought better of it. "I really don't know who exactly you mean, Charlie. I'm trying to remember."

He sighed, still looking straight at me, as if deeply disappointed.

"They live in the old white house right behind Harkness." Harkness was the name of the dorm he'd lived in sophomore year. "Now do you remember?" I shook my head. "Mr. and Mrs. Anderson. Maybe you never met them. Lucky. You're real lucky, Mike. Just like you're real lucky to have such good friends. Chip for example. And Eva. She's such a *nice* friend," he sneered.

"Mr. and Mrs. Anderson," he continued. "They're, I don't know, maybe fifty. Mid-fifties, something like that. He's a big, strong man. Like a big bear. Big shaggy eyebrows. Business man. Mr. Business. And he talks . . . like . . . this." Charlie demonstrated, his elastic actor's face and arms imitating a solid, no-nonsense middle-aged man.

"And she's a proper housewife. Garden. Church. Everyone loves her. 'Oh! How *are* you Charlie? Come on in!'" He did a grotesque imitation of a middle-aged woman's high voice. It might have been funny. But while he was doing it, Charlie's mouth maintained its horrible grimace, showing through like a hole poked through a mask so the wearer can breathe.

"'Come on *in* Charlie! Oh don't sit there; you'll get it dirty! Let's go on down to the basement where we can sit down and talk a bit.' They're evil people Mike. 'Come on *in* Charlie! Come on *innnn*!'"

"What—" I began.

"They molested me," he said. It was warm. The heated air was intimate.

"Do you remember," he continued, "that year in Harkness, I had John and Dirty Ray staying in my room for like two months?" I did remember. John was a teenage drug dealer whose brother had killed a gas station attendant with a screwdriver the year before. Charlie had done a large painting of a screwdriver and given it to John as a present. John loved it. Two years later, after I graduated, I'd hear from James that John had held up the same gas station, shot someone (not fatally), got caught on tape, and was doing ten to fifteen. Ray was a huge blond hippie.

"Mike, do you remember we used to get in fights all the time? 'Play' fights?" I remember sitting on Charlie's bed. Charlie was painting in the corner. Ray was breaking down a quarter-pound of weed. John leapt in and grabbed the scale. "Give it back John." "Fuck you Ray." Ray grabbed John, they stumbled over Charlie, Charlie, grinning, got up and began beating Ray with a broom.

"And you remember that broom?"

"Sure," I said.

"Well do you remember the time John held me while Dirty Ray pulled down my pants and stuck the broom handle up my ass while James filmed it?"

Strangely enough, I did kind of remember that. It didn't seem very unusual at the time. I was in and out in those days. Even then Charlie was not an everyday guy. I don't think I actually saw the broom-handle incident, but I remember people talking about it.

"Well, when you put it like that, Charlie."

"Put it like what?" he whispered. "It was rape."

"*Rape*'s kind of an intense word, Charlie. You'd wrecked Ray's bike or something, and he was mad, and afterward you stole a bunch of acid he had or something. I don't know, *I* couldn't have hung out there all the time. But you guys were all friends. Crazy stuff like that was always happening in that room."

"I know," Charlie said darkly.

"But now," I said, trying to be sensitive, "thinking about it, it does seem kind of awful."

"I know," Charlie muttered. "It was especially awful for me," he continued. "Because the Andersons constantly molested me.

"They'd take me downstairs. She would hold both of my hands. Soft at first, but then tight." He demonstrated, grabbing my wrists.

"She'd have hot chocolate. Mountain Dew. But not too much because I'd have to go to the bathroom." I had a bad thought. "Mr. Anderson would wave to me if he saw me on the street. 'Hey how are ya, Charlie!'"

Granted, the Dirty Ray incident, taken out of the haze and smoke of Charlie's dorm room two years ago and placed in the strong spring sunlight, didn't look too good. But it would be insane to believe that big, strong Charlie had been molested two years ago by a middle-aged couple living behind his dorm.

"Only two sips of Mountain Dew. But I'd have to go to the bathroom anyway."

Could he be talking about something that had really happened to him? Maybe in his childhood? Maybe in another old white house? Had the white of another white house gotten stuck to the house behind Harkness? Or could it be possible that a couple who had molested Charlie when he was a child was now living here in Ohio?

"They said if I ever told anyone they'd kill me. Well you know what, Mike? You know what?" I shook my head. I was very aware of everything that was happening. "Maybe I should kill them. I've got everything I need. I've been watching their house. I know when they go to sleep."

"Charlie, I—" He cut me off. His eyes were white all the way around the iris.

"No, why should I go to jail? Let them. I'm going to go to the police. I'll show them where it is. The basement." Half a foot from my face, his intense white eyes stared through me.

"Charlie—"

"Because I don't know if I can take knowing they're out there anymore, Mike."

I had another bad thought. More than likely there was no other white house in Charlie's childhood, no evil older couple anywhere. It would be insane to believe what Charlie was saying. It would be insane to believe what Charlie obviously believed.

This wasn't the first time. Cash. Andy. Funboy. Dorsom. All my life I've been drawn to extrasensory people. People who see through things. Charlie's too-white eyes kept staring through me. Sweat shone on his cheeks. I was drawn to people who wanted things. "I'll kill them, Mike." What did Charlie want? There was some red in his eyes now, and they were full of tears. Andy and Dorsom are dead. Cash is in an institution. I don't know where Charlie is. There is no end to wanting. When you have senses that go through things like a chainsaw, one day you'll look around and there will be nothing left.

To write is to study the self. To study the self is to forget the self. To forget the self is to be open to all things. As I'm writing this, I occasionally stop to look out the window and remember so I can write a little more. Sometimes, now for instance, the tree outside my window stops my look. Like a raised hand, palm outward.

I convinced Charlie not to go to the cops by telling him I'd help him get the Andersons. My attitude in those days was that if your friend started acting like Charlie was acting, it was your job to keep him out of the asylum. Besides, I couldn't be sure it wasn't just some kind of bad trip. It was impossible to tell with Charlie. He *came* to college declaring that acid no longer had any effect on him. On the way to the car, we ran into Chip and Eva, who looked like they'd been arguing. Eager for help, I asked if they wanted to go for a ride with us. They did.

Chip in the passenger seat, Charlie and Eva in the back, me driving. Charlie was caught and held in triangular space. Quieted. He stared out the window. We set off through the dusk. Eighty degrees, windows down, "God Only Knows" by the Beach Boys on the stereo.

Chip was smiling and tapping his feet. I looked through the rearview mirror. Eva had a soft smile on her lovely face and was swaying gently. Charlie was bone white and looked like he was about to throw up.

"Turn that fucking music off!" he snapped. "God only knows? God only goddamn knows?" I turned off the music.

"Are you carsick?" I asked gently.

It was too late to turn back. ("I don't want to ruin our little trip," Charlie said ominously.) I'd been planning to drive to a quiet bar a little way out of town where we could all just relax and talk Charlie down out of whatever he was going through. I now decided that would be inappropriate. There was a forest preserve on the way, and while it technically closed at sunset, no one ever got busted for being there. When I was feeling down, I often took walks by the lake. I had fond memories of the place.

"I absolutely agree that your feelings about this are very valid," Charlie was telling Eva as we pulled in, "but I just have a tiny question about whether it's healthy, not for us, but for you." As the disastrous premiere of our play approached, Eva had been trying to drop out and get her understudy to take over her role.

"How is it not healthy for me?" she asked.

"Maybe it is, maybe it is," Charlie smoothly answered. "Maybe it is healthy for you. I just wonder if you are really going to do it. There's a big difference between wanting to do something and actually going ahead and doing it. I don't know how you get past that difference. I really don't. I want to work with you on it." Charlie was a great director.

I nodded in the rearview mirror, wanting to encourage Charlie's interest in healthy things.

"You know, what Charlie says makes a lot of sense, Eva," I said. "And he's not telling you to do one thing or another. He's just talking generally about some potential problems with action in general."

Charlie nodded vigorously. "That's absolutely right, Mike. You have a clear sense of your options, Eva. Probably a clearer sense than anyone in this car. And you know which one you prefer, which is really very healthy. We're just trying to clear away some of the things that can come between deciding to do something and doing it. Some of the garbage."

I was very satisfied with this kind of talk. Confidence building. It built a healthy sense of camaraderie without raising any potentially thorny issues.

"I'm not saying there *are* going to be problems in this particular case," Charlie continued. "I'm not saying there *are* any problems at all." I nodded around at everyone. No problems.

"You're not saying anything at all," Chip said dryly. "Of course Eva can't quit the play. It opens in two weeks. She's the only one who knows the lines. Her 'understudy' Allie has never even been to a single rehearsal. I don't know why you can't just say what you mean for once, Charlie." I was extremely disappointed by Chip's attitude and tone. I parked the car.

"You're a very superior person, Chip," Charlie said. "You remind me of Mr. Anderson."

"Who's Mr. Anderson?"

"OK let's get going," I said loudly. "Chip, do me a favor and get the beer out of the trunk. Charlie, can I bum a cigarette?"

As we walked to the picnic benches, Charlie was humming "God Only Knows."

When we got there, opened the beer, and looked around, we were all suddenly overwhelmed by space. The vastness of space seemed literally to push the words back into our faces. It was a clear spring evening; you could see the stars, the distant hills over the lake, the acres of grass stretching toward the highway. There was even a house in the distance. One of those uncanny middle-Ohio houses. An ordinary suburban house missing a suburb. Sitting in a vast empty field. Folded in on itself like an ear. Focusing all that silence, all that emptiness. The horrible little kitchen windows looked out over acres of dead or living grass. It was easy to imagine Mr. and Mrs. Anderson living in such a house.

SIX

WHITE OUT

Chip graduated that May. Eva and I would be back the next fall. We'd be living together, too. But for the summer, Eva and Chip were living in his apartment in SoHo. I flew in from Chicago to spend a week with them in July. As soon as I walked through the door, Eva hugged me, her face shining. Chip gestured toward the dining room table, where there was a shaving mirror with several white lines on it.

"What's this, coke? You know I don't like coke," I said, dropping my bag.

"No," Chip said.

"What, the other thing?"

"Yes." Eva stood in the corner, watching me. Chip was in the doorway, watching her watching me. I stood against the wall. The mirror with the white thing lay on a table in the center of the triangle.

The first time is magic. What does that really mean? Let's start with another, more familiar kind of first-time magic. I love pop songs, and the first time you hear a really great pop song is magic. For instance, today is Saturday. On Tuesday, I bought a CD by a band called Gnarls Barkley, which several people had recommended to me. And Kelefa Sanneh, my favorite music critic, in his column for the *New York Times* called track two, "Crazy," the best pop song of the year.

So I put it in my car's CD player with a sense of anticipation. The first time you hear a song, it isn't very clear. That is, you don't recognize its shape. You can't, because you've never heard it before. Listening to "Crazy" for the first time, I didn't recognize the throb of the bass before the vocals start, because I didn't know the vocals were about to start. On a more microscopic level, I didn't recognize the bass as a throb because I didn't know the bass would keep repeating the same note throughout the entire song. I loved it, absolutely and instantly, but I didn't love the tripping way Cee-Lo sang "live life" in the line "My heroes had the heart to live life out on a limb." When I heard "live," I didn't know "life" was coming. When I heard "limb," I didn't remember the line had begun with "My heroes." I wasn't sure the line was over. I didn't know what exactly I was hearing. It was the first time I'd ever heard it.

I got an instant joy from the song. I was smiling after ten seconds. But what I listened to, what made me smile, wasn't exactly the shape of the song. I wasn't sure what its shape was. That shape would gradually come into focus as I heard the song again and again. Already by the second listen, I heard the throbbing bass before the vocals start. By the fourth, I loved the tripping way Cee-Lo sang "live life." And now, after hearing it maybe thirty times, I know the song's shape. And I really like it; it's just an amazing, perfectly crafted pop song. I recommend it to everyone I know.

But the magic has vanished. The song's shape is very clear to me now. If you played three seconds of it I'd be able to identify it. This clear, perfect song stands where the magic used to be. I no longer feel there is a new hole in the world, and that every future thing is streaming in from it. That hole has been plugged. It's been plugged by the song. By the throbbing bass, by Cee-Lo's tripping singing stutter. The shape of the song is the fossil of the magic. Good-bye "Crazy"! But what am I saying good-bye to? The CD is still in my player. I still listen to it sometimes. Then good-bye to the invisible, inaudible "Crazy," the magic, first-time "Crazy," the angel "Crazy."

This is what "the first time is magic" means with most things. As you become more familiar with the shape of a song or a face, the magic sensation you had the first time slowly drifts away from it. The magic drifts away from the thing, as if it only ever had an accidental, lucky connection with it. The song is still there, but the magic is not.

This is not what happens with dope. This is not what junkies mean when they say "the first time is magic." Just the opposite. The first time magic evaporates from "Crazy." The first time magic burrows deeper and deeper into the white tops. It sinks into the molecules of the dope. The first time you do it, the magic isn't so strong. But as time goes on, it gets stronger. With "Crazy," I lost the magic as the song got clearer. With dope, the magic got so strong I couldn't see the dope. Now, all I can see in dope is that first-time magic. Pick up a white top, it's like picking up a white phone, and the angel of the first time is singing down the line.

So if you ever see a junkie gazing lovingly at a needle or a vial of dope, it's not like a miser looking at his money or a voyeur staring at porn. The vial of dope you see isn't there for the junkie. To him, it's a little pane of clear glass, and he's watching his first time through it. It's the most personal thing in the world. It's not like a voyeur staring at a picture of nameless naked bodies. It's like a prisoner looking at a photo of his family.

It still doesn't last, the first-time dope magic doesn't last. But it doesn't last in a different way than "Crazy" doesn't last. The magic of "Crazy" grows old and dies and decomposes in me, pretty quickly too. I bought it Tuesday. Friday I was sitting in my car wondering if something was wrong with the volume or the treble. "My heroes had the heart to live life out on the limb." I last longer than the magic of "Crazy." I don't last longer than the magic of the white tops. If you're out there, and you've experienced the first-time magic of the white tops, then don't worry: It's not going anywhere. It's not going anywhere you're not going. You're not going anywhere without it.

So I did it. Up the nose through a straw. Then we went up the stairs and out on the roof. This is kind of hard to write about. My legs felt funny as I went up the stairs. I wondered if I was dying. I emerged on the roof, late afternoon mid-July in New York, the city spread out across the ten directions, heavy gold clouds in the blue sky. I wondered if the funny feeling I had was good or bad and then it was doubtless.

A single cloud moved through the blue sky. I was on my back looking up. My eye was a glass box, and inside it there was no time. I kept the cloud inside it. I wish I could show it to you. I never imagined this could happen. A breath entering my nostrils coiled over the nerves, losing all dimension. This was the end of desire. The end of wanting. The end of fear. The end of desire. I had carefully preserved some precious memories from my childhood. Those memories seemed to promise a great happiness at the end of things. I had taken them as signs from the invisible world, and made a private religion of them. Lying on my back on Chip's roof, all the memories of my childhood turned white one by one.

Until that afternoon, those memories had been my most valued possessions. They aren't in this memoir because they don't exist anymore. All that remains are different colored frames around the same white picture. The same picture of white. Like the Candy Land story. I release them like white balloons. Good-bye, childhood memories! I don't need you anymore. While I was lying on the roof freed from time, from desire, from loneliness, from change, the white was freed from that afternoon and began traveling into the future and into the past. The white tops looked into the polished, carefully preserved surfaces of those early memories as if looking into a mirror. "You were waiting for me. When you were three, what did you see from the carseat? You saw me."

Once you know that marvelous white immortality, there is no place, no image, and no face in your past or your future that doesn't turn toward it. A beautiful girl or boy, a pleasant beach, a lovely building: A distant glory glows around those shapes. Their far side faces the white sun.

I should probably say that my experience with the drug, although rather common, is by no means shared by everyone. For many other people, the dust inside the white tops is strangely inert. It doesn't do much to them. My friend Dave, for example. In Dave's case, dope's power seemed strangely confined to the time he did it. While it was in his system, he thought it was marvelous. But the next day he could only remember a kind of sleepy feeling, and had no wish to do it again.

I was completely baffled by this. As an experiment, I got him to do it one more time. He did it, and as soon as it started to take hold he started saying how wonderful it was. I gave him a pen and paper and forced him to write down what he felt. "The best . . . I love it . . . immense, spacious." That evening, while the drug lasted, he also remembered the other time he'd done it, and how wonderful *that* was. The next day he awoke saying that it was just like taking sleeping pills. I showed him the page he'd written the previous night. He read it over. He remembered writing it, but he felt no connection to the words or the feelings they described.

"I must have been high," he said, and threw it out. He also would have thrown out half a vial of dope if I hadn't been there. A pervert.

How do you explain this? Addiction science is extremely primitive, and talks vaguely of "predispositions." Granted, if you are foolish enough to even try the white tops you've got some kind of predisposition, to stupidity if nothing else. But what about people who try it, love it, and then just forget about it? The literary writers have done little better than the doctors. William Burroughs, the author of *Junky* and *Naked Lunch* and an addict himself, for example, claimed that anyone who used it would get addicted. His error flows from the common mistake of equating addiction to the drug with the physical dependence that is one of its less pleasant side effects. This is foolish. Any old lady who takes OxyContin for two weeks will develop a dependence and suffer some withdrawal symptoms. When the doctor takes her off it, she'll feel like she has a mild flu for a couple days, then she'll forget about it.

Unless it got into her memory. Then she'll go to doctor after doctor after doctor getting scripts. Then one day the pharmacies will put it together and she'll be cut off. Then she'll make her way, through seven or eight different contacts, each one a little lower, to Dominic's, where I'll meet her. 2001. Her name was Betty, she was maybe sixty. She drove a Lincoln.

What's the difference between Dave and Betty? Some people, the Daves, must have a kind of memory immune system. When a Dave takes the drug, the memory immune cells sense the white moving into the memory system and go to work. They bind to the white, disrupting its ability to travel in time. The white dust is confined harmlessly to the present.

For the Bettys, there is no memory immune system. They remember what it was like. All their memories remember what it was like. Their future remembers what it was like.

So are you a Betty or a Dave? Either you'll try it and forget about it, or you'll try it and forget about everything else. I'm 100 percent Betty. Full-grown, meat-eating, red-blooded Betty. I mean white-blooded. And the stuff was white this first time. It came in a little vial with a white top. That was the "it" brand in Alphabet City that summer. Chip had done his research.

It might seem like I'm kind of obsessed by the first time I did dope. No shit. If you're writing a book like this, and you don't use at least this much space writing about the first time, you're not being honest. That first time follows you around. It doesn't stay in one place. It goes everywhere you go and does everything you do. In fact, my first time is here with me right now. Say hello, first time. Hello. A number of other people moved through the roof as afternoon turned into evening and then into night. Seth. Ann. Ashley, I think. Charlie, definitely. No one has ever said, "I went to a party the other night. I'm not sure if Charlie was there or not." You're always sure. Charlie was also living in New York for the summer. Like me, he should have graduated in May, but had another semester to go. He'd heard I was coming into town and came over. I remember his face rising over me like the moon.

"Hey, Charlie."

"I'm very disappointed in you, Michael," he said. "Just look at you. A beautiful summer day. You should be out playing baseball like all the other little boys and instead you're lying on your back on this filthy roof. I bet you couldn't even stand up if you wanted to. You're a lazybones. Laziness has eaten into your bones."

"Sorry, Mom," I said, putting plenty of space between the sounds. My smile started in New York and ended in Philadelphia.

"They're going to call you 'Noodle-Bones' at school," Charlie continued. It was easier for him to keep going than to stop.

"'Look at lazy Noodle-Bones draped over that stick. He got so lazy his bones turned to mush. He wouldn't listen to his mother.' That's what they'll say. And then you'll cry, and you know who will come running to help you? No one."

Charlie took a drag of his cigarette and resumed his middle-aged woman's voice.

"No one will help you. And then they'll rape you. They'll rape you all day long."

"It's great to see you, Charlie," I whispered. If I were Charlie I would have stomped on my head. What can you do with a worthless boneless Betty? Flat on her back in the middle of the day. And Charlie was a puritan. He wouldn't have touched that shit for a million dollars. He thought we were completely insane. And he was insane himself.

"So how is it?" he asked in his normal voice. He looked disgusted with my reply. Then he wandered over to smoke a joint with Seth.

Eva's short body lay perpendicular to my long body. From the sky, we looked like a clock stopped at three-thirty. I was glad she was near me. I don't remember exactly where Chip was. The magic triangle was broken. Six months of pressure and joy and tension and desire had precipitated the white tops into our world. I don't think any of us would have done it otherwise.

Well, maybe we would have, but the fact is we didn't. It was three-thirty. The triangle was broken. Eva and I were involved.

Chip was still around. In fact Eva was still living with him. But it was different. What mattered about him now was his absence. We'd make love in Chip's absence. In Chip's absence, we'd live together; we'd fight and laugh and hurt each other. Chip's absence was like air to us. Without it, we couldn't breathe. It turned out we couldn't breathe in it either, but that took longer to discover.

We lay for hours in Chip's absence, getting used to it. Her hand found mine.

"It's just incredible the cloud really pass me some water thanks thanks."

The first time you do dope, it feels kind of good as it leaves your body. A kind of tickling, like moving an arm that has fallen asleep.

I wish I could find every pebble of gravel, every grain of dust and cigarette butt from that magic first-time roof. I'd bottle it all up in white-top vials. I'd have old-time junkies selling their wheelchairs for a hit of that shit. Dominic, Dorsom, and Betty would rise from the dead for a free hit of that, and I'd give them a free one. I'd give them one for free. Then I'd hold up another and make them answer my questions.

"Dominic, tell me what it's like where you are now."

Silence.

"Tell me or you can't have a vial."

"It's empty, Mike. Like hailstones on mountains. Please just let me have one more. Just one more, you can't imagine . . ."

Chip was setting up a Ouija board when Eva and I finally got up. Everyone else was gone except for Charlie, and Charlie didn't look happy. Chip's soothing voice was falling over him like coils of rope.

"It'll be fun Charlie, relax. It's just something to do, like checkers." Charlie shook his head. He was wearing his sky blue suit with a thick fuzzy brown tie. It was night so there weren't any colors.

"I don't know if that's such a good idea, Chip." He looked worried. I couldn't tell if he was just being dramatic or if he actually believed in the mystic powers of the cheap Parker Brothers Ouija board. Probably both.

"Something bad might happen." If Charlie hadn't somehow let slip that he was afraid of Ouija boards, Chip would probably never have pushed it. Charlie's fear excited Chip. It was like an aphrodisiac.

"We'll just try it for a bit, and if we don't like it, we'll stop," Chip said soothingly. We took our places at the board's four corners. I scratched idly. Dope makes you itchy. Sometimes you start itching and forget to stop. Henry said one time he got so high he itched and itched and itched all the way to China. He only had one arm when I met him.

"What do we do, Chip?" Eva asked. He produced the planchette.

"We close our eyes, we ask the spirits a question, we all put our hands on this, and it'll move around the board stopping at different letters." It was still very hot on the roof. The sun had gone but it had gone into black, fuzzy bodies. The square roof buzzed with the heat. A discarded beer can glowed black with heat. I looked out over the city. The spaces between the lights looked like stuffed mouths. In the blackness, Eva's black fists looked like full cheeks. Electricity traveled two inches from the top of my stomach to the bottom of my throat.

Charlie sighed. "If we're going to do this, we should do it right." He threw his head back and closed his eyes.

"Everyone clear your mind. Close your eyes." The two were the same for me. Eva giggled. Opening my eyes I saw Chip's hand snaking between her thighs. Charlie's teeth glowed black in the no-light.

"Who are you, spirit?" The tips of our fingers gently touching the planchette, we pushed it in circles.

"Who are you, spirit?" We pushed it in circles. Eva moaned softly. I opened my eyes and looked at her. She looked directly into my eyes. Her mouth opened. Chip's forearm rose from her crossed legs.

"Who are you, spirit?" The planchette buzzed softly under my fingertips. It stopped circling and jutted across the board. Charlie's eyes snapped open.

"M." Charlie was in control. And maybe someone else. Charlie was like two helicopter blades spinning so fast they looked like one.

"O." The planchette jagged and squittered. Chip had only one hand on it, the rest of us had two.

"M." A little electric twist started in me and crushed itself out on my stomach walls. "I really have to go to the bathroom," Eva said. Her cheeks were flushed. She swayed her hips a little into Chip's forearm.

"Y." "Do you have to go special bathroom, Eva?" Chip's smile started in the bones of his face and headed southeast, toward Philly.

"I." Three weeks before I had a dream that Chip came into my room in Big Five holding a grocery bag filled to the top with white powder. I didn't want any. We argued. He gestured wildly. He dropped the bag, a white cloud rose up from it, and I inhaled it accidentally. Chip laughed. "You're going to die." I stumbled outside to the street. The sun white on the pavement, no-time rising in my eyes. I dropped to my knees, dying, and woke up.

"T." "Oh God!" Charlie said. "Oh God," Eva whispered.

"Mommy It," Charlie hissed through gritted teeth. "Fucking Mommy It. I've had nightmares." He lurched up, shambled over to the edge of the roof and began retching and barfing. As soon as I heard him retching, a thing came loose in me. Tears filled my eyes and sweat popped out on my forehead.

"I'm going to be sick." I got up, swayed, and then threw up on the roof three feet from where Eva sat red-cheeked and open-mouthed with Chip's stiff forearm rising from her crotch.

"Oh my God!" She propped herself up on her hands and threw up into the spot where I'd been sitting. I was still going. I felt like I was throwing up toes and knucklebones. I felt like the skin on my feet was coming up.

"I hear dope makes you sick the first time," Chip said, standing up and looking distastefully around.

"But I didn't do any!" Charlie wailed from the edge of the roof.

"The spirits made you sick, Charlie." The air was thick with retching. I couldn't get enough. Steady streams of puke. I was backward hungry. Starving. Oh God, was that red in my vomit? Was my ulcer back and bleeding? I threw up fresh yellow gruel over the old. I couldn't see it. I frantically started digging in it with my hands to see if I could find that red streak again.

"Hey, Eva," I moaned. "Come over here and see if I'm throwing up blood." She crawled over on her hands and knees. I pointed at the colored mess and she instantly threw up on it.

"No!" I yelled. "Now you've covered it up. Help me dig it out." I put my face three inches over the muck and began trying to peel back the layers with my fingers. It was subtly differentiated, like the changing colors of a Gobstopper, or the rings on a tree, or the gremlin bubbles on a wet Mogwai's back. When you get Mogwais wet they multiply. That's where Stripe came from.

I was frantically trying to think of things to keep myself from throwing up. I thought of Eva's pussy. I threw up rolls of dead skin in seltzer water. I threw up dry birthday cake. There was nothing left. Yes there was! My teeth! My parking tickets! I was vomiting up everything connected with me. My shoelaces! Candy Land! My first cigarette! Charlie ran over for some idiot reason, slipped in the three-foot vomit slick, hit his elbow and threw up sideways onto the Ouija board. Eva was crying and laughing and hiccupping and vomiting.

The smell suddenly rose from the hot roof in a tidal wave. It knocked Chip back, who'd been resisting, and he dropped to his knees and threw up. I was still going. It was a vomit orgasm. I was being pulled through sensitive holes in liquid form. Time and space started to come apart. It was like the formation of the earth, the birth of the continents, the beginning.

It was still. Charlie was snoring. Eva, exhausted, was still propped up on her elbows breathing heavily. Chip stirred behind us.

"I'm kind of horny," he said.

"Oh God!"

"I can't help it," he continued. "Eva, you look hot even with puke on your lips." He wriggled nastily behind us. My cheek was pressed against the hot roof and my eyes were closed.

"You look even hotter all nasty like that." Chip was a famous pervert.

"You're a potty hotty, Eva," he went on. "Baby want to go potty with you. Baby gotta go bathroom. Baby gotta go special bathroom."

"Gross, Chip." She stayed motionless. I felt disgusted and a little jealous, but what could I say? She was technically his girlfriend.

"You know what?" Eva said thoughtfully. "Even when I was throwing up I didn't really feel sick. Like it was happening to someone else."

I thought about this for a little bit. I didn't really feel anything. I started to say something but then I stopped. I felt like I'd forgotten something important, but I didn't know how to put it, and I didn't really feel one way or the other about it. Best just to rest.

I looked at the cooling vomit slick. Fuck it, if I could somehow reach back and get my hands on that shit I'd bottle it up too. Sell it in white-top vials. I'd use it to make the ghosts answer my questions. Do you remember me, Dominic? Do you remember your first time?

SEVEN

FUNBOYS

Last night I woke up at 2:00 a.m. covered in sweat. As I write this, I teach at the University of Michigan. I spent the last week working on the introduction to the academic book I'm writing and it's a little tangled. It's not clear as day, put it like that. It isn't crystal clear. My position in the department is unstable. Uncertain. I feel like everyone hates me. My own former advisor doesn't understand what the hell this book is about. It's about the philosophy of the price system. He says, what is that? I try to tell him haven't you ever felt you were part of a giant nervous system?

I'm biting the hand that feeds me. I can't help it. It's my inspiration. I moved here to Ann Arbor recently and the new friends I've met aren't exactly top shelf, put it like that. My old friend Alix called. She just moved to Seattle and complained about her new friends. "All they care about is money." She's going sailing with them on Sunday. My friends here are more likely to have wheelchairs than sailboats.

I have to get out of here. I'm thirty. I hate Ann Arbor. I have to get a new job this fall and the market is terrible. And I didn't move here so recently. I've been here over a year. I've broken up with two serious girlfriends in the past eighteen months. I hate it here. I'll never get a new job. People will think I'm crazy. I am crazy. I'll be stuck here slipping lower and lower in the department, finally falling out. I'll be sticking up gas stations with a screwdriver.

They won't let me have a gun, are you kidding? They know my record. They say it was expunged. Bullshit. Plus I'm not breathing right. It's the humidity. Yesterday I think I saw one of those old tenured professors shuffling down the hall holding his toothbrush. I'm supposed to pitch my secret late-night insights about the price system to these people? They just want somebody to prove to them that they are never going to die. They want magic tricks.

I'll give them one. Are you kidding? I'll do anything. I'll switch things up. How about that? Originality is highly prized. The unexpected. I'll write a brilliant article telling them exactly when they're going to die. The day and the hour. It'll be pretty soon, too. They'll love it. Creepy? You just don't know; they'll eat it up! You have to know how to talk to these people. You can't go around treating them like princesses. They won't respect you.

"Did you see that young Clune's brilliant new paper? It says I'm going to die next month. Really die. Think about it. The end. He's a genius." I can't deal with these academics. And the people outside the university are forty times worse. They'll attack you in broad daylight. A normal job? They won't even let you write in peace. Hell no. The real-world bosses stand right over you while you type.

"What's this? A letter? A word? All we deal with here are numbers! Figures! Just write down the numbers. Is that so hard? Just look at the numbers on this sheet here and type them in that space there." The bitter reality of the price system I'm in love with! It's ironic.

But my vision concerns the future. A beautiful, pure economic world is hatching inside their cubicles and calculators. The vast nervous system of the world insect. Their own heads are the chrysalis. Can you see the slender antennae of the idea of my book? Waving over the cubicle? No? The bubbles on the Mogwai's back? The Gremlin's scaly finger on the chainsaw? The eviction notice under my apartment door? The Final

Girlfriend? I see our squat shadows on the horizon. In the future. We're both three hundred pounds and bald. We're eating quietly at Ponderosa. "Are you going to finish that?" Is this why I got clean?

By now I'm throwing myself around on the bed. I'm sweating. Panting. Twisting. Turning. Moaning. Anyone looking in would think I was fucking someone. But I don't have a girlfriend now. We broke up. I'm fucking myself. I need to relax.

I must be going crazy. "Is this why I got clean?" Ten days ago I saw Cash for the first time in months. I'm worried about my introduction. Cash was sallow, skinny in the fat places, fat in the skinny places. Sick. Stuttering. He never used to stutter. Mumbling about fire prevention. Hardly making a pretense. "I kind of sleep a lot." In hell. In white hell, white frosted eyes. White lips, white freezing tongue. I'm a little apprehensive about a footnote, I'm wondering about phrasing. He's dying. He's been where I've been and never got out. "Is this why I got clean?" Where's my gratitude?

Gratitude. I lay awake in the dark. Gratitude. The very word is like a bell, tolling me back from me to the quiet room. The clean sheets. Gratitude. The darkness. Gratitude. The sound of my breathing. The sound of the fan, turning slowly, gratitude. Gratitude. I lie there until I'm transparent. Until the clean sheets below me can see the ceiling above me. Until they can see it clearly. Until the sound of the fan is alone in the room.

This morning I arose refreshed, smiling for no reason. This is why I got clean. I didn't know it then. The cure keeps working also. Growing. I said the first time I did white tops lasts. The cure lasts too. The way out of the white out. It gets stronger. At first I saw only one way out. Now I can see more ways. That pine tree outside my window, for example. A hundred little branches at least. And each little branch has sixty green needles. That's six thousand.

Where was I last night at 2:00 a.m.? Where am I when I'm knotted and tangled up in myself? The roof at Chip's? The future? Candy Land? Who knows? But every road leads out of it. Everything. In a little while or a little longer. Thousands of exits. Pine needles. The sound of my breathing. Gratitude. Gratitude takes time. It's the fruit of experience. It still feels new to me, I haven't had it for that long. Gratitude came only after I'd passed through all the other feelings.

Actually I've only had two other major feelings worth mentioning. The first is the White Out. I met that on Chip's roof. The second is Fun. I met Fun one year after the white out in SoHo. Eva and I had been traveling in Africa, celebrating our graduation from college. When we got back to the States, I moved to Baltimore to start grad school. Eva moved to New York. I missed her at first, but soon I met someone else. In Baltimore, I met someone who could really score. A connection. His name was Scott, but he insisted I call him Funboy.

"They call me Funboy," he said, "'cause I get raw bags of fun." He wasn't being poetic. Dope was the only fun. And the best dope was "raw," as opposed to "scramble," which was cheaper and more heavily cut. "Raw bags of fun."

Well, maybe he was being a little poetic. The raw fun came in vials, not bags. Funboy called them bags because the first time he did dope, in the distant past, it came in a little plastic baggie. He was twenty years old, three years younger than me.

"OK, I see him. Now slow down." I slowed down. Funboy was in the passenger seat. He peered out the window at the knots of people leaning on walls, sitting on the row houses' narrow porches, pacing the corners. Funboy didn't sell any dope himself. He was a connector, one of the drug world's many wires linking paranoid dealers with ravenous addicts. The street dealers all knew him. The addicts would give him a vial or two for taking them to cop. If you were new in the city, like I was, and tried to cop on your own, you'd get burned. Funboy made connections. Of course sometimes the wires got crossed. And if anyone along the connection got unhappy, the electricity went through Funboy. He looked like he was a little burned inside.

"What's up, Red, you on?" Funboy stuck his head out the window. The heavyset black man on the corner shook his head.

"It's hot right now. Ten minutes." We rolled off. I gritted my teeth. Ten minutes could designate any length of time. I had no patience. And I didn't even have a habit yet.

"You'll be the worst dope fiend ever, Mike. No patience."

"I'll never be a dope fiend," I said. His eyes kind of slid around.

"Just don't do it three days in a row." Three days, that was the magic number. Don't do it three days in a row and you won't get addicted. Ridiculous, with that white hole swelling in my memory. Suddenly Funboy yelled and turned up the radio all the way.

Oh baby I like it raw.
Oh baby I like it raw.
Oh baby I like it raw.

"Yeah! I like it raw too!" He raised his fist out the window. The popular rap tune was his theme song.

"You know, Mike," he said thoughtfully. "I only get raw dope. That's because raw dope is the best. Scramble dope is cheaper, but it's got a lot of cut. Now how many dope fiends do you think only fuck with raw dope?" I shrugged. "Less than 10 percent? Probably less than five. That means I'm in the top 5 percent." He stared out as street after street of standing, stumbling, stooping Baltimore junkies flew by.

"Look at these fucking scramble dope fiends." We pulled up at a red light. A middle-aged woman stood on the curb next to our stopped car. Her mouth hung open.

"Fucking scramble dope fiend." Funboy spoke it slowly into her face through the open window as the light turned green.

"All right, man, isn't there anywhere else?" I was a little tired of driving around. I lit another cigarette. I don't smoke anymore. In my diseased memory, the cigarette is as thick around as a baby's arm. Its white skin is as deep and rich and full of the future as a baby's. Funboy looked uncertainly at the sun.

"Well, there are other spots, but these red tops are really the best right now. Plus, I like to support that corner." Ten minutes later we were back. Red shook his head.

"Too hot out here. We getting everybody together at the park."

"All right," Funboy said. "Make a right, then a quick left, Mike."

"OK, Funboy." It kind of felt good to be ordered around by Funboy. "Right! Left! Right! Left!"

"Yes, sir!" I was a soldier in the army of fun.

We parked at a lot adjoining a small city park and got out. We walked through a clump of trees and into an unbelievable scene. There were at least fifty or sixty junkies milling around in the green space between the park's path and the busy street. As I stared, another junkie came up the path in a wheelchair. Two more came out of the bushes to my left. It seemed like all of Funboy's top 5 percent were here. Some were wearing ratty jeans and faded Metallica T-shirts. Some were wearing ratty jeans and faded Bob Marley T-shirts. Some were wearing ratty jeans and faded "Baltimore Reads!" T-shirts. It was a diverse crowd.

"We can't just wait here with all these junkies!" I whispered. "This is totally obvious. The cops will definitely see this from the street. It'll probably be on the news." Funboy shook his head.

"You sure don't know Baltimore. This is why I moved back here from Seattle." He wandered over and sat down next to a middle-aged black man in a suit, a woman in a faded Beatles T-shirt, and a sixteen-year-old white girl in a McDonald's uniform.

"Oh hey, Funboy," the girl said. "Waiting on that raw?"

"You know me, Melissa. I only fuck with raw," he said. She smiled.

"Me too. Here's a coupon for a free soft-serve cone," she passed it to him and he took it.

"You know," the Beatles fan said, "there's nothing like raw dope. Maybe I'm funny. I could get scramble near where I live, but I take the bus all the way out here. I guess I gotta have that raw."

"They better hurry," the suited man said, checking his expensive watch, "I have to be in court in an hour and a half. I'd go downtown, but I really only mess with raw dope."

"How'd Richie's case come out, Louis?"

"Pretty good, Funboy," the suited man replied, "when you consider what we had to work with. We were able to plead it down to manslaughter, but in the state of Maryland—" Louis was cut off by a sudden surge through the crowd. Everyone was standing up and moving. We pressed forward with the rest.

"Get over! Everyone get over quick or you won't get served!" Members of the dealer's crew, identifiable by their plain white T-shirts and confident alert movements, were directing the crowd across the street. Traffic stopped, honking, as a jerky stream of junkies walked, ran, trotted, biked, and wheeled across the busy street to the block of row houses. A hundred yards down the street to our left, I saw a stream of about thirty people crossing the road in the other direction, toward the park. I grabbed Funboy's arm and pointed. He shot them a quick glance.

"That's just the line for ready rock." Ready rock was Baltimore slang for crack.

Across the street we were herded down a block and a half and into an alley. There must have been almost a hundred of us by now. The crowd spilled out one end of the alley into the street. "OK!" voices rang out. "Everyone just keep still or you won't get served." The pushing and moving ceased instantly, like the current had been shut off. I pushed three twenty-dollar bills into Funboy's hands. We stood still for maybe five minutes until one of the crew came by and served Funboy. Then he turned to me.

"How many?"

"None," I said. He looked startled.

"He's with me," Funboy explained.

"Man," the dealer said, "if you're not buying don't be getting in line. These extra motherfuckers draw the heat." We took off.

I looked back as we crossed the street. The knot in the alley was coming apart as little threads of two or three furtive junkies peeled off and disappeared.

We climbed back into the car. I turned the air-conditioning on full blast and we pulled out, looking nervously for cop cars. Cop cars are white on the outside. On top they have big red and blue organs for sensing fear. You have to stay calm. That's why Funboy insisted on fixing right there in the moving car. I hated that. But I admired his dexterity. When he was done, he sat back. Then he yelled and turned the radio all the way up.

Oh baby I like it raw.
Oh baby I like it raw.

"I only fuck with raw dope," Funboy said. "Because. Raw. Dope. Is. The shit." He called out the dope spots as we passed them. "White tops . . . green tops . . . ready rock . . . black tops . . . scramble . . . scramble . . . scramble." We were getting into downtown. Mount Vernon Square, St. Paul Street. People drank tea under café umbrellas, strolled under sun hats, picked up change from the sidewalk. Outside the Atlantis, young broke junkies lined up to audition to be strippers. Outside the Walters, old rich junkies walked their poodles. The sun lit up fake and real jewels on old and young women. There were red awnings and blue awnings in the air, and red tops and blue tops on the ground. There were people climbing in and out of buildings with no windows. And the alleys were even more crowded than the streets.

Swinging Baltimore in the late nineteen-nineties! There was no place like it. I've taken Ecstasy in Dublin, been clubbing in London, seen art shows in New York, talked with Charlie in Cleveland, gone shopping in Tokyo, overdosed in Amsterdam. But there was no place like Baltimore in the late nineties. Everyone knew everyone. You felt like you could walk in any door and find someone who was selling what you wanted. There were beautiful parks. There were liquor stores and ice cream trucks. There were no Nazis. It was my kind of city. Well, there was one Nazi.

"I'm a Nazi, Mike," Funboy admitted, as we rolled up Charles.

"Really," I said.

"Yeah, I hate niggers."

"What about Jews?"

"I don't know any Jews." I thought about this. It didn't make sense.

"How can you be a Nazi if you don't hate Jews?"

"Because the niggers rule the world. They keep us down. They stick together. They're smart and crafty and they run shit. It's a nigger conspiracy out here. I mean, you're not blind. Look around. What color are the dealers?"

"Black," I said.

"And you saw that crowd of fiends out in the park. White and Asian and Mexican. But the dealers? Everyone was black."

"Wait," I said. "There were lots of black fiends too. What about Louis? He's black."

"Yeah," Funboy said, "But he's a lawyer. An Oreo. Black on the outside, white on the inside." He pondered. "Most black fiends," he said, "are white inside."

I decided to try a different approach.

"You know, Funboy, most people see it differently. If you look at the country as a whole, you'll find that black people don't actually dominate it. In fact, on average they tend to be poorer than whites. Because of a history of racism, many blacks are forced to live in inner-city areas infested by drugs. They don't have access to the education that would enable them to get good jobs. And because of this lack of opportunity," I concluded, "some of the smartest and most ambitious are forced to become drug dealers."

Funboy snorted. "Forced to become drug dealers." He looked disgusted with me. "Forced to drive Mercedes and fuck hot bitches and get all the money and all the dope. And what do you mean, black people have to live in the part of the city where there's drugs? I'd do anything to live in that part of the city! A dope spot within walking distance? Are you kidding? But I can't live there. The niggers would kill me. They're forced to live there, yeah right. You just try moving to Edmondson Avenue!"

"But I wouldn't want to move there."

"That's 'cause you're stupid. People come from all over to visit that place. Best dope in the state for sure. But they won't let no white people move in there. They wouldn't give white people the opportunity. That's why I hate niggers. White people work all day in some shitty suburb, then take their paycheck down to Edmondson or Druid Hill or Greenmount. Like slaves. Niggers run the world. You're blind."

"But they really don't, Funboy. You're not being—"

"And all the rappers are black!" he yelled. "How do you explain that? Practically every fucking one of the rappers is black! DMX, Jay-Z, Master P. Sure, they let Eminem in. One. A token."

"What about the president, Funboy?"

"A token," he said, "like Eminem. You just keep talking that shit the niggers teach you in grad school, Mike, while you stand in line waiting for Red's dope." He imitated my voice. "'Niggers are poor and oppressed! Please let me get one, Red! I'll do anything!'"

He resumed his normal Funboy voice. "But one day there will be a revolution." He looked dreamily out the window. "A Nazi revolution. Then the slums will be filled with white people. And I'll be right there."

Although Funboy was a Nazi, some of his best friends were black. Tony, for instance. Tony Rolls, or Tony K., or Carey Street Tony.

"Cool," Tony said. He was looking at a poster for some shitty band Funboy was in.

"Yeah," Funboy said. "We're playing at the Otto Bar next Sunday."

"How much do you get?" Tony asked.

"Almost nothing." Funboy set down the guitar he'd been strumming. "Pretty much nothing. Enough to get high. Kind of." Tony let the poster fall.

"Bet you get more than I get slinging for Red, man." He lit a cigarette. He had "Carey" tattooed in Chinese restaurant letters down the back of his left forearm, "Rolls" tattooed down the back of his right. "I worked it out. If you add up all the time I spend waiting on the damn corner and helping move the stash and shit, it works out to about eight dollars an hour."

"Yeah," said Funboy, "but you also get crazy free red tops, man." He laughed. "I work 24/7 and *all* I get is free red tops. You're eight dollars an hour ahead of me."

"If y'all be lovin' those red tops, then why the fuck," a low booming voice uttered, "is you here then?" The enormous man shuffled in and sat heavily down on the couch. He tossed two white paper squares on the coffee table. They landed on an open porno mag, next to a pair of nunchaku, an overflowing ashtray, a fork sticking straight up from the wood, an open box of Domino sugar, and a Polaroid picture of a baby with an open mouth. A pit bull was chained to one of the table's frail legs. Four or five pairs of new-looking Nikes lay scattered around the floor.

"Cool, Howard." Tony scooped up one square, tossed me the other. A chain hung from the ornate wooden mantle. The apartment, overlooking Druid Hill Park, had some nice plasterwork on the high ceilings. Probably built in the twenties. Now this was the worst neighborhood in Baltimore. I didn't want to be here, but it was late, and all the drive-through raw spots were closed.

"If you gettin' all them red tops," Howard repeated, "what you come see old Howard for?" He grabbed an inhaler off the table and started hitting it. He probably weighed four hundred pounds. Tony picked up the Domino sugar box and poured a little sugar into his palm. While Howard continued to wheeze and pump the inhaler, Tony took a wad of tinfoil from his pocket. He unfolded the tinfoil and gently tapped some yellowish powder on top of the sugar in his hand. Using his index finger, he mixed the powder in with the sugar. I stared.

Howard recovered. His eyes were watering.

"I think I seen you in that movie you was talking about. Wasn't your hair a different color then?" He stared at the girl sitting next to me. Sara. She was cute, with milky skin, a lithe gymnast's body and bright dyed-red hair. I met her through Funboy. She smiled at Howard. "Uh-huh."

Tony held his palm full of sugar and yellow powder out to the dog, who began eagerly snuffling at it. Howard looked over with molasses eyes. There was no yellow in the white at that distance.

"Toss me that box," Howard ordered. I passed the sugar to him, leaning over Sara. He poured out a handful of sugar and tossed it in his mouth.

"I seen lots of movies, you know," Howard said. "I love movies. I'd like to direct. I think I'd be real good, 'cause I know what people like. What was it like acting in the movie, baby?"

"Wow, it was *so* awesome!" She sat straight up like an alert schoolgirl, an enthusiastic smile on her face.

"Some people think all movies is the same," Howard said. "Wai-Chee, my nigger down at the video store, don't know. 'It's the girls, Howard, not the director.' But you know when he comes to order new ones, he be asking me which ones and shit. I love a good director. I spot 'em in the first shot. I like the way they be getting them in position, not just any way, but like a statue." Howard demonstrated, shifting his grotesque bulk, arching his back, and opening his mouth in fake ecstasy. "You see, baby, what I like to see is when the girls—what the fuck is wrong with my dog?" The pit bull was snuffling and foaming. Funboy stood up.

"I just *loved* doing that movie," Sara said loudly over the dog. "At one point, they made me close my eyes. I wanted to keep them open, but they thought it would be more passionate." Howard lobstered over to his foaming dog. The dog made a wet inside cracking noise and lay still, breathing slow and rough.

"Did he eat something? Did y'all see him eat something? Did he eat something up off the floor? Did he eat some dope off the floor? I know didn't no dope do this."

"Ain't no fucking dope on the floor," Tony drawled. He rose slowly.

"Yeah, ain't no dope on the floor, Howard." Funboy pushed his long blond hair out of his blue Nazi eyes. "Where is the dope, by the way, Howard?"

"It's not on the floor," Tony said. He pretended like he was looking for it. "I just don't see it on the floor. Gotta be some-where else. Where you keep all the dope, Howard?" Sara lit a cigarette and stood up with smiling eyes. Howard seemed oblivious, still crouched over his dog, fat belly flopping, mutter-ing. He was all over, shapeless fat poured over five or six square feet. Funboy moved out into the hall.

"Where the hell you going?" Howard turned and stood up like spilled water poured back into a glass. Phantom guns moved outside the dark windows. Tony was whispering into his cell phone.

"Nowhere, Howard!" Funboy said in a high-pitched school-boy's voice. "We just gotta go now."

I stood up, clutching the white square of paper. It was more like a lump. My hands had sweat right through it. Howard turned, wheezing. Tony closed the cell phone.

"Get at you later, Funboy. Peace, Mike, Sara. Howard, I'ma chill for a minute. You look hungry. You want some more sugar?" Earlier that day, Tony had performed a little rap for me. He said he kind of practiced rapping while he stood all day on the corner of Edmondson and Denison. "Niggers got to not see me / Niggers be turning up casualties," Tony rapped. He'd laughed, showing white teeth. He had a white heart, too. Funboy said he had a serious habit, kept alive by multiple wires going multiple places. One lay sparking in the dog's throat. Tony was going to chill for a minute. I was kind of excited to leave.

Out in the car, as Sara, Funboy, and I sped away, I really let Funboy have it.

"What the hell was that about, Funboy?"

"Nothing, man."

"What do you mean, nothing? What did Tony do? What is Tony going to do? Did you know he was going to . . . to fuck with Howard's dog?"

"He was just playing with the dog."

"Oh, that's just bullshit." The whole situation was sour to me. I wondered if I had committed some kind of crime just by being there. I wondered who Tony had called, what he was doing now. "What if something happens to Howard? Will I be connected?"

"Everyone's connected to everyone," Funboy replied.

"Come on," Sara said. "Be serious. Mike's scared."

"I'm not scared!"

"Look," Funboy stifled a yawn. "Who knows what Tony's got going? Stay out of it. It's between him and Howard. And maybe Red too. Just forget about it."

"Well, I'm never going back there," I said. "Safety is rule number one with me, Funboy. Remember that." From now on, it was strictly drive-through dope shopping. After two weeks, I was beginning to realize I could no longer blindly go wherever Funboy led.

"Hey, don't order me around," he said. "You're lucky I cop for you. Most people I cop for give me four or five vials. You only give me one and sometimes none. You don't have any fucking money, so quit acting like I work for you."

He paused. "We're friends."

He was right. I didn't have any money. The first time he'd taken me to cop I'd given him sixty dollars, the second time twenty, and then I was broke. We had nothing in common. Did just not giving him money make us friends?

"We are friends," I said.

"That's precious," Sara said. I looked at her. The passing streetlights fell on her bare arms. I felt the square of dope in my shirt pocket. Right then I had a lot of needs, but also a lot of ways. I confess plainly that events have controlled me. I wasn't 100 percent sober, either.

We pulled up to my apartment building. Right across Charles Street from the Homewood Campus of Johns Hopkins.

Apartment 606. "It's kind of bare," Sara said. She had a tattoo on her lower back and she'd been in a porno, but I could tell the rubies in her earrings were real. Funboy said she only dated rich guys. I'd made an effort to act superior, but my car was a cold fact, and my cheap bare apartment was another. I was a little worried that she'd bail when she realized I was just a broke grad student. She didn't.

I was feeling kind of excited. I took out the white paper square of dope and looked at it. It was a white tunnel. At the far end of the white tunnel, I saw the white cloud from the afternoon on Chip's roof. The cloud spooled out into the room. There were a couple lit candles. Funboy passed out on the couch. Sara and I crouched under a candle. I spread open a book on the eighteenth-century painter Fragonard and showed it to her.

I was obsessed with the French master. The luxury of ancient Europe. I'd been dying to tell Sara about him. It would impress her. It would bring us closer. Something Howard said had reminded me. The book was open to a full-page color image of *The Swing*.

"Is this what you study in grad school?" she asked.

"No. I just like it." The pink dress of the girl on the swing spread out like a rose. Her shoe flew off, revealing her naked foot. Her lover crouched below her on the grass, his thin arm pointing at the center of her spread dress. Behind her stood another man, pulling the ropes that moved the swing. Sara's lazy finger swirled down the girl's rose spirals.

"Look at their faces." Fragonard's round, open-mouthed porno faces. Pasted on the bodies like a fish's fake eyes. Fake openings. Fake shock. Blood and feeling ran smoothly under those faces, finding their real openings below. Their real faces: the girl's rose center, the man's jutting arm, the servant's tense rope-hand. Sara's shocked mouth O'd open. The servant's hand pulled down on the rope hard. The girl's naked feet turned in opposite directions.

Sara's naked foot rose from the floor, pointed up at Funboy's open mouth. His closed eyes. His sleeping arm hung over the couch, pointed into Sara's center. My tense hand pulled down on the rope hard. The girl's head went back on the swing. Behind her stood another man.

"Can you look at me when you do that?" White tears ran up her rose face. My body turned white in her fake shocked eyes. Sara reached over my chest to pick up her earrings, carefully placed inside her tiny shoe. She turned her head and fastened them. Funboy made snoring noises like a dog snuffling sugar.

"Those rubies are beautiful," I said. She gave me a funny look.

"They're totally fake."

I looked at them more closely. She was right. They weren't even red. They didn't even have any facets. They were pink plastic dots.

EIGHT

SORROW

When I woke up, Sara was gone. A brief note and a twenty-dollar bill for her share of the drugs. One o'clock. It was a Sunday in September. I stretched and yawned. The yawn went on, my eyes were a little watery, but otherwise no symptoms. I'd done dope two days in a row, not three. I walked into the apartment's other room.

Funboy was snoring and snuffling, his arm hung over the couch. *Probably hasn't slept for days,* I thought. He looked awfully thin, stretched out in the daylight. I'd have to remember to get him to eat something. It was a little chilly in the apartment. It could still get pretty warm during the day, but the humidity was gone. The air was getting thinner. The day's heat hung in it like oil in water. Before something disappears, it separates from the things around it. I opened the blinds. The sun's heat pulsed in the cool room.

I gently pressed Funboy's shoulder. He turned and coughed, and sat up. He was only twenty. "Whoa," he said. He sat up, rubbing his eyes. He was shivering. He reached under the couch's cushion, took out a wadded-up sock, unrolled it, took out the half-empty vial, and started looking for his works.

I never met anyone who said they liked Funboy, and it seemed like most people in Baltimore knew him. I was alone with Tony for exactly two minutes the day before. Funboy had gone to the bathroom. "Dude's a lame," Tony said. Even Funboy's mother, who I would meet in Canton later that year, didn't like him. "Let me ask you something, Mike. Why the hell do you hang out with Scott?" My friends from New York, who I introduced to him when they visited, didn't like him. Chip asked frankly if he was retarded. Funboy would rip me off six or seven times, but it was never for that much. I kind of felt like I deserved it. I ran into him twice after I got clean too. I think I was the only one who liked him.

He'd had his leg broken. There were knife scars on his side and his arm. His nose had been broken. He'd been to juvie and then to jail. He'd been an addict since he was fifteen. I started doing dope when I was twenty-one. In the middle of getting high, in the middle of the night, I often felt as if I'd forgotten something important. Funboy didn't. His arms looked terribly thin in the sunlight. His eyes were empty. There's nothing to be done about that. Compassion does not restore a human form to those who have lost it. Everything living dies, everything changes.

And things aren't as bad off on their own as I used to think. It's insane the way some people try to turn their memory into a hospital for every sick thing they've ever seen. I know better. I'm not a safe place even for something as desperate as Funboy's thin right arm, with the small knife scar, the smaller burn mark, and all the tiny track marks. But if he's still alive somewhere, and needs some help . . .

"Howard's dope is pretty tight," he said. "He gets it from the same place as Red." He wiped his nose and looked around with slow eyes. In some ways Funboy was like a blind person. His eyes always pointed in a different direction than his body. He stood up and walked toward the door, eyeing the couch. He was humming the tune to "I Like It Raw." The tune only had two or three notes. The tune wasn't the point of that fucking song.

"Shut up, Funboy!"

"Damn, Mike, what are you so pissy about?" I guess I'm just sad.

When we got outside, Funboy looked lovingly at my dirty Grand Am before getting in.

"I love this car, Mike. It's the only place I feel safe sometimes." I nodded, not knowing what to say. I guess I loved it too. Two years later, I would take fifty or sixty pictures of that car with Cat's camera over the course of an autumn. I found a pile of them when I was cleaning out my apartment after I got clean. No people in the pictures, just the car. Under sunlight, in the rain, parked under trees or streetlights.

"Where do you want to go, Funboy?" He fiddled with a lighter and looked out the window. The blue September Baltimore light isn't good for you. Funboy throbbed in it. He didn't know shit.

"I want to go with you," he said. I couldn't tell if he was joking.

Well, he definitely wasn't joking, if by "joking" you mean sarcastic or ironic or humorous. Funboy didn't get into that. But a lot of the things he said didn't mean anything. I looked at him. You couldn't tell anything by looking at him. I dropped him off in Fells Point, then headed straight to the airport.

My stepmother's sister had died, and I'd agreed to come back for the funeral. I didn't really know her well, but she'd always been nice to me, and I could tell her niceness wasn't a front or a fake. It was sincere. It went all the way through her, like the taste of oranges goes all the way through an orange. Even the peel.

Barb (that was her name) had been hit and killed by a drunk driver. Barb and Lori, my stepmom, had been closer than any two people I'd ever seen. War prisoners get close like that. For them it was childhood. On the plane I felt restless. I kind of thought about ordering a drink. It was before noon. My sister picked me up from the airport.

"Kind of fucked up, huh?" she said.

"Yes, well, it's good to get out of Baltimore for a little bit. Perspective. There's a lot of interesting people in Baltimore. My friend Funboy, for instance. I don't think it would be a good idea for you to come and visit me any time soon."

Jenny shot me a strange look. "I meant about Barb, idiot."

"Oh, yes. Well, these things happen. One day you're here, the next day you're gone. Gone but not forgotten. Can I borrow twenty dollars? I can write you a check."

I looked out the window. "I'm probably the best graduate student in the university. I might not be the smartest, but I'm the fastest." I moved my finger rapidly around in the air. "The thoughts go through my head so fast. Some of my fellow students, the ones that went to Harvard and Yale for undergrad and were Rhodes Scholars and all, they're not so stupid. They're pretty smart. They probably have more actual thoughts than I do. But my thoughts move so fast. One of my fast thoughts gets to all the same places as twenty or thirty of their slow thoughts, and it gets there faster. You can ask me something if you want."

She didn't feel like asking me something right then. OK, maybe later. I felt it was very important to be able to communicate with people. We pulled up at my stepmother's parents' white house in their deep-fifties Wonder Bread suburb. We went in the front door and Jenny offered appropriate condolences while I nodded. Lori's father gave me a beer. He asked me how grad school was. Lots of people milled around looking dazed. My own father came up, hugged me, and told me how much it meant to him and Lori that I was able to make it.

"I wouldn't miss it for the world," I said. It occurred to me then that I had made a decision to be there. I remember thinking that was strange. In those days, things just seemed to happen by themselves.

I sat down in an open chair around the kitchen table. One of Lori's uncles was telling a story. He was a grizzled white-headed guy. I'd met him when my dad and Lori had gotten married. He'd been a captain in the Navy during World War II.

"The one thing I could never stand on my ship was a homosexual," he was saying in his firm, matter-of-fact way. "Nowadays it's 'cool' to be homosexual. All the high school boys think it's cool to act like they are homosexuals. They think it's neat to dress and walk like they are homosexuals. Well, I assure you things were very different in 1942. It was not 'cool.' We had a homosexual aboard my ship in 1942. We were escorting convoys out of Iceland. At night, the homosexual was going around to the different bunks and jumping the men. One night they'd had enough, and they threw him overboard. In the morning we called roll, and he was gone."

"Gone but not forgotten," his wife said solemnly. Barb had been thirty-six. There were pigs in a blanket on a plate in the center of the table. Exactly the kind of detail, I thought, that someone suffering from intense sorrow would notice. The kind of thing that would burn deep into your memory. I stared at one pig in a blanket in particular. A particularly juicy one.

After waiting an appropriate amount of time, I went to the bathroom. I knew Lori's mother had some kind of intense arthritis, and sure enough, in the medicine cabinet I found a bottle of Percocet. A bottle of now and laters. I took three for now, three for later. By the time we got to the funeral parlor they started to take effect. The effect was deeply disappointing. A very faint white light, coming from the crack under a closed door. Nothing like raw. (I like it raw.) I remembered taking Percocet before, and it had always given a really intense and satisfying buzz. Something had changed.

After a time we left in a convoy to go to the funeral parlor. I made Jenny stop at a gas station so I could get cigarettes, and then had to borrow money from her to buy them. The attendant yelled at me for lighting up next to a gas pump. When we finally walked through the door of the funeral parlor, I saw the father standing in the middle of the hallway. His powerful hands hung limply at his sides. He was crying. His solid square face was cracked and broken. Like someone had swung a baseball bat hard at the center.

"What am I going to do?" he said. "What am I going to do?"

The funeral parlor had deep brown carpeting. The walls were wood paneled. There was an oil painting of a house on one. Lori was standing at the entrance to the chapel. Her white face shuddered, opened and closed and opened around a single long sob. I walked toward her with my arms half-spread, mumbling condolences. She gripped me bone tight.

"What am I going to do?"

I sat in a pew and watched the procession of people file past the open coffin. Several had to be supported. One woman's face looked like water going down a drain. The low sound of crying erased the edges of every other sound. Whispers, footsteps, thoughts, purse snaps, and even a faint singing rose and sank in the crying. It was a sea of tears, everything floated in it. Minutes floated by.

The Percocet, after opening a tiny white hole in me, closed up like a wound. I grew restless. I looked at the brown wood-paneled wall of the chapel. Outside, the day was going off like an alarm. Cars shot out of alleys. People stood in lines at counters. They looked out windows. The tubes of outer space hung down through the gas sky. Letting in a little nothing. Inside the millions of suburban houses was something worse than nothing. Couches connected to carpets connected to refrigerators connected to televisions.

The soft sounds of crying in the chapel sounded suddenly dry to me. Like a constant dry cough. The world was thirsty. It was thirsty for escape. It had died of that thirst.

My father nudged me. It was my turn to kneel before the open coffin and look into it. I walked up, knelt down, and looked in. *This is what a human face looks like,* I thought. *I have some perspective now,* I thought. *No, this is what you look like after you die,* I thought. *To someone else. This is what you always look like to other people,* I thought. *This is what I look like to my father and Funboy and Eva,* I thought. *This is who I really am,* I thought. My thoughts moved fast, like I told Jenny. One connected to another connected to another connected to another. Something worse than nothing. After an appropriate amount of time I stood up and went back and sat down.

I thought of telling Jenny to drive me out of there, but I knew nothing would be different anywhere else. I didn't know where to score in Chicago. And even if I did, I couldn't do it. It would be three days in a row. That would make me an addict. So I decided to just stay put. Better to turn in the slot I was in than to twitch out in the open. I closed my eyes and imagined a white hole opening in the middle of things. I imagined a white flood rushing over the desert world. I opened my eyes. There were white holes everywhere, but they were all dry. The father's caved-in face, Lori's open and shut and open mouth, Barb's parted lips.

White tops are white. I guess death is another meaning of the color white. Barb's white face in the coffin.

In some ways, this association is misleading. I'd already overdosed once (in Holland with Eva), and I would overdose again. You could describe my behavior in a general sort of way as suicidal. But I never really believed I was close to dying, or that I could die, or that I was dying. Maybe I was too close to see it. Or maybe in white time, death is a difference that doesn't make a difference. Think of Fathead, or Henry. Junkies tend to be drawn to metaphysical schemes in which dying is like moving a piece on a checkerboard, or like moving from one room to another, or even like moving around in the same room.

The reality of death is something you don't see until you are cured. When you can see it, it's a sign you're cured. When you are cured, you can see the difference death makes. It divides one world from the next. It divides each living moment from every other. Change. Wonder. Peace. Surprise. The fact of death is the deep source of health. But in white time, it's a white line in a white room. I crossed over from Chicago to Baltimore about ten days after the funeral.

I hadn't planned to stay for so long and I wished I hadn't. But it was just one thing after another, hanging around my dad's house. When it got to be the time in the day when decisions are made, I'd usually be kind of drunk. I was doing a lot of thinking about certain problems my new lifestyle in Baltimore had confronted me with. For instance, if I did dope three days in a row, I'd be an addict. I believed that. It made sense. Don't feed Gremlins after midnight, don't do heroin three days in a row. Who would do heroin three days in a row? An addict.

But I wondered how you were supposed to count three days in a row. I wondered if the first day you did it was "one." Or maybe the space of time between the first day you did it and the next day would be "one." And then the next day would be "two." And then the next day would be "three." So if you started on Monday, Friday would be the first day you'd have to stop to make sure you didn't turn into an addict. Right? It was pretty confusing. When Funboy said, "Just don't do it three days in a row," he made it sound so easy. Of course, it was pretty obvious he'd failed at not doing it three days in a row. You could count it any way you wanted.

I wanted to take advantage of my time in Chicago. I planned to go to the art museum to see if they had any Fragonard paintings. I wanted to check out some bookstores. I wanted to visit some old friends. My fast thoughts ate holes in my plans. I wondered how to turn my thoughts into weapons. I had a drink of orange juice mixed with gin. I called the department secretary and excused my absence with reference to the death in the family. I lay on the floor for a little while. Then I called to change my ticket and asked Jenny to give me a ride to the airport the next day.

White and gold clouds of fun hid Baltimore as the plane descended. The region had been in the grip of a late heat wave for the past week. I stepped out into the heavy Baltimore air. All the lethargy that had sogged my bones in Chicago turned into something rich and strange.

I'm putting down roots in this city, I thought. When the first colonists arrived in Maryland, they thought it was a weird paradise. They were amazed at the lushness of the vegetation. They remembered stories they'd heard of the lands of the Aztecs far to the south. My vegetable nerves swayed in the invisible Baltimore waves.

In the heated air, the difference between land and sky dissolves. Especially if there's any sun. Then the Baltimore color goes all the way through, like the taste of oranges goes all the way through an orange. Life is a brick of solid gold. The murder rate goes up like a thermometer, showing the power of this new atmosphere. The Baltimore murder rate stayed above three hundred the whole time I was getting high.

I'd saved a half vial in the glove box of my car for my return, and I did it in the darkness of the parking garage.

I drove out into the center of the day. The Baltimore streets can go dead in the middle of the afternoon. It wasn't even a Sunday. I drove through the stately empty streets like they were Aztec ruins. It wasn't just me. The drone of ancient sleep passed through my bones. The alien shapes of plants and buildings lay in ninety-five degrees of heat. No definite outlines, no borders. Baltimore. Anyone who knows will know.

I bought a Coke at the corner store, then entered my building. My legs inside my jeans got sweaty from the short walk. It was devil hot. I checked my mail in the ornate decayed lobby. A thick pile fell out of the box. Bills, bills, bills. I picked out one of the oldest. The paper envelope looked a little yellow with age. As I filed through the rest of the pile the envelopes turned threatening shades of orange and red. "Response Required!" "Overdue!" "Turn off notice!"

When was the last time I'd checked my mail? It was a Monday, I remember, because I'd been coming back from Ferguson's seminar. Was that the day before I left? The day before that? Let's see. I'd been gone for ten days. (Gone but not forgotten.) If today was Wednesday, then I left on a . . . Do I start counting backward from today? Is today "one"? Or is yesterday "one"?

These questions led to another: When had I last paid my bills? I couldn't remember. OK, try to remember what I'd been doing the last day I paid my bills. I couldn't. I tried to remember writing out a check, putting a stamp on an envelope. I concentrated. I saw my pen move across the check; I saw myself licking the stamp. It felt like I was making it up. That wasn't a good sign.

When I got off the elevator at the sixth floor, there was a smell in the hallway. At first I thought it was just me. I was high, after all. I ducked back in the elevator, went up a few floors, came back down, and got out again.

The smell was still there. It was pretty strong right outside my door. It wasn't really a good smell, but it didn't smell like chemicals, either. Not gas. I couldn't identify it. Not smoke. *Why fool yourself?* I thought. It smelled like shit. I opened the door.

The smell was abominable. That was the word that came to mind. It wasn't a word I typically used. The smell used it; it was the smell's word.

There were clouds of tiny flies in the apartment. It was probably a hundred degrees in there. I flicked the light switch. Nothing. The power had been cut off. In my dark mailbox the bills had been warning each other about this for weeks. Now it had happened.

There was a green beer bottle sitting on the floor with five cigarette butts floating in three inches of liquid. Normally one would have smelled that. But it had no smell. Its smell was just erased by the foulness coming in waves from the kitchen. The odorless beer bottle was unreal, just a picture. Like something in a movie.

I walked forward into the apartment and turned straight into the smell. It was hot death. It was obscene, perverted. Full of lies. The smell pulsed and pumped out of the refrigerator. I stared, stunned and frightened, at the white refrigerator, sagging on the filthy floor. In one hundred degrees of heat. Its metal edges went soft and flabby in the heat waves. The evil smell gave it a life. It was alive. I stood there for a while, the dope heavy in my calves and feet. I was afraid to open it and look inside. It had changed.

I stared at it, transfixed. The color white can also mean heat. Intense heat. White heat. The fridge was like a square white sun. The blinds were all closed, and the horrible ten-day-old heat of the apartment bent the light. Look at the fridge. Tiny flies poured from an opening in its back. Look at it. The indent between freezer and refrigerator looked like a thin-lipped white mouth. Unsmiling.

And the abominable smell went right through me. My nose belonged to it. My nose was full of its fly life. I was gone. The smell smelled itself in me.

Stop. I pulled myself together and opened the refrigerator door. A half jar of mayo, four bottles of beer, and a two-pound package of ground beef. Scott and I had opened it to make hamburgers, but then the dope came on and we didn't feel like eating. Now the dead meat was alive with maggots. People used to think maggots spontaneously generated in meat. They'd leave meat in a tightly closed cupboard and open it a week later and it would be crawling with flies. They couldn't understand how the flies had gotten in. They believed it was magic.

I don't remember how this phenomenon was eventually explained, but I felt an ancient feeling when I stared at that two-pound black-and-purple fly womb. I didn't feel too objective. I didn't see this as what happens to meat left in a fridge in an apartment where the power has been shut off during a heat wave.

Looking at the living fly meat, I believed in a devil. I was like a child learning a new lesson. The meat had been dead. But that was a trick. Death is just a thin shell around more life. Worse life. Death is alive. There is no difference between death and life. I shut the door and the fridge's white face stared back at me, flies rising from its head like fast thoughts.

NINE

PLEASURE

Through no fault of my own, my apartment had become infested by maggots. Workers with gloves and masks had to come and take the fridge away. The company that managed the apartment was pretty angry. There had been complaints about the smell. The fridge had to be replaced. They only calmed down when they found out I had nothing to do with it. I carefully explained how the whole mess was my subletter's sole responsibility. My subletter's crime. I'd sublet my apartment to an irresponsible person for the last month. Why beat around the bush? He was an animal. One of the maintenance people had seen him a number of times over the summer. Entering and leaving the apartment, in the company of vicious scumbags. He was tall, thin, and pale, with dark hair and blue eyes.

Yes, well, he looked like me. There's no denying it. We always feel that people who look like us on the outside will be like us on the inside. We feel we can trust them. That's where racism comes from. Well, I've learned my lesson. I'll never trust anyone who looks like me again. He didn't leave any forwarding address, he just cleared out. He still owes me rent money. If you see him, let me know. We're all his victims.

The undead meat smell lingered after the fridge was removed. "It smells like your mom's been in here," Funboy remarked. But a little time removes all smells, the smell of death, the smell of birth. A little time, applied to the stain, removes the stain, then removes what was stained. More slowly. By the time this smell had gone, I'd learned how to kill time for good.

By late October, time still ate away at the bricks and boards of my apartment, but it stopped when it got to me. Time stopped at the lenses of my eyes, at my eardrums, my toes, and my fingertips. With all my bad math and sick memory, I'd finally fucked up and done dope three days in a row. Now I could feel weeks and months and years collapsing inside me, turning to white dust.

I felt like laughing. I wished I'd done it three days in a row before. October 1999 to April 2000. The museum of pleasures. It's time to think a little about the pleasures of addiction.

In October 1999, I realized what I'd been doing. I'd cast a spell on the world. The spell worked. White tops. Time killers. It's a wizard pleasure. It lasted for roughly six months of calendar time.

The museum of white pleasure. I still have it. It sits on my desk as I write, like one of those glass globes. When you shake it, white dust covers the little house and people. I'm there. Funboy, Todd, Nancy, and Andy are waving. Six months, curved like a globe. The needle that pierces it from the north, will emerge in the west. Emerge changed. White power. Those whom I love, time shall not touch. It's like a poem. No weapon raised against me shall prosper. It's like a prayer.

Pleasure, ancient spinal animal pleasure, comes from gaining control or losing control. Losing control and gaining control. The pleasure that began for me in October 1999 was the pleasure of gaining control. The first power granted me was the control over spirits, over numbers, over the words and thoughts of the dead. I discovered it late one night, sitting on my ratty couch reading *Walden*. I was wondering what I'd gone to grad school for. I was supposed to be learning how to think in Baltimore. History, literature, philosophy.

I was reading *Walden*. An assignment from a seminar I was taking. I'd just gotten back from a dope run with Funboy, and as the white dope wheel turned inside me, the words from the book dropped through the spokes.

The words lost their old familiar shapes in the turning dope wheel. The most naked clichés, shapes as dull and public as a post office—"Each man steps to the beat of a different drummer," "Wealth is the ability to fully experience life"—I saw them melt and run. Everything was melting and running, and my new dope thinking had a place for everything. I saw myself writing a new history of the nineteenth century. Of the twentieth century. The twenty-first. Close up, my new history was grooved and tunneled like a beehive. It had slots for every melting sentence from the past and future. From a distance it looked like a star.

In the timeless space of dope I discovered that time is the great enemy of thought. Trapped in time, a thought is shapeless. Its far end is hidden in an unknown past; its near end is lost in an unknown future. The business of the thinker is with the part that passes overhead. The conduits, the wire or metallic hollows going from there to there. Skulls, gold, bubbles, names, and viruses fill the chambers, empty the past of everything solid and carry it all to be reassembled in the future. The present is crisscrossed with tubes and wires. Put your hand on any present object—this wooden desk, *Walden,* a ten-dollar bill—and the hum of the traffic of solids, liquids, numbers, and words vibrates under your fingertips.

Time means that every solid shape is in motion. The teacup I hold in my hand is a bullet shot out of a gun. It's no wonder that it's so impossibly hard to think in these conditions. It's no wonder that maggots grow in fresh meat, that an electric bill is overdue as soon as you open it, that the first time you try something you're already addicted.

But all that was over now. The timeless space of dope was like a magic picture frame. In it, the shapes of thoughts, sentences, and phenomena grew solid outlines, stood still, and let me copy them down in my essays. My stalled graduate student career took off. I found my star shape in every volume in the archives. I couldn't read enough. My professors took notice.

"You have an interesting mind," they said. "Send this to the editor of this journal." The editors liked it too. I wondered if they did dope themselves. I became certain of it. I imagined myself at the age of the oldest, sitting in my spacious office, the walls lined with my books, and a crystal bowl of raw dope on my desk. Funboy's portrait over the doorway.

October, November, December, January. Isn't it nice to sit down with a good book and take the phone off the hook while a fire burns in the fireplace? Wouldn't it be even nicer if the fire was burning the future and the past, and now nothing could ever touch you?

I'd always wanted a place outside the world. Candy Land with glass fields and sidewalks, so you could rest your head on your hands and gaze dreamily down through the clouds at the world below. I was building Candy Land. Each book in the piles around my couch was a square of glass pavement.

The tall windows of my apartment looked out over cold streets in November. With the chill, and the end of time, a new elegance had taken hold everywhere. Nothing would grow again, but that was fine; there was so much to catalog and reshape and light up, even a thousand years wouldn't be enough. I had a thousand years. Just then my friend Todd showed up at my door. He wanted to talk. I put on the teakettle.

"I feel as if the next frontier for the theory of sexuality is bestiality," Todd said. He was writing an article on the history of sexuality. I laughed.

"No, I'm serious, Mike," he was smiling. "You know, when you've got a little dog, and you want him to come in for the night, and you put a little dish of water at the back door, and he comes in? What is that?"

"Bestiality," I said.

"How about when you've got a little white horse, and you set him down on the counter, he's pawing at the tiles, and you bend down, and you let him run up into your nose?"

"Bestiality," I said, bending down and sniffing a line of horse off the counter. "But what does it have to do with sex?"

"Losing control," he said. "Every kind of losing control is sexual. Plus everything about animals is sexy."

"Why losing control?" I asked, ignoring the part about sexy animals. "Dogs and horses are tame animals. Isn't that gaining control? Both of those examples are examples of mastery."

"No, they're not," he said quickly. "All you do is let the animals in. You open your home, your nose, to the animal, and then the animal is free inside you. The dog slinks around the china, sniffs the glasses on the dinner table."

"But you let the dog in because the dog is tame."

"Being tame means that when you tell an animal to run inside your house, the animal runs in."

"OK, but all this is pretty abstract. Bestiality is just when people get turned on by animals."

"That's an oversimplification. Bestiality is not necessarily about being attracted to the animal's body. Not at first. First you let the animal in. The idea of the animal gets loose in you. It makes new openings. The animal trots and nuzzles and bites and makes new sensitive spaces. At night, when you're sleeping or watching TV, the animal rewrites your body from the inside out." He paused, lighting a cigarette.

"You wake up one day and your body is covered with paw-shaped holes, horn-shaped holes, hoof-shaped holes. Each one is red and sensitive and horny. The animal has made you animal-ready. It's a process, like falling in love."

What could I say to that?

Todd was smart and rich and handsome, in a kind of androgynous way. Blond, blue eyes, slim, medium height. Every grad school had wanted him. When he'd visited Johns Hopkins, an important professor from Chicago had given a lecture. A bunch of the professors had asked questions, trying to trip her up. Todd had calmly raised his hand and asked a question that she said "opened new vistas."

Whatever. But he was super-smart, and I felt like I needed new friends like him. Blond, blue, androgynous. Blue-white skin when he was high. Then he looked like a tall JonBenét Ramsey. And he talked about bestiality. The third point of the new triangle was a real girl, which kept everything in perspective. Her name was Nancy.

She was smart and lovely, with dark hair and fair skin. Well-dressed. Her parents had raised her as if they'd been richer than they were. Phantom mansions and Bentleys shone in her gestures. She wasn't above a little dope, either.

That fall, she and Todd and I were often together. We'd stage elaborate dope-doing times, with candles and music, and me pretending that I only did it on those occasions. It was easy to pretend. Ice was growing in my veins. Any discrepancies would disappear down the white holes of our weekends. Of course there were some awkward moments. But on the whole I was happy. I spent the white nights writing and reading, the soft white afternoons drinking tea with Todd, or Todd and Nancy.

Or just Nancy, for instance. It was snowing a little.

"I worry about Todd, Mike. He seems so vulnerable, as if he could be easily lost."

"We should mark him in some way so we could easily find him, if he does get lost. If he had one eye, for instance, or one arm . . ." She laughed. I didn't like this talk of Todd's tenderness. It seemed like the beginning of a crush. She was worried. She wanted to take care of him. A nasty nurse's crush. Nurse Nancy pushing Todd around in a wheelchair. Todd and Nancy. An animal with Nancy's legs and Todd's head. Bestiality. That would upset our little triangle. I knew; I had experience. Plus I had other plans for Nancy.

"Still," she said, "he seems to like dope a little too much. You and I, Mike, we're different. But I can see it being a problem for him."

"You know, you're right," I said, looking troubled. "Last week he asked me if I could get him some. Just to do on his own. Help him relax after his seminar. I refused, of course, but . . ."

"Oh, I'm glad you didn't, Mike. You mustn't! Promise me."

"I promise." We sat in her living room talking about philosophy, and Milton, and rap. It grew dark. She was drinking wine;

I was drinking tea. When the white light dimmed I went to the bathroom and tipped a little white powder onto the sink, sniffed it up, and flushed the toilet. When I came out I told her some stories.

"And then he told me that after the revolution, the slums would be filled with white people!" Nancy laughed merrily. I told her about how Funboy and I had stolen guitars from a music store and almost got caught. I told her about my stepmother's sister, and fell silent for a few seconds, while she contemplated the depth of my hidden feelings. I told her about Charlie.

I began talking about Marx. I told her a joke about Queen Elizabeth. She laughed until she coughed, her cheeks were bright red, and her eyes were shining. I wished I were on the ceiling, looking down, the better to admire my performance.

Then she ruined it all. She took my hand. I stopped in mid-sentence. She kissed my open mouth. When her tongue pressed into my lip I could feel her heart beating. This was not what I'd planned.

"Come on," she said. Her hand slid down my leg and back up, and back down. My rebel body responded. She kissed me. I kissed her. I pinched her nipples. She put her tongue in my ear. I massaged her inner thighs. I turned, bent, kissed, rubbed, and kissed again, thinking frantically all the time. What was I going to do? Dope doesn't stop you from having sex, but it makes it absolutely impossible to stop having sex. No finish. You can't come.

I knew this. I'd been planning Nancy's seduction for weeks. But it wasn't supposed to be tonight. I was going to make very sure I didn't do dope the night we finally hooked up. But the dopeless night never came, and now it was happening. I was pulling her hair; she turned around to look nasty at me. The mirror showed an animal with four legs and two heads.

I had total control over it. Total control over my mind, her body, and the situation. The one thing I couldn't do was the one thing I needed to do: lose control. The most natural and ordinary thing in the world, a kind of sneeze. A little muscular spasm, seven seconds of uncontrollable shudders and my triumph would be complete. But I couldn't do it. And I couldn't not do it either. She'd know something was up.

She didn't make it easy.

"I want you to come on my face."

"Um, I don't want to ruin your sheets. I love this color."

"Never mind the sheets!" It had been a half hour easy. She was going all out. Everything she could think of. She could have used a wrench and a vise; it wouldn't have mattered. I noticed the snow sifting down through the dark windows. I looked at her back when she was facing that way, her breasts when she faced this way. She was red-faced and sweating like a sailor. She was stronger than she looked. I had to admire her effort. I was afraid she was going to have a heart attack. There was no putting it off any longer.

"Oh God!" I cried. "Oh it's happening, oh baby! It feels so good! Aaaarrggghh!" As soon as I'd said it I realized how fake it sounded.

"Oh Jesus yes!" My best wasn't good enough. The room fell silent, the really bad kind of awkward silence it usually takes more than two people to generate. Saying the wrong thing at a funeral, for example. This was a fifty-person awkward silence. Maybe a hundred. Nancy lay still in it. I hadn't been wearing a condom. She hadn't let me. For men, successfully faking an orgasm requires either a very drunk woman, or technology. I had no technology and the exercise had sobered her up. She lay looking at me strangely.

"That was really awesome," I said. Just ride it out. I was still as hard as a rock. The room was dark but my pupils were tiny pinpricks. Nancy wasn't an idiot.

"Good-bye, Mike."

Gaining control and losing control. One night that fall I dreamed I was JonBenét Ramsey. My white, white face floated in mirrors, in silver bowls, in huge, dark eyes. I put my tiny white hand in someone's huge red hand. He followed me wherever I went. I could make him do whatever I wanted. I had total control. I stopped. He stopped. I knelt down. The vast dark bulk above me halved.

I charmed my follower's huge hand like a snake. It moved toward me, fingers spread. I pointed at it. It stopped. It started moving again. I pressed against it. It kept coming. I pushed. The tiny muscles popped and wore out all along my arms and back, and still the hand moved toward me, the fingers closing. I saw myself in the huge white and red eye like the white dot at the center of a target. My white face. The eye closed on me like a trap.

Gaining control and losing control. Perhaps they're the same after all. One makes more sense than two.

But that was an anomaly. I started telling people Nancy had raped me. I said it as a joke at first, for the shocked laughs. Then I kind of believed it. She wasn't too pleased when it got back to her.

But that was just a misunderstanding. Not important. I really don't know why I even put it in here. At the time, I hardly even noticed it, with all the new things I was learning. The little things, for example. I never knew about the cancer of the little things. Checking my mail, doing laundry, opening a car door, closing the door. I never realized how sick it was making me. Picking up the phone. Buying milk. I was a sitting duck. Walking across a floor or down a path. Driving somewhere. Waking up. It was killing me. It's killing all of us. Some diseases you never know you have until you get the cure.

I got the cure. It came in white-topped vials. Sometimes they had red tops. The cancer of putting gas in my car in fair weather or foul without being high was history. The cancer of sober morning, the cancer of sober evening: history. The cancer of being vulnerable to constantly changing feelings. Exposed naked on the cliffs of your natural brain chemistry. Alternately scorched or frozen. Some days you're happy; some days you're sad. Fuck that.

Human life is like a Greek curse. Pushing a rock up a hill. Everything good is changing into something bad. And what's almost worst, everything bad is changing too. Smiling or crying for no reason. On purpose or by accident.

When you're human all things conspire against you. The terrible feeling of a sheet brushing against your naked skin when you've got a cold. No price is too high for escape. Stalin's agents had cyanide capsules hidden in false teeth. I was the agent of the white revolution, and I had white tops hidden in my glove compartment, my desk drawers, my shoes, my allergy medicine bottles.

Perfect safety. Perfect freedom. Perfect comfort. Straight months of the invulnerable high. It closes all those doors, the doors that let in what you hate and let out what you love. The accordion doors of the lungs, the traitor heart mixing pain and time-poison with your blood. The hand door, the eye door.

Dope gives me a new, dope body. Closed like a fist. Of course I'm a little constipated, but that's a small price to pay for total protection. No way for the time-poison, the change-poison to get in. I'm like a ball of metal. A thick spike of oxygen melts slowly in my center, where the lungs were. A white heart. I don't know what the white heart does. It gets me high. I imagine it looks like a lump of dope. Like two big sugar cubes in a glass of milk.

And the way the world looks from deep inside the dope body! From high atop the white tower. The world. It would break your human heart to see it. Everything so smooth, gleaming so smoothly. So beautiful, so deep. My dope eye doesn't have any bottom, and I see into the bottomlessness of things.

Eyes open for ten minutes without blinking. The world has a perfect geometry. The buildings above in the snowfall are all arcs and moons. The way ahead is all squares and triangles. Sleep is like the back of my hand, nothing mysterious. Same with death. Nothing to fear.

And when I wake, I've saved a half vial. I wake with that itching and twitching, the old human body thawing, the old creaking doors opening, letting in the time-poison, the human lungs starting up again. A little cold sweat on the forehead.

But it's just tingles of anticipation. Savor it for a few minutes. I can stop it anytime I want. Withdrawal lasts only as long as I let it. Make a cup of tea. Let my limbs ache and let sweat come out on my forehead. Watch my body stutter and shake like a zombie coming back.

And remember it like a prayer: This is the sickness of human life, the sickness I've been saved from.

Then do that half vial. Here comes the perfect world. The essay, where I left it. The thoughts have been burrowing while I slept. The morning is like a star that swallowed itself. Bright dust in space. And it still costs just ten dollars to keep my white metal angel body alive for another day. My exoskeletal astro body. My astro lungs, white heart, and hard, decorative marble genitals.

Nobody better fuck with me. Funboy got a foot up his ass when he came sniffing around. He owes me forty bucks. See you never, Funboy. I was copping from Tony. I always knew where to find him. I wrote my essays with ten dollars in each nostril. Todd came around in the sweet, deep afternoons. Am I making myself clear? I floated like an astronaut in the white world. I was in graduate school. Listen to the voice of the teacher:

"Our work at this institution concerns interpretation. Interpretation is the art of becoming open to the past. You wish to become a historian? To discover the past? Endeavor to become the future of the past you wish to discover. Endeavor to remember it.

"The documents we work with in this institution are not messages. Do not think of them as messages. They are not communications from one person to another. They are more like fossils than messages. More like the tools of an ancient people than fossils. Primitive and clumsy. Ridiculous, out of place, a scandal in the modern world.

"Henry David Thoreau's *Walden,* for example. Delivered into your hands. Do you understand this document? Do you understand the past? Is your memory strong enough?"

Dear reader, I floated like an astronaut in the white world. October 1999. I sat on my ratty couch reading *Walden* for my seminar the next day. Imagine me there in my white space suit, heavy sound of mechanical breathing, my white eyes dim behind the glass shield of my helmet, the book spread out before me. I unhooked the ropes of words from the lines on the page, strung them between my bookshelf and the stars in my window, and they began to glow.

TEN

BLOODLESS

What's left of you when you change? Is there a part of you that doesn't change? And if there isn't, how will you even notice when the change comes?

I can't say for you. I kind of noticed. I noticed I'd changed. At first I was relieved. I was relieved I couldn't feel certain things. Like the boredom of waiting for my car's gas tank to fill up. I couldn't feel it. That was fun. Then it was fun, but a little spooky. Like putting a two-inch needle through your arm and not feeling it. Or feeling good. Then I caught a glimpse of myself in the mirror.

It wasn't what you might think. I wasn't shocked by my white lips or red nostrils. I didn't get freaked by the astronaut suit or the silver visor.

It was very quiet.

I was getting ready to teach class. I brushed my teeth, spat, and looked up into the mirror. I saw my body, my face, my eyes and lips there in the mirror. I also saw my bathroom wall, my sweater, the edge of the light fixture, and the back of the faucet. All these things (nose, wall, eyes, faucet) looked the same. The things looked the same as each other. I looked the same as the things. I didn't see a difference between my face and the back of the faucet.

I'm not saying my face and the faucet somehow lost their proper forms or colors or melted into each other or something. Enough LSD or Robitussin can do that. I'm talking about a genuinely strange experience.

There's a simple human feeling people get when they see themselves in the mirror. I don't mean when you worry that your teeth look yellow or your hair looks flat. I'm talking about something beneath that, something basic.

There's a simple basic difference between seeing your own hands or eyes and seeing a metal faucet. It's not a sharp difference, like discovering the person sleeping next to you is a dead horse instead of your girlfriend. It's not a big feeling, this felt difference between your hand in the mirror and the faucet, but it's there. You're reading this, you can see a fringe of yourself, your hand or maybe your hair, around this page of words. See?

Maybe you notice it, maybe you don't. But when it's gone you feel a little strange. A certain distance. I felt a little distant from myself. From that distance my hand and the faucet looked about the same. The way houses look from outer space. Black dots on black dots. Which one is yours?

Where had I traveled, to get that distance from myself? And did part of me stay behind, to notice how strange it all was? What was left of me when I changed? Where did it stay? And if nothing was left, then how could I even tell I was different? You see what I mean.

Because I'm not saying this change was totally obvious. I'm not saying I stopped caring about myself or anything. I'm not saying I stopped being able to walk around, or teach a class, or fall asleep, or read a book, or recognize a familiar face (even my own). I mean, I could still function very well. Pretty well. For a long time, another year or so, I was able to function just fine. It's not like I had to get on my hands and knees to get across a room. (Not often, anyway.)

But humans have certain, almost invisible adaptations to this world. We're made for these minutes and seconds and seasons. We're sensitive to differences that don't seem to matter, and are hard to describe. The human body has a grip on this world. The white body, the white eye, the white mind: It just doesn't have the same grip.

I stood looking at my face in the mirror. It looked the same as the things. Not bad. Not good. A lot of white, though. Maybe it was the lighting? The metal faucet looked white too. There was an odd spreading brown bruise on my thumb. How had that happened? The phone rang. I threw up into the toilet and went back to bed.

What was there in bed? Memories of my computer game. I'd been playing a game called Civilization. In it, you try to take over the world. I set the difficulty level to "Easy." I was playing the Germans. I had tanks, and my rivals, the Egyptians, were still using knights on horses.

As I lay in bed shaking from the bad dope I imagined line after line of horses meeting my tanks. I imagined the staccato of the tanks' machine guns, then the heavy boom of the big tank guns, then the machine guns, then the dying horses, the bullets biting the knights' faces, the boom of the big tank guns.

What happens when a tank shell hits a knight charging at full speed across a muddy field? A white fire. Bullets coming through the thick sunset, the thick Egyptian dusk. Like Morocco. Eva's eyes swam up through the dusk like death kisses. Catching white knights unawares.

I imagined my capital, Berlin, surrounded by lush jungle. I had built the Eiffel Tower in it. It was the number one city in the world. The dope I was doing now was deep brown. It even tasted brown. I also had the number two, three, and five cities. Egypt had number four. Thebes. Brown like coffee. Do they smuggle dope in coffee? My hands shook. My legs were scratched to hell. My tanks approached Thebes inexorably. The valiant, doomed Egyptian knights sallied forth. The phone rang again.

The bullet-air was like a mouth chewing on the knights' white swords and brown horse faces. Today was a Thursday. I had two hundred dollars of unusually deep brown dope on my dresser. It was making me sick. When I took it I got nauseous and threw up and lay in bed waiting for it to wear off.

As it began to wear off the nausea subsided and the first little shakes and fevers of withdrawal started. I got up and took shaky steps back over to the dresser and stared again at the bad brown dope. Can your eyes get bruised? Can you get bruises on your eyes? I did some more of the dope and the withdrawal shiver vanished.

I threw up again. I crawled back to bed. Do you know what immortality is? When you have tanks and they have horses, and death is a length of brown carpet between your bed and the dresser. Death is the toilet handle. Death is closing your right eye and opening your left eye. Then death is waiting. Alive and waiting. Then death is opening your right eye and closing your left eye, then it is waiting again, and then it is throwing up.

Then, standing gasping over the toilet, I heard them. Through the thin body haze they appear: the immortal pixilated brown computer dope tanks.

Before children arrive at the stage of wanting to be firemen or soldiers, they pass through the stage of wanting to be fire trucks or tanks. Unkillable red trucks, unkillable brown tanks. I was sunk in the mud of that stage, the heavy brown treads of the dope tanks churning my memory to mud. And killing hundreds of thousands of people. The phone rang and rang and rang and rang.

Each time you call a dope fiend who doesn't want to talk to you, that fiend's hate spins down through time and memory and kills a living person.

In this way, when I was six, I learned of the death of one of my neighbors. She died behind the white face of her house. It got her there. Hate out of the future surprised her when she was lying down for a little nap after lunch.

She was a nice older lady. She wore white gloves and a blue dress. She had a nice car. My mother called us into the kitchen.

"Kids, you know how I told you Mrs. Nichols was sick?" We nodded. I shifted from foot to foot smiling. I had been in trouble for something earlier and was now perfect.

"Well, Mrs. Nichols passed away last night. God took her. She was old. She lived a good life, and she is in a happy place now." I looked up at my mother and saw a half smile on her quiet church face. It was clear to me she didn't know what she was talking about.

"How does that make you feel, kids?" While Mom was talking, my sister was creeping. Now she stood far enough away from me that Mom could just barely look at both of us without turning her head. Then Jenny crept a little farther away.

"Jenny, come back here! I want to talk to you kids." Jenny crept back. Mom looked expectantly between our faces.

"Mrs. Nichols was our friend and neighbor," Mom continued. She looked at us expectantly. Mrs. Nichols. A happy place now. A thing like that. What could one say?

"Who," I asked, "is living in Mrs. Nichols's house now?"

Who indeed? Friendly pairs of houses faced each other across our quiet street. Our house faced Mrs. Nichols's. The enormous white face of Mrs. Nichols's house still turned toward us. After Mom dismissed us, I sat out on our steps and looked back at it. My friend Dan rolled up on his Big Wheel.

"What're you doing, Mike?"

"Nothing. Mrs. Nichols passed away," I said.

"Who?" Dan looked puzzled. He lived eight houses down from us. Living so far away, I didn't expect him to have heard of her.

"Nobody," I said. I tipped my head back and looked at the white clouds, the blue sky.

"My teacher has arth-rit-is," I told Dan, pronouncing the big word slowly. He went to Lincoln public school while I went to St. Mary's Catholic school across town. My first-grade teacher's name was Sister Pancraceous. My parents thought her name was funny. Sometimes when she dropped something my mother would laugh and say, "Goodness gracious, Sister Pancraceous!"

"My grandma has arth-rit-is," Dan said. "Her hands always hurt." I nodded.

"My teacher told us that she got arthritis because she used to fidget when she was a kid," I said. "She said if we keep very, very still we won't get arthritis."

After lunch one day, Sister Pancraceous told us how to prevent arthritis. The whole class practiced sitting very, very still together. I remember looking curiously at my own limbs. *They want to move so badly,* I thought. Dan looked worried.

"How long do you have to keep still?"

"Not that long," I said. "And you can save it up. Every minute you keep very still you are saving it up for the future."

"Is that what you are doing now?" Dan asked.

"Yes. I just want to save up a little bit today."

I tilted my head back and looked at the sky again. I was unaware of how strange it was for a child to stare at the sky. I was six. My looking was tuned to human faces. To the little or big people faces of toys, shoes, televisions, Mom, chocolate bars, houses.

Looking into the sky, I felt like anything could happen. The sky was like a face that had come apart. The clouds rose in Mrs. Nichols's windows.

Dan climbed off his Big Wheel and sat down Indian-style. He stared hard straight into the grass. After he had saved up maybe forty seconds of stillness he started plucking single blades of grass and counting them.

"One . . . two . . . three." I watched him. He wasn't just picking any blade.

"What are you doing?" I said, crouching down next to him. He had an intense look of concentration as he scanned dozens of grass blades. The day had clouded over. The outside was like a room now. It was people time again. Who lived in Mrs. Nichols's house? I poked Dan on the shoulder.

"Look at this one," Dan said. He held a blade of grass between his thumb and forefinger. I bent closer.

"What's different about it?" I asked, puzzled.

"Look at it." Gripping the slender pale-green blade firmly between the thumb and forefinger of his left hand, he pressed the tip of the fingernail of his right pinky against a tiny place in the blade.

I looked closer and saw the grass blade was made up of hundreds of strands, like a white sheet is made up of hundreds of white threads. Dan was pointing to one of them. His little finger shook with the effort.

"You see it?" The single strand he was pointing at had a faint red color. There was a slender red strand in the grass blade. I followed the thread of color up and down the blade's two inches, to where all the strands ended in a shiny green sheath.

"I see it," I whispered. He nodded, and opened his left palm. There were two other grass blades in it. Each had one of the red threads.

"They're red-blooded," Dan said.

"Blooded," I whispered. I plucked a grass blade and held it against the sky. The blade was woven of strands that were white and yellow and brown and yellow-white and white-brown and white-white. I was surprised I had ever thought grass was plain green. Dan looked at me disapprovingly. He took the blade I was holding out of my hand and threw it away.

"Look for the red-blooded ones," he said. He continued to search. "Four," he said. "Five," he said. I got down on my hands and knees and started to look.

I never found one. I saw the blood every time he showed me one of his. Every time he patiently pointed it out with his shaking pinky I could see it. But I never found a blooded blade of grass myself.

All summer on clear days Mrs. Nichols's house looked at the sky. On overcast days it stared blindly out, with a milky film on the windows.

And from time to time that summer, sitting on the grass with Dan while he slowly counted, I would be seized with panic. It was like a test. Why couldn't I find any? Why couldn't I see the red-blooded ones?

I thought then it was bad luck. I think now it was my bad habit of looking at the sky. I stared at the sky and I think there were things I missed because of it. Who taught me that habit? The person who lived in Mrs. Nichols's house after she died taught me. It taught me to look at the sky and now I couldn't see the tiny thread of red in one out of a hundred grass blades. I couldn't see the really small things, the things you can't see from the sky even with a ghost's eyes.

I could see the larger shapes. The shapes you might remember from twenty or a hundred years out. Something as big as a house, sure. And I could see the colors of the future. White, and sometimes brown.

I lay undead on my bed with white sheets made of white threads, looking down into the past. Dogshit brown dope on my dresser. Had this happened before? I wondered. Or was it just the memory disease? It makes things seem like they happen twice. The phone rang. When I got up to get it, the line went dead. I went back to bed. *Maybe it was me,* I thought. *Prank calling myself from the future. A future of hate.* Just then there was a crack as my bedroom door swung open at a thousand miles per second and Henry stood armless in my doorway. Half-armless. One-armed.

"What the fuck?" I said.

"Your door was open," Henry said. His inhuman form rose where it shouldn't have, leaning there in my bedroom like the Eiffel Tower. Or the Leaning Tower of Pisa. He looked at the dope on my dresser.

"Don't even," I said.

He shuffled over to the dresser and started doing magic tricks over the dope, honking softly, rambling.

"You shouldn't just leave your door open, Mike . . . beautiful pile you got here . . . just a little too close to the edge of this dresser, huh . . . deep brown, huh . . . this is just going to blow away standing at the edge like that . . . not going to jump are you, little fellow . . . just let me help you there."

He carefully adjusted the dope pile, moving it a little to the left, a little to the right. I thought I saw a straw between his fingers for a second and then it was gone.

The dope pile looked a little different when I finally got over to it on my bloodless brown dope legs. But I had to admit it was safer. Farther from the edge of the dresser. Henry was like insurance. Sometimes you have to pay a little to save it all. I looked at the smaller pile with love and hate. Henry excused himself and went to throw up in the bathroom.

"I didn't leave my door open, Henry," I said. "How did you get in?"

"It's that nasty brown dope you got, Mike," he said, sitting down heavily on my bed. "You shoulda told me but it's OK. It happens. Damn Nazi dealers. Poison you to make a buck. The secret is to take it in little doses, just enough to hold off the jones, until you can get your hands on some good stuff."

"I didn't think you knew how to get to my place, Henry," I said.

"Kurt dropped me off," he said.

"For what?"

"You don't remember?"

We stared at each other. I don't remember. Then we were in the car. I was driving. We stopped at a nice brick house in Guilford where Henry scrambled up to the door and handed a bottle of Oxys to a nice middle-aged woman and then came back to the car with the money. Then we went to Edmondson Avenue and scored six red tops. I fixed in a gas station bathroom off Route 40 just outside of downtown. Little phantom mouths flowered around my neck, releasing ten thousand years of pressure in a gust of brown gas. I looked into the bathroom mirror through the brown mist and the condensation and the claw marks of devils and I smiled.

When we slid out the gas station east toward Fells Point, several seconds were missing from every minute, and five or six words were missing from every sentence.

"Ye—es," Henry said.

The sun hung at the summer angle that turns the feelings of mortals away from the sadness of eventual death, toward the sadness of endless life. Squirrels, dogs on leashes, white ladies, pigeons, snitches, and stray cats moved or stood along the sides of the road as we passed.

"Roll it out," I said to the wheels beneath me. "Roll it out."

"The cap-ital of California is Sacramento," Henry recited. "The cap-ital of Arizona is Arizona City."

An unreal high had its knife at my heart, and when we went over a little bump it pushed in the tip a little. I thought, *Damn, there's more to this shit than just how you feel about it.*

"The cap-ital of Texas is Texas," said Henry.

When we got to Dom's, the door was ajar and we pushed on in. We were feeling a little like cowboys and a little like explorers. Relaxed like cowboys, but still looking for drugs, like explorers.

"Yoodle-ey-hee-hoooo," Henry said into the bright heart-attack darkness of Dom's place of residence.

"Up here, pardner," said Dom with his voice.

We tramped slowly up the stairs. Henry went into the big open room at the end of the hall, while I swung into the bathroom. Dom was there, next to the mirror with his chin up, looking like he was shaving, unsteadily guiding a needle into his neck.

"Let me shed some light on the subject, Dom," I said, pushing open the rag that hung over the bathroom window and revealing a neck that looked like a broken foot with the toes missing. "You're going to kill yourself doing that in the dark."

"I think I already did, son," he said, pushing the plunger home. He straightened up, blinked a couple times, pushed the rag back over the hole, turned to me, held out his arm, and said:

"Shall we?"

"Such a gentleman!" I said, as he escorted me down the hallway.

Henry was sprawled full on the floor in the big room, with his head and face lifted politely and even elegantly up toward his approaching guests. He pulled himself up to a sitting posture as Dom and I took our seats on the floor.

"We're glad you're here today, Mike," Henry said, "because today—"

"—is Henry's birthday!" Dom said. They both beamed.

"Happy birthday, Henry," I said.

"Got somfin' for you, Henry," Dom said. He turned behind him and rooted around in the pile of newspapers, empty cigarette packs, unopened condom packs, and gas-station hot-dog wrappers until he emerged with something long in a brown bag.

"What is it?" we breathed.

"A beer!" Dom unsheathed the twenty-two-ounce beer and placed it in the center of the room. We all craned over to look at it.

"A beer!" I said.

"A beer," Henry said. "Look at that." He looked at Dom, who turned shyly away.

"You shouldn't have, Dom."

"Well," Dom mumbled, "I figured what the hell, a birthday only comes along once a year."

"I guess it's been so long I tasted a beer, I forgot what it tastes like!" Henry said. He picked it up gingerly by the neck in his single hand, and turned it a little in his palm. He did this by ungrasping his hand so the bottle would slip a little, turning as it slipped, then gripping it again. Grip, slip, turn, grip.

"Bud, too!" He said. "That's a good brand."

"The best," I said. "Say what you like about Bud, it's a very good beer. Everyone knows that."

"They got all kinda ads and shit," Henry said. "When's the last time you seen an ad for Old Milwaukee?"

"I just thought that one looked nice," Dom said. I could tell that now he was thinking maybe he should have got a forty, or even a six-pack. Maybe he was even getting a little sad about it. Henry looked at him.

"I just love it, Dom," he said. "This is the best birthday present anyone has gotten me in as long as I can remember." He paused. "Matter of fact, it's the only birthday present anyone's gotten me since . . . since I was a teenager." Henry's eyes were bright. He set the bottle on the floor and pushed it out to the center of the room.

"I want all of us to share it," he said.

"No, Henry," I said. "It's your beer, you drink it."

"That's right, Henry," Dom said. "It's your birthday, this Bud's for you."

"No," Henry said firmly, "everyone gets a sip."

He nodded to me. I looked at Dom, who shrugged. I picked up the bottle gingerly and unscrewed the cap. Budweiser's famous life-giving brown bubbles moved slowly behind the real glass. I sipped it, and as the potent warm juice dropped down my numb throat into my nonfunctioning guts I thought about beer. About how it was the universal beverage of good times and celebration.

I wiped my lips and passed it to Dom, who shook his head. I gave it to Henry. He drank deeply. Then set the bottle down and wiped his lips with the back of his uniarm. He was smiling, smacking his lips. After a few seconds his smile disappeared.

"Beer sucks," Henry said. "You gotta be a fucking retard to be an alcoholic."

"No shit," said Dom immediately.

I spit the piss left in my mouth out onto the floor.

Dom reached out with his huge bear arm and knocked over the bottle. The beer pooled out in long dirty streams collecting ashes and dirt and dried blood until the streams turned to black marks and stopped moving. We all started laughing. We laughed and laughed, sounding like vacuums trying to suck up tennis balls, laughing, laughing, our long dry tongues lolling back into our throats, laughing until the unabsorbed beer sprayed out of my nostrils and out of Henry's half-toothless mouth.

When the laughter had died down and Dom had stopped talking and moving and almost stopped breathing collapsed in a pile in the corner—when that happened I leaned over to Henry, who was still smiling.

"Can I ask you a question, Henry?" I said.

"Anything, Mike," he said. "It's my birthday."

"How did you get into my apartment today, Henry?"

Mrs. Nichols dies when I'm six. I look at the sky. The phone rings when I'm twenty-five, lying on my bed alternately sick from dope and sick from no dope.

Why did these things happen? What caused them? Did Mrs. Nichols's death cause me to look up at the sky when I was six? Did my odd habit of staring at the sky when I was a kid cause me to become a junkie? And then, lying sick from bad dope, did my hate at that goddamn ringing telephone drop down through the past and kill Mrs. Nichols?

I'll admit that these cause-and-effect chains are pure speculation. Does fidgeting cause arthritis? Sister Pancraceous fidgeted when she was a kid, then she got arthritis. You want to correct her? Punish her? A nice old lady like that? A nun, for God's sake.

It's not like anyone really knows for sure. Cause and effect is a famous mystery. One thing happens, then another. There's an empty space between. No way to tell for sure. Connect the events as you like. Sister Pancraceous fidgeted, then she got arthritis. Simple as that, a straight line.

I prefer circles to lines. Mrs. Nichols's death caused me to become a junkie, and my junkie hate came out of the future to kill her. She deserved it, in a way.

Sure, I want my life to look realistic, just like anyone would. But cause-and-effect questions don't always have realistic answers. Think about it. What came first, the chicken or the egg? Dom or Henry? Life or death?

I had stopped working on my dissertation, but I still sometimes scribbled little bits and pieces before I went to sleep. Not about the big questions. Practical writing: "Don't Do Dope Today!!!" "Dope Kills!" "Get Help, I'm Worth It!" I left these little notes for myself all around my apartment. I was like a slogan writer for D.A.R.E. I also wrote a poem around that time. I still have it.

JULY

Dumber and harder to remember
The summer turns itself into
Those two junkies you were sure
Wouldn't make it through the winter:
Dom and Henry, Henry and Dom.
And they are living in that house
Stripped down to that bone,
With that light on those boards.
Those plain and simple four:
The two that they are and the two they are not.

Henry found a bit of what he calls unloosening glue
Drip drip from the pipe under under
The sink. Gets a bit on his fingers gets
Unstuck from the thing, and then the other,
Then his grip comes loose going up
Like smoke rings.
And Dom burned a hole so deep in his wrist
He hides quarters there for emergencies.

If this is death, I don't want to die. July.
The one time of the year
When the same unendingness of undeath
Is better
Than the monotonous Dom/Henry, Dom/Henry
    changes of death

ELEVEN

THE PEOPLE

In Baltimore they call cops "knockers." We had to watch out for the knockers. Cops dressed like junkies. Undercovers. They were hard to spot. I asked everyone I knew about their favorite way of detecting knockers. It was a survey.

"So how can you tell a knocker?" I'd ask.

"It's easy," Funboy said. "Knockers're black. But the dope boys got it twisted. That's why some spots won't serve white fiends."

"It's easy," Tony said. "Knockers always white. That's why we don't serve white boys. Except you, Funboy. And you."

"It's tricky," Henry said, "but I got the trick. Knockers always look you right in the eyes. Their eyes knock into yours. It's why they're called knockers."

"Knockers don't look at the dope right," Dom said. "They look at it the way you might look at a beer. Or at Henry."

"Knockers drive Toyotas," Todd said.

"Knockers have white teeth," Fathead said. "Don't shoot till you see the whites of their teeth."

"Knockers mostly snort dope, they never shoot it," Funboy said.

"If you ask a knocker if he a knocker, a real knocker gotta tell you," the teenage dealer said looking at me. "You a knocker, motherfucker?"

"There are fake knockers and real knockers," Henry said. "The fake knockers cover for the real knockers. They send 'em through and everyone freaks. Then they go and everyone chills. Then the real knockers come."

"Knockers talk to the helicopter cameras with their finger moves so watch how they fingers move," Chico said. He was one of Funboy's friends.

"A knocker got me." This was a girl I met at the Center for Addiction Medicine. "I can't tell you what it looked like."

"If you ain't a knocker I wanna see you do that shit in front of me," the dealer said.

"Knockers smoke Winstons," Karen said. She stayed at Dom's until the knockers got her.

"You can tell fake knockers 'cause they look more like knockers than the real knockers do," Henry said. "Real knockers look just like us."

"You can tell knockers by their money." This was a pimp named Phil who hung around Dom's. "I can pick the knocker bill out of a roll every time. I trained my girls to get the trick to hold up the bills before each date. If I catch a bitch with that knocker money I beat her."

"Some knockers don't even try to bust you," Fathead said darkly. "They just buy your dope with that knocker money. Marked money. It's like that dye they give you at the hospital so they can see all your veins. A dose of that knocker money and your whole system lights up for the goddamned knockers."

"Knocker money is like AIDS," Dom said.

"I saw you *snort* it," the dealer said. "I ain't see you *do* it. Knockers snort dope too."

"Knockers look *too much* like junkies," Henry said. "Dirty jeans. You know, Metallica T-shirts with holes. They look more like junkies than junkies do."

"So what do junkies look like?" I asked Henry.

"Junkies don't look like anything," he said.

•

Over time, the odds of getting gotten by knockers are 100 percent. Even if you educate yourself on the many signs and symptoms of knockers, it's just a matter of time. And those signs are themselves misleading. Trust them too completely and you might find out they're traps.

Because the signs only work most of the time. Most of the time the knockers will have good teeth and look you straight in the eyes. Most of the time the knockers will drive Toyotas. Most of the time the knockers will be white. Most of the time the knockers will be black. But sometimes they won't be.

The awful truth is that a knocker can come in any shape. And there's something even worse. It's hard to explain. It's hard to find the right words. But sometimes the knock gets loose from the knocker. It gets loose in the air. It gets unshaped. I know it sounds strange. But you can have the knock without the knocker.

I started to pick up loose knocks during the fall of 2001. The first time was when I was standing in my kitchen staring into space. Dispersed. Then I felt the knock.

"What the fuck was that?" I said. I kind of went into myself, like a spilled glass of water going back into the glass. That knock humanized me for a second. I was all there.

Then I felt it again.

Someone's in here, I thought. *A person is in my apartment.*

I listened to the air.

"Oh God, they're in here," I whispered.

I shut myself up and took control. I gripped my wild heart hard in my willpower. Willpower. I will not get got. Or gotten. I was standing in the kitchen. A plaster wall separated the kitchen from the open main space of the apartment. The front door opened into that space. The invader was in there. That much was certain. He wasn't in here.

There was a window to my right. It shone like a mirror. It faced the open space. I saw the reflection of the edge of my couch in it. I saw the reflection of my white front door. The reflected image was so bright and clear I could see the chain was off my door. Why did I leave the chain off? I saw the reflected top of a little pile of garbage. Then there were the faint half shapes of unknown reflections. I examined each one in turn. Any one of them might be part or all of a knocker. Then there were the shadows.

I heard the boards of the living-room floor creak under the shifting weight of the invader.

I swallowed slowly. My throat hurt because the little punching bag in the back of my throat was swollen. The only way out of the kitchen was through the open space occupied by the knocker. The only way out of the apartment was through the front door.

How had this happened? What the fuck had I been doing before this? How long had I been standing in the kitchen spacing out? I pressed my long junkie nails deep into the flesh of my palm. Deeper. Ow. Good.

I began to peek around the wall. I did it like this: First I gently dropped down onto my knees. Then I stretched my whole body out flat along the floor. The very top of my head rested against the very edge of the wall. My plan was to slowly push my head out bit by bit until enough of my eyeball was out to let me see into the living room.

I soon realized the flaw in this plan. It had to do with the size of my head. The distance from the top of my head to my eyes was at least two inches. Two blind inches of me would be exposed to the invader before my eyes were out. The geological pace of head movement I'd planned would minimize the chances that the invader would notice the small dark object growing at the foot of the wall. But if he did, that same geological pace would seal my doom. It would give the invader plenty of time to tiptoe up and crouch down, waiting with a sharpened needle for my eyes to appear.

A long needle directly into the center of my eyeball! I'd feel it somewhere in my spine. Not in my eye. The instant nerve damage would send the pain skipping randomly into my body. I'd probably feel a sharp pain in my foot and then I'd be dead.

So I put the side of my face against the wall. There was less than an inch of face space between my right eyeball and the right end of my head. If I can put it that way. I was still lying flat on the ground. To edge my head sideways out of the wall to peek into the living room while I was lying flat on the ground. That was my battle. The battle was with my neck. I had to raise my head until it was at a near ninety-degree angle to my body. It hurt like hell, but what could I do? It had been a terrible risk to lie down. I could not afford the commotion standing up would involve. Even if I spent half an hour doing it. My knees, for example, creaked terribly. So I craned my neck up and started to move my head slowly out of the shelter of the wall.

It was at this point that I began to feel terrified. I admit I lost my nerve. The new closeness of my eye to the edge of the wall, to the open . . . it was too much for me. A minute at the most and I'd be looking out at . . . what? Maybe a face. Maybe an ex-face. A face that had gone into things. The way smoke goes into furniture.

I put my hand over my lips. To make sure they would not move.

"Oh fuck," I said.

With horror, I felt my lips moving under my hand. I couldn't even say something mentally without moving my lips.

"That means I'm retarded."

I must have said that out loud. I could practically see the vibration in the air.

Then, in the sudden sublime decision of total feeling, I pushed myself out of my hiding place and scooted out of the kitchen into the bare floor of the living room. I scooted out by rapidly paddling the floor with all four of my limbs. Surprise, motherfucker!

I caught the damn knocker off guard. I surprised him so much he disappeared. Nothing of him remained but the ghost of a knock. I lay there on the floor while the knock slowly evaporated from the ceiling and the tops of the walls. Everything looked different. I noticed the two old cigarette burns on the couch, the off-white color of the walls, the unplugged phone sitting in the middle of the floor.

So this is what it's like to be here, I thought, looking around at the world.

I stood up rubbing my neck and picked up the handwritten note that the knocker had left on the couch.

Dear Mr. Clune,

We have been contacted by your family and asked to check on you. Your father has called our office and expressed his concern at not having heard from you in several weeks. Receiving no answer to repeated knocking, we entered your apartment to leave this note. We also wish to remind you that October rent is now four weeks past due and your November rent is due in two days. Please contact us and your family as soon as you receive this letter.

Sincerely,
The Management

Needless to say, I made no reply to this bizarre and inexplicable communication. I didn't know what all the sentences meant, but the gist was clear enough. It was some kind of knocker trap. I didn't have the time to decode it. Or the energy. I was tired. My neck hurt. The little punching bag inside my neck hurt. I wanted to disappear.

I took down my dope utensils and a half-full red top from a hiding place that I'm not going to reveal. I wanted to do a little dope. The desire to disappear was inside of the desire to do a little dope. The way one color is inside another color in a Gobstopper. The outside of my desire was white, but the inside was clear. I wanted to disappear. I licked on my white desire wanting it to come clear. In a manner of speaking. I mean I did the rest of the dope and now I didn't have any more.

I looked around my apartment. It was pretty clean. In fact it was pretty new. I'd moved in two months ago. I'd moved out of the last place in the middle of the night. It was starting to look like I'd be moving again. The only question was whether it would be a daytime move or a nighttime move. I'd done my job. The ball was in the knockers' court.

I picked up the phone and called Cat.

"Hey, do you want to go get something to eat?" I said.

"Oh," she said, "I'd love to."

"Great," I said. "Where would you like to go?"

"It's so sweet of you to ask me. You're so sweet, Mikey."

"I just haven't seen you in a few days," I said modestly. "I just thought it would be nice."

"Of course it would be nice," she said. "Of course it would."

"Then great! So where do—"

"But I can't," she said.

"Oh."

"I'm sorry," she said.

"Ah."

"Yes."

"Of course. Well."

"Sometime, though," she said.

"Yes, sometime soon. Well, good luck on your project!"

"What project?" she asked.

"Weren't you just telling me? The castle thing? Never mind."

"You can be so funny sometimes, Mikey!"

"Did I ever tell you the one about the Queen of England on *The Price Is Right*?"

"Oh yes! You can be so funny!"

"How about the one about the Big Baby?"

"I love that one," she said.

"Yes, well, I'd better let you go now."

"Good-bye," she said.

I felt refreshed by this conversation. Refreshed, and a little bit exhausted. It wasn't every day I got to speak to a person. I opened my wallet for maybe the twentieth time that afternoon and looked inside. The two green shriveled low-denomination knocker bills were still there. I fished one out and held it up to the apartment's thick brown light.

"You little cocksucker," I said.

There was a "one" in each of the bill's four corners. Plus a "one" in the center. Plus some other ones in small print at the bottom. There were ones all over the goddamn thing. One is the loneliest number. I put it back in my wallet next to its friend. Two is the loneliest number in the world. Even lonelier than one. Nothing on earth is lonelier than two one-dollar bills.

I decided to pace a bit. Pick up the pace. The apartment had a kind of thick softness that cried out for vigorous pacing. Like a cat with thick fur, begging to be rubbed. I could pace back and forth across the living room all day and there would be no sign. Except a little something on the carpet. A kind of smudge. But no sign anyone could point to with confidence. Especially if I didn't let any blood drip. And there was practically nothing to cut myself on, anyway.

Of course, accidents happen even in the safest places. Even in hospitals. But the apartment was nice and soft and furry. It invited endless pacing.

The desire to disappear was somewhere inside that pacing. Like the tiny face of the young Hitler in that famous photograph of a crowded square in Vienna at the outbreak of World War I. Do you know that photo? Go get one of your Hitler books out and have a look; it's in there. What Hitler books? Yeah, right.

Now let me show you my bedroom. Immaculately clean. Especially the top of the dresser where I'd snorted all the dust off. In fact, most of the surfaces of the apartment were pretty well snorted clean. Periodically I'd have a little dope-flow problem, and would go around snorting for little specks of dope that might have gotten lost.

I bent over, looking carefully at a corner of the dresser. What was that? I rolled up a one and snorted at the corner for a couple seconds. I sneezed and straightened up. With my hands behind my back, I continued my pacing tour of the apartment.

Ah. The "office." My pride and joy. A corner of the bedroom, really. But my computer was there. I'd gotten a new computer early in the fall. Don't ask me how. Don't be too nosy. Miracles occasionally happen, even in an addict's life. A new computer had come to live with me. Call it proof. Proof of my unshakable intention to finish my dissertation. Proof of my faith in the future. And a willingness to take risks.

I picked up the camera I'd borrowed from Cat and took a picture of it. Then I got the two books I'd recently stolen from the Hopkins bookstore and posed them carefully next to the computer. I took another photo. I wished Cat were there to pose next to the computer and books. "Girlfriend with Computer and Books." I became angry.

"Goddamn it!"

The desire to disappear was inside my anger like a bone is inside a fish. Supporting it.

I fell down a little bit. I picked myself back up off the desk. A burnt spoon was kind of stuck to the bottom part of me. I peeled it off. It was sticky. I took an antidepressant. I believed in them and so did my doctor. I counted some of my accomplishments on one hand, then I ran out of fingers. I needed the other hand for balance. OK, you've seen the office.

Now back through the bedroom. Here in this plastic bag are some vitamins Dom sold me. He told me they were Percocet. A new generic kind of Percocet. I'd stared sadly, unbelieving, when he held the bag out. He looked embarrassed.

"There they are, Mike. Real good Percocets. Forty dollars. These babies will really help you wean yourself off dope. That's how Ron Howard did it."

I looked at him sadly. I looked at the vitamins. They looked scared and naked in the plastic baggie. There's something obscene about vitamins in a plastic baggie.

"I'll give you five dollars, Dom. It's all I got."

"OK," he said.

He gave me the bag. I never saw him again. I took one vitamin a day until they were gone. Now we're back in the living room. I can't stay long. It's almost time to go to Chicago to kick dope forever. Just a few more minutes. I can't kick in Baltimore. This is where the TV used to be. This is where the VCR used to be. This is where the cable box used to be. I'd done a little minor dealing early in the fall and had some extra money for a while. I'd bought some cool things. I looked at the space where the TV used to be.

"From money you came, and back to money you went," I said sadly to the TV hole. "Money to money."

This chair is where I sit when I get tired of pacing. And this square of carpet beneath the western window is where the autumn sunlight disappears. I took a photo of it. There was still light left. I looked up. Reflected in the bright window I saw the part of me that shows up in mirrors. A brilliant white outline, with a clear center.

Later that week I had to meet with my advisor. I'd sent him the chapter I'd been working on. I had high hopes for it. Every time I read it over it seemed to mean something else. I took this as a sign of its intellectual richness. Now I stood outside his office door with a clean shirt on and my freshly washed hair still damp. I knocked.

"Come in, Michael!"

I trooped in and sat down, looking at him expectantly. He had my chapter on the desk in front of him. I noticed he was avoiding my eyes.

"So what do you think?" I asked.

"It's . . . interesting," he said.

"Thanks," I said. "Do you think the ending is clear enough?"

"The ending?"

He looked down at the chapter. He frowned.

"Well, to be frank, Michael, it needs a lot of work."

"It is a draft," I said.

"Yes. In fact it might be best to just put this . . . draft . . . aside for a while."

"Put the ending aside?"

From deep down in my relaxation, I was a little shocked. That ending was good.

"No," he said. "Not the ending. The whole thing. Just put the whole thing aside. Just forget about this whole chapter." He peered at me. "You need a new perspective. And some rest. Are you getting enough rest?"

"Oh," I said. "I've had a cold."

"Ah," he said.

In December, I flew out to Chicago for my father's birthday. The occasion inspired me to try to kick dope. Well, maybe *inspired* is the wrong word. But I'd gotten clean before in Chicago, and I thought I might as well try again.

It couldn't hurt. My habit had gotten a little out of control. I'd been self-medicating to control my disappointment at my advisor's lack of support. I was disappointed in Cat, too. And now my fellowship checks, frequent supplemental checks from my father, and a whole lot of stealing were no longer enough to support my habit. My habit was on crutches. I needed a change. I went to Chicago with ten bags of dope and one bag of hope.

The second day I was there I sat in my father's living room watching TV with him. The dope I'd brought with me was already gone, and I could feel withdrawal starting in the goose-flesh of my legs. I decided today was not the right day to kick.

"Hey, Dad," I said. "I think I might, you know, go out for a little while."

I stood up.

"It's my birthday," he said, looking up at me.

"I know it's your birthday. I'll be back soon."

"Where are you going?"

This wasn't like him, I thought. He was usually so easygoing.

"I want to get something to eat," I said.

"There's food here."

"I feel like a hamburger," I said.

"There's hamburger meat here."

"Dad, come on, I'm just going out for a bit. I'm twenty-six, you know."

He looked at me.

"Michael," he said. "I don't ask you for much, do I?"

"No, Dad," I said.

"I help you out with money when you need it?"

"Of course, Dad, I'm very grateful."

"I don't ask for much?"

"No, Dad, you really don't."

"Well," he said. "I'm asking you for one thing now. This is my birthday. And I want you to stay here with me today on my birthday."

"And not leave the house at all?" I asked.

"Just this one day," he said.

I shifted from foot to foot.

"Dad, I—"

"Just this one day," he said.

He was facing the TV again now, an angry look on his face.

"Dad, I—"

"Go on," he said.

"I, um—"

"Go on!"

I left.

You might think that my father knew. That my advisor knew. That Cat knew. But they didn't, not at that time. I know they didn't, because when they did finally find out, they were all surprised. Of course, they told me, they'd known *something* was wrong. They didn't know quite what it was, but they got a funny feeling around me. Something a little off, that they couldn't put their finger on.

Naturally, I was careful. If I had to be around people who I didn't want to know about my habit, I used great care. Showers. Clean shirts. And just enough dope to keep the withdrawal away. So it wasn't obvious, unless you knew what to look for. And most people don't. So my family, my professors, my old friends noticed only a slight souring of the space between them and me.

Of course, there was probably a healthy helping of denial on their side. People don't want to think someone close to them is a heroin addict. They want to be fooled. So they collaborated with me, in a way, in hiding it from them. Not asking me certain questions. Suggesting excuses. "You look tired. You must be tired." But part of them remained unfooled. Their senses, their bodies, their eyes startled and shied away from me. Like horses shy away from vampires. I noticed it.

After I got clean, I asked my friend Cash, who I'd had intermittent contact with all the way through my junkie days, if he knew.

"No, man," he said, "I had no idea."

"Well you must have thought *something* was up with me," I said. "I mean, you had to have noticed something."

He thought for a while.

"Sure I noticed something," he said.

"Well, what?"

"I just thought you'd turned into a complete asshole," he said. "It happens, you know."

In Chicago the street name for police is "people."

"Look out for the people."

"Did you see the people?"

After my father's birthday, I'd decided to stick around, wait for the right time to kick. But the right time never came, and instead of spending my days kicking in my father's basement, I spent my nights there, writing "Don't Do Dope" signs. Really tiny ones, so my stepmother wouldn't find them. Really good ones. "Don't Do Dope" matchbook scraps. "Don't Do Dope" on a half-inch piece of McDonald's napkin, with fancy designs on the Ds. I got so good I could write "Don't Do Dope" twenty times on the back of a stamp.

I spent my nights writing. I spent my days copping dope in the projects on the Near West Side of Chicago. Ogden Courts. Roosevelt. The shells of Cabrini-Green. Moving fast. Ducking the people. At 10:00 a.m. about a week after Christmas, I was standing in a dope line, doing a little dance to keep warm.

"The people will be here soon," the little gangster said as I got to the front. His eyes moved in the ski mask's eyeholes, his leg jumped in the ten-degree morning, he handed me two baggies.

"The people was here twenty minutes ago," said the lookout as I passed him.

"The people are getting close," said a woman, standing in the breezeway with a tiny kid on her arm, sniffing the air.

"The people are here," the glassy junkie next to me said.

He dropped his dope and went right. I dropped my dope and went left. The people started coming through the tenement's modernist archways.

There is deep folk wisdom in calling the police the people. None of us were people. In our world the human shape dissolves. The apparatus of the state is required to prop up the human form.

"Here come the people!"

I moved along the wall, face melting in the heavy wind of no-dope.

"Hey, you there!"

I kept moving.

"Are you fucking deaf? I said stop."

I stopped. Only the people expect you to take these face noises seriously. I turned my hole toward the people. The people swiveled their human faces toward me.

"OK. Where's the dope?"

"I don't have any."

"We'll see about that."

A big person came over and started patting me down, going through my pockets, feeling under my belt and in the tops of my socks. My human flesh materialized under the hot people fingers. When it took its hand back I sagged formlessly against the tenement wall. The person grabbed me by my human shoulders and looked into me.

"Where is the dope? Look at me when I'm talking to you."

I tried. I was out of practice.

"I said look at me!"

It wasn't just my lifestyle, either. Evolution has made these face-to-face meetings obsolete. Unnecessary. Unpleasant. In the distant tribal past all communication took place in face-to-face encounters. Then came drums, money, drugs, writing. Panic and desire sounded through jungles in drumbeats. Panic and desire dispersed across continents in markets and caravans. Panic and desire dispersed across time through white molecules of opium. Humanity received new, possible bodies. Communication spread beyond the face-to-face.

Since then, direct communication between people-heads in the present has been mainly used for religious and police purposes.

"Please place your right hand on the Bible and repeat after me."

"You may now kiss the bride."

"Look at me when I'm talking to you. Where is that goddamn dope?"

The people seemed to enjoy my confusion. They flaunted the expensive obsolescence of face talking.

"See," they seemed to say, "we've got so much time and money we can afford to just stand here talking to your face."

But when they really want to know, they don't stand around talking into faces. When narcotics agents want to measure the effectiveness of their policies, they buy a bag of dope. They listen to the price. A high price means they're winning a little, a low price means they're losing a little.

When the dealers want to control an area, they spiral out through cell phones, little scraps of paper with digits written on them, numbers on high school bathroom walls, U-Hauls and station wagons, color-coded vials.

And when the junkies want to travel through time, when they want to erase the present by joining the immaculate white past and the immaculate white future—the way you fold a sheet in half—they buy a bag of dope.

Dope is information. Just like prices on objects or the code traveling through fiber-optic cables. The dope molecules carry information to the brain's memory glands, where time is manufactured. At every instant the addict inhabits at least two times at once: the first time he did it and the next time he will do it. Right now is the switchboard.

What is true of time is also true of space. At every instant the addict is in several different places at once. Blood circulates within the borders of the skin. But the addict's need for dope opens his mind-body system to the world. To the circulatory system of the world dope supply. The addict's veins and nerves spool out through prices on bags, fiber-optic cables where dealers' voices peel away from their bodies, airplanes landing in empty fields. The dope body spreads out like an open fire hydrant.

So when the people stand looking at the addict face-to-face, they don't see much. They don't expect much. An addict doesn't fully materialize in the present. When I looked in the mirror back in Baltimore, I got an odd feeling that I wasn't really seeing myself. Because I wasn't really seeing myself.

The people looked at me. They snorted in disgust.

"OK, beat it!"

They turned their bright people faces off me. I walked back over to where I'd dropped my dope when I'd first heard the people sounds. I felt the people faces sweeping the area, lighting up the dirty pavements and graffiti pillars. My dope lay in a shallow crack of shadow between two long people looks. I bent over and pretended to tie my shoe. I picked up the bag, stood up, and walked off quick.

"I don't believe it. Hey, smart guy! Get your ass right back over here."

I dropped the dope again and turned slowly around into the sharp human facelight.

"You just couldn't help yourself, could you? Carl, go pick up that bag he just dropped. Unbelievable. No willpower at all."

Addiction has nothing to do with willpower. It took enormous willpower to pick up that dope right in front of the people. If anything, the problem is too much willpower.

"I said come back over here! Damn, Carl, it's like talking to . . . Hello," the person waved his hands in front of my eyes, "is anybody at home? Is anybody in there?"

Now he was getting warmer. Because, of course, I wasn't really in there. To pass through addiction is to come to terms with not being where you are. More and more people are entering the modern world by passing through addiction. Perhaps in the future everyone will have to pass through. Like a gateway. Leave your human body on this side, and pick up your possible body on the other.

"Are you listening to me, junkie?"

Kind of. But the people like you to be all there. 100 percent there. They're old fashioned. They like to look at you and know.

"Gimme your wallet. All right, let's see here . . . Michael Clune. That your name, junkie?"

So they took me to jail. Jail is kind of like a forest preserve. It's a space for preserving a form of life that mostly died out long ago. A life form without connections. Without money or dope or cell phones. The people like to see you down there in the jail. You remind them of people. All the junkies and dealers standing around in the bullpen talking to each other like people. Biting on each other like people. Like the people.

They brought me and the other one in and talked to us in separate rooms. They were trying to find out something about some dealer called "Rabbit."

"Is Rabbit the one who sold you this shit?"

"Is Rabbit still around here?"

"Does Rabbit wear a red bandanna?"

"Is Rabbit the guy we picked up with you?"

I answered yes to all the questions. Especially the last one. "Yes!"

I'd known the guy a few weeks. I liked him. Black guy in his forties. Always complaining about the cold. His street name was "Tiger" or something. Some name a six-year-old would pick. I'd never heard of Rabbit. I knew the guy busted with me wasn't him. The people probably knew too. But I thought it was important to demonstrate my complete willingness to rat anybody out at any time. I could imagine what the people would say.

"You know, Carl, I was wrong about that kid," one person would say. "I think we got us a real good one here."

"We sure do," the other one said. "I mean, if he's willing to rat out his friends for things they haven't even done, just think what he'd do if he actually met someone who did something!"

"Maybe he's worth more to us free," the first one said. "Maybe we should turn him loose. Give him some money. A car. A badge."

"Maybe some dope, too. I mean, he's got to blend in . . ."

"Yes, he's Rabbit," I said again. "He's a big-time dealer."

But the people didn't commission me as a secret narcotics agent. They lost interest in my answers even before they finished asking the questions. People are like that. Easily distracted. Sometimes they get depressed all of a sudden. The people who'd been questioning me kind of sat back mumbling to themselves. I think they were talking about New Year's. It was New Year's Eve.

"And then Molloy calls in sick and who do they bring in but me. Any other night of the year, fine. But this is New Year's Eve and my girl is . . ."

"Yeah, Carl. Well today I was sitting in my squad car and got the call . . ."

"I have tomorrow night off, but right now I gotta . . ." Now. Today. New Year's Eve. This was the talk of people confined to a single time and place. The talk of the people. Finally, they seemed to remember me.

"OK, it's back to the cell with you, buddy."

At least they called me buddy. That was a small victory.

"You know," I told my buddy as he was walking me down. "I'm really going to quit this time. This arrest is just what I needed. Soon I'll be a person again."

"Yeah whatever," he said. "That's what they all say."

He was right. The cure doesn't turn junkies into people. Who would give up dope for that?

TWELVE

LOVE

That was eight years ago, in Chicago. *Hey, smart guy! Get your ass right back over here.*

These days I follow the law. Almost eight years off dope. I even go to NA meetings now. I finished my dissertation five years ago. Got a job in Ann Arbor at the University of Michigan three years ago. Now I've moved again. I'm living in Florida as I write this. No shirt, no shoes, no service. I think they have a law against feeding the alligators, too, but that's about it. And no one follows the first law except me. Only me. When I get out of bed in the morning, I put on my shirt. Then I put on my shoes. Then I ask for service.

While I was in Ann Arbor, I finished the introduction to my academic book, and a university press gave me a contract for it. I went on the job market and got flown out to a few different campuses to give job talks.

At one of them, a prestigious department at a great university on the West Coast, my old friend Cash tried to kill me. He didn't succeed, obviously. It's an open question how hard he really tried. He was drinking a lot of Robitussin, for one thing. A lot. He had gotten hold of some guns somehow—aren't felons supposed to not have guns?—but his ability to use them was questionable. It's a long story. When I got back from California, I withdrew my candidacy with a shiver of relief, and ignored the shocked and angry emails from the faculty there. And the demented and angry emails from Cash.

My hopes of leaving Michigan dwindled. An Ivy League school flew me out for an interview, but they ended up giving the job to someone else. I was number two. I watched the Michigan snow pile up.

Then, out of the blue, I got this great offer from a university in Florida. Good money. Low cost of living, better weather. Not very prestigious, but big things were happening down there. When they flew me down to the campus, the chair told me all about it.

"The state has made a big commitment to the university, Michael," he said. He was smiling. "Our department is currently rather small, but it has just received a tremendous amount of money. You will be the first of an anticipated thirty new hires. If you come here, you will have an opportunity to shape the growth of this department into a powerhouse in the discipline. You will have a degree of input enjoyed by few junior faculty anywhere."

I like the sun. Ann Arbor has fewer sunny days than Seattle. I signed on the line. I flew down again in April and got a great place in a cool part of town. In early summer I said my good-byes to my friends in Michigan, the movers picked up my stuff, and I drove down to meet them. I like driving. Tennessee, Kentucky, Georgia. It got hotter.

Soon after crossing into Florida I stopped and got some gas. It was hot as hell. I went inside the store and got a twenty-ounce Coke. I went to the counter and the lady rang it up.

"Sixty cents," she said.

Only sixty cents? I looked at the bottle. It seemed perfectly good.

"Really?" I said.

"Sixty cents," she repeated.

Why did they feel like they couldn't charge at least a dollar for it? Every other state I drove through did. Even Kentucky. I looked at the lady behind the counter.

"Sixty cents?"

She smiled weakly back.

In Florida they just don't have the confidence to charge a dollar. "Who do we think we are?" they say. Sixty cents. That wasn't a good sign. They don't have any state income tax either. I picked up a couple newspapers and scanned the headlines.

STATE SLASHES UNIVERSITY FUNDING

GOVERNOR VETOES UNIVERSITY SPENDING BILL

UNIVERSITY IMPOSES HIRING FREEZE

I felt like someone had punched me in the throat. I quickly skimmed the story. "State revenue projections plummet . . . governor vetoes tuition hike . . . legislature demands universities admit more students." The perfect storm. "'We're at breaking point,' says University Chancellor."

Were they going to take away my new job already? I should have gone to California. I could have bought a gun. Yes, Cash. Two can play that game. I'd be more than a match for him. Especially if he'd been drinking. Catch him slipping and BLAM! See his tiny head coming around the corner and BLAM! Creep up on him while he was sleeping, shove the gun in his mouth, and BLAM! I was freaking out. I called my old friend Dave.

"Well," he said slowly. "They can't fire you. You have a signed contract."

"Thank God for that," I said.

"But they can squeeze you to death. First they'll cut your travel money. Then they'll cut your journal subscriptions. Then they'll tell you to teach more classes. It's the same story at state universities around the country."

"What is?"

"Everyone wants to cut higher education. For the Republicans, cutting funding for higher education is like being tough on crime. You know how it is in Congress." He imitated a southern senator's voice.

"The American people need to know the kind of trash that is being taught in our universities today. Here is a textbook that says that Abraham Lincoln was a homosexual. And this book says that Shakespeare was a homosexual. This book says that Norman Rockwell's art is gay. Norman Rockwell! This is a picture of Santa Claus by Norman Rockwell. Does that look gay to you?"

Of course it looked gay to me, but maybe that proved Dave's point. He did have some good news about Cash, though. After some soul searching, Cash had figured out he didn't have to quit drinking after all. He was just doing weekend binges now, and his liver felt fine. The one undeniable problem, however, was that every time he got drunk, he fell. A lot. He'd wake up with his head bloody and covered with bruises.

This was a problem, but hardly an insoluble one. Cash had discovered a solution. Now when he felt that itch for a drink, he would put on a helmet. They made good lightweight helmets for motorcyclists. Dave left me with the touching image of Cash sitting alone in his apartment, slowly strapping a helmet to his head, turning on some quiet music, and pouring Aristocrat whiskey into a coffee mug until it started to spill over the edges.

I hung up and walked around my new neighborhood wringing my hands. Why had I come here? All they care about in this state is cutting taxes. I looked at the self-satisfied Floridians. Middle-aged women with ankle bracelets. They should be very highly taxed to pay for higher education. An Italian guy with oil on his muscles. He should be forced to face the fact that Lincoln was maybe gay. And that he is definitely gay. A smirking septuagenarian getting out of a Mercedes. Where did he get that car? What did he need with it? He should be taxed to death. Through the plate glass I saw a couple jolly Republicans sipping mojitos. I imagined them being slowly taxed to death.

I stopped at a café. I ate some chicken that was dry in the center and wet at the edges. The sun was setting when I got out. I walked back through the orange light. At my new apartment I sat on the floor amid all the raw matter. Everything was there. What was I supposed to do next? I had no habits here. No routines. Nothing to blunt the world's sharp edge.

When you've lived in a place for long enough, you hardly see it. That starts to get to you. Michigan got to me like that. I felt like I was getting old among appliances and carpets and lighting fixtures I knew like the back of my hand. The back of your hand isn't interesting until it's gone. I wanted to move to a new place where everything is interesting. Where I don't feel so numb. Where I see everything as if for the first time because it is for the first time. I moved.

And now, sitting in the middle of a strange floor piled with unpacked boxes, I longed for the thick, comfortable cobwebs of habit. Ten or twenty years of habit. Enough habit to bury all these terrible surfaces. I wanted them invisible. The way living in a place for years almost makes it disappear. You don't notice it. Everything was too bright in Florida. The new shapes were too sharp. They got stuck in me and I couldn't relax. What is that coming out of the floor? A door stopper of some kind. It's weird. I don't like it.

A sunbeam hit the alien tiles below the bay window. Sunlight didn't come through my windows like that in Michigan. The sunbeam came through in a strange way. I followed its track with distaste. It lit up the inch-long black antennae of a monstrous brown-and-yellow insect.

The thing looked at me. It was maybe a third as big as me. Give or take. The shock of Florida had obliterated my sense of perspective. The insect was an uncertain size. I couldn't tell whether I should step on it like an ant or kick it in the side like a dog.

I hit it with a three-pound literary theory book. I had to throw the book out afterward. One chapter of the book says Shakespeare was probably gay. I slept with the lights on. I heard dinosaur bugs moving in the walls.

When you wake up in a new place, you have to find yourself out there among all the unfamiliar things. In the air-conditioned bedroom, with orange light coming through the beveled glass, it takes a while to distinguish what's you from what's not. The hand that feels cold, the leg that feels sore. I pulled myself together. The bugs and the new furniture went to one side of the world and I went to the other. I got out of bed and looked in the mirror. I was covered with skin.

In the afternoon my new television broke and I decided I should go to an NA meeting. I had been to one in Florida before, when I'd visited in April, but I forgot how to get there. Plus this was a different day of the week. At least I thought it was. My Internet wasn't working. I found a meeting schedule in my glove compartment. The meeting was at 8:00 p.m. I puzzled out the directions on a map.

The meeting was near the airport. Everything spreads out near the airport. You can see distance in the sky like birds. The buildings look like they could go too. The air is the color of a wishing well.

The meeting was in a place called the Church Without Walls. I guess the name means that it's the kind of church you're still inside of even when you're outside. Even when you run outside the church and keep running you're still in it. That kind of place. It was ninety degrees when I got out of my car in the vast parking lot. The visible form of the Church Without Walls is a six-story office building done in mirrored glass.

The lobby was deserted. No sign where to go. The floors and even parts of the walls were done in expensive marble. The parts of the walls that weren't marble were expensive wood. There was a cheap drop ceiling. I opened a door and saw a big empty room filled with folding chairs that had been spray-painted gold. On the wall in big gold letters it read:

AS HE COMMANDS US

Perhaps they hadn't finished doing the rest of the message. Or maybe we were supposed to focus on the *way* he commands us. How he commands us rather than what he commands us is important. The whole area was like that. There were even signed pictures of famous people on the walls. Mariah Carey. Cedric the Entertainer. You can go there yourself if you want. The doors aren't locked. There was no sign of the meeting.

I walked back outside and scanned the parking lot. I saw two figures on bicycles getting bigger. When they got close enough for me to see their hair I knew they were going to the NA meeting.

"You here for the meeting?" one asked me. I nodded.

"Then let's go." They picked up their bikes and walked in. I followed them. We took an elevator up to the third floor. The elevator was slow.

"They did a real nice job with this wood," one guy said, rubbing his hand along the surface.

"Yeah," said the other, holding his bike like a video-game gun. "Real nice."

When the elevator stopped, we stepped into a corridor of plush carpet and signed celebrity photographs, mysterious gold stenciled messages ("Let Us Begin"), phantom machine guns, wood-paneled walls, cheap drop ceiling, and a small glass case on a pedestal containing a shining object or objects. At the end of the corridor was a door. The first bicyclist opened it. We stepped through and the Church Without Walls ambience abruptly vanished.

We were in a small gray room half-full of serious working-class people. The people were milling about talking in low voices. Their faces were familiar from old newsreels of radical union meetings in early twentieth-century America. There were five or six rows of metal folding chairs, a giant metal coffee maker from the nineteen-thirties, a large metal table from the nineteen-thirties, and several other items from the nineteen-thirties, including the thoughts inside everyone's heads, including my own.

"It's good to see you, brother," a man in a painter's suit said heartily, slapping one of my companions on the back.

A woman stepped up and handed me a pamphlet. It had the NA logo on the front.

Two men, black and white, walked in, each holding copies of The Book.

"We keep up the struggle together," an elderly worker with steel eyes was saying to a young man to my left. "No one can do it alone, we need The Group."

I had found The Group. I had stepped through a time portal in the wood-paneled, gold-painted, celebrity-eyed Jesus of the twenty-first century into the steel, concrete, and communism of the thirties. These time portals lie in every city, town, and village of America. Nearly all of them are concealed—with diabolical irony—in churches. Lenin would smile. There are NA meetings in hospitals and schools also. We use only our first names.

"And what's your name, brother?" the old guy asked me.

"Mike," I said. Nothing else about me was real, and I slid effortlessly into one of the two million chambers of the world-wide struggle. It began to turn.

There were slogans in the air. A middle-aged woman without any nonsense straightened a pile of pamphlets on the table. I moved to help her. Security, solidarity, honesty, open-mindedness, willingness. The five steel principles of NA. The Twelve Steps. The Twelve Traditions. The two books. The two million members.

NA's roots are in AA, and AA was forged in the nineteen-thirties. The era of the worker's struggle. The decade of the five-year plan. Unflinching opposition to the fascists, the bosses, and the opium of the masses, which in my case was opiates, but for Bill W. was alcohol. The earliest AA posters depicted a gigantic concrete man ascending twelve enormous steel-gray steps. I saw a reproduction of it in rehab.

Seven decades of sports and cheap electricity have pulverized the worker's movement in the West. In the East, the Soviet dream vanished overnight in one of the sudden, inexplicable, and absolute ruptures in world history that make a mockery of statistics and provide the last best evidence of the existence of a god or gods. Churches without walls soon rose in every city, patrolling a world without slogans, without solidarity, without honesty. Strikes lost their romance. Long lines lost their romance. The endless waiting in government buildings lost its romance. The leader you could lose yourself in disappeared or turned retroactively into a criminal.

The very idea of the group became loathsome, and class feeling was replaced by an obsessive disgust with the image of the stranger. The man in a raincoat in the back of the theater. The man in front of you in the grocery checkout line with both of his hands stuffed down his pants. The tax-exempt retiree stuffing his face in the McDonald's drive-through. Even his fingernails have stopped growing, but he keeps eating.

A little while ago, I read a newspaper item to the following effect: Eight men were arrested yesterday in the adult bookstore the Love Shack on 11203 S. Dale Mabry Highway in Tampa and charged with lewd conduct and resisting arrest. The men had surrounded an employee of the store and were masturbating when the police arrived. The store has a history of similar past incidents, and nearby residents and businesses repeated their demand that the store be shut down.

My girlfriend, to whom I read this item, responded: "Eight people masturbating together in public? Are they part of a team?"

This story and her response illustrate more eloquently than any statistic the fate of the group in contemporary America. From the labor union march to the group masturbation team. Today the glue of group solidarity is the corrupt semen of perverts. The Catholic Church, for example. Or the Boy Scouts. Or *Three's Company*. I grew up in the Catholic Church, going on Boy Scout campouts on the weekends, watching *Three's Company* reruns every day after school. But even this kind of indoctrination couldn't stop me from falling in love with the idea of The Group.

It was a private love—the secret afterlife of communism. It started in 1989, the year communism went underground and began hiding inside the children. I was in eighth grade. That year I read *The Communist Manifesto* with my best friend, Sid. We memorized the slogans. In history class I looked enviously at the long lines of anonymous gray marchers in the grainy documentaries shown to us by our alcoholic Catholic school history teacher. Through the static of the ancient Catholic school television, the marchers were marching. Marching for food. Marching for revolution. Marching for marching. At lunch the other boys in my class lined up to touch the huge early breasts of the sluttiest girl in the school. I stood in line with them, squeezing my eyes shut when it was my turn and imagining red flags.

During my college years, I came to love Comrade Stalin. It wasn't easy, working slowly backward from the terrible statistics of his crimes to the fantasy uncle of the nineteen-thirties, but I did it. The pot helped. I thought of him late at night, when Eva had gone to sleep. His crimes left a splinter in my love. It was a rugged, mature love. A love of this world.

Then as the harder drugs took hold, I would sit alone in my first apartment in Baltimore, high with no music on, and go back over the history of the first and only pure communist state. A history that was also in a way my own ideal past. In a fragile way. The hardest drugs took hold. I lay on my bed in 1999, and up through the dark, squat chimney of the Yeltsin years, I could see the little white clouds of my imaginary communist youth. Through the chipped, cracked lenses of the Clinton regime, I could still make out the brilliant outlines . . .

The warm afternoons and tender tears of Khrushchev's years in power. Then the cerulean blue of the Brezhnev era. The tranced apartment blocks, like a magic syllable repeated to bring good fortune. The bust of Lenin in the state grocery store. Great Lenin's eyes smiled down benignly: This was socialism.

We listened, but we didn't hear! Oh Comrade Stalin, Comrade Lenin! We heard but we didn't listen! And when I passed into the deeper blues of the heroin nod, there were tears in my eyes.

So you could say I was receptive to the atmosphere of NA. In a way only slightly more twisting than the usual paths of history, Lenin is responsible for my recovery from addiction. For my recovery, and for the recovery of who knows how many countless others? The revolution moves in strange and fragile ways.

But the meeting was starting now, and I took my seat with the others, relishing the bite of the steel folding chair in my lower back. A large poster on the wall read KEEP COMING BACK in big group-effort letters. A large black man stood up in the front of the room.

"My name is Melvin and I'm an addict."

"Hi Melvin!"

"I remember when I came to NA first I couldn't be around nobody. Walked into the room and thought y'all was looking at me funny. Them folding chairs made me itch, and I got up and left most as soon as I sit. Like I been bit. But then I started to go to jail every time I got high. Every single time. I'd open up the lil' baggie and officer friendly would come up out of it with the handcuffs."

Laughter from the group.

"I love the group today. It keeps me and I keep coming back. When I first get into recovery my home situation wasn't so good. The cops had a whole list on me. When they drive up to serve me for child support or for missing a court date or for God knows what else out of the notorious past my girl would ring this big bell we had on the porch. And I'd sneak out the back door and go lay down in the swamp back there. Then she'd ring it again when they were gone. One time she fell asleep and I was out there all night, one big mosquito bite listening to helicopters that weren't there crying thinking, *Lord, just let me go get high one more time.*

"But when I come back in here to the group y'all told me *Meeting Makers Make It* and *One Day at a Time* and *Keep Coming Back.* And I did. And now it's been six years, and that bell don't ring no more, and I'm clean and it's all due to this group right here. Keep coming back."

He sat down to an appreciative rustle. There was a silence thick with the firm breathing of the group. Not like the weak thin breathing of strangers at a bus stop. Or the watery panting of a masturbation team. Or the hopeless breathing of a funeral or a jail cell or a bank lobby. The man in the painter's suit raised his hand.

"I don't have much to share today. I just wanted to say that I'm grateful to be clean and I'm glad to be here with you people tonight."

"We're glad you're here too," the group said.

"I'm Helen, and I'm an addict," a thin, blonde girl said into the group, and the end of her sentence already sounded richer and faster and stronger and better than the beginning. "I, uh, I guess I never liked being around other people that much. People they . . . they act like . . . like, people." She giggled like it was a private joke, but there are no private jokes in the group and everyone was laughing.

"I didn't feel comfortable in every situation. And I kept taking these little pills. At school the teacher's mouth would move and I would laugh. And they would get angry. Or sometimes they'd laugh. But really, you know, I didn't understand. Anything they were saying, you know. My relationships were like that. And now, it's been, God. I don't know, like ten months. And I can say these things to you and you. You just act like . . .

"I don't know what I mean."

She meant that her whole fucked-up body and mind was making the group and everyone in it stronger and more relaxed, including her. But not her more than anyone else. Not more than me for instance. She smiled and was quiet.

After a moment an obese woman with an "I Love My Home Group" button began to speak.

"My name is Ebony, and I'm an addict."

"Hi, Ebony."

"Lord! I am grateful to be here at my home group tonight. I get excited when it's my home group. I wake up and I say, 'It's Wednesday today; I'm going to my home group tonight.'" She shuffled around in her folding chair and fanned herself with one of the readings.

"I been through it this past week, y'all. And some of you in this home group know that. Y'all helped me get through it. Your love and support. I won't never forget that. It was my sister's service this week. It was the first time I been together with my whole family since I been clean. Now, I have never in my life gotten together with my family and not been high. And I did not get high this week. I did not have the desire to get high this week. I did not have the thought to get high. And I am grateful for that.

"But you know, my whole family came down. People coming from Georgia and Tallahassee. Aunts and uncles and you name it. And you know some shit had to happen." She shook her head and we laughed.

"I love my family but you know I hate they guts and only here in this group can I say that. 'Cause there's no hate in here. And it makes it easy and makes me not ashamed the way I feel about my family. Because in here it's all good. Like you was my family. No you better than family. The group, the NA group. People in here you ain't got to convince of nothing. Group people. I'm just saying this just to be saying. Like I was to talk about how I could cut my uncle's ears off with a butter knife. It don't matter. I ain't have to use no drugs, and when I called some of the people here on the phone when I felt crazy with my family every minute under my damn feet, y'all answered.

"If you sitting here new in recovery, what you need to know is that there is a lot of love here. And I love every single one of you. It don't matter who you are. I love you. The love here is strong. I felt it the first time I came to this meeting. This room, these chairs. That table Sandra sitting at. I still feel it. The love in this room is strong. Helen. My heart is full here tonight. And this home group has a special feeling here tonight. And it does have a special feeling every time I come here. And I will keep coming back."

I noticed that all the tension had drained from my body.

The basket had been sent around, and a voice out of the group told us that the group had collected nine dollars and fifty cents to help with expenses. It told us if we didn't have any money don't worry about it and keep coming back to the group. Like Soviet communism, NA has many slogans, each with a strange potency. "Don't Pick It Up and It Won't Get in

You" is a charm against mind devils. "One Day at a Time" is a charm against the devils of time. But "Keep Coming Back" is the master slogan. So is "Meeting Makers Make It."

We got up and stood in a circle with our arms around each other while someone recited the Serenity Prayer. Ebony was to my right. A guy with a tattoo of a knife on his neck was to my left. His eyes were closed. He was wearing a button that said "I Love My Home Group."

I closed my eyes. The love here is strong. I stood in the circle with the waves of it vibrating in my skull and my legs and my tongue. Twice a week at least I stand up and get exposed to the love rays of the group. It disperses the hard lines of my body. The thought lines shift, waver, and melt.

That love isn't the kind of love where you need to know a whole lot about the people you are in love with, either. What they look like, even. It doesn't really have a lot to do with the people. When it's really strong, the people blur in it. Like Ebony said, it seems to come more from a place, a room, a day of the week, than from the people who come in the room alone from the endless eviscerated capitalist century outside, and who go out alone later.

In that room the hard strange surfaces of Florida opened. Gold spray paint and Jesus and Mariah Carey and linoleum lined the opening. The group stood in the circle together and when I looked across into Helen's open eyes it wasn't like looking at someone. It wasn't hard like that.

I drove back up the highway with the windows down and the love slowly fading. Past tenements and shopping malls. Orange clouds hung in the hot black sky. I'm past thirty now. As I drove I remembered another night. In Baltimore right after I'd moved there. Eva and I were high, driving fast, Guns N' Roses on the stereo. Laughing. I smiled, remembering. Wondering also why still. And for how long. Eva's eyes, the streetlights through the windows. Surfaces less solid than smoke. How long can they last? How long will they keep coming back? It already seems like centuries.

I drove fast, remembering the Baltimore billboards, the humid trees, Eva's floating hair. Remembering how the lights came on in the heavy Baltimore night. I was watching what I was doing as I drove but I wasn't. I wasn't really seeing the Florida highway as it curved up over the buildings and into the orange and black sky. The Chevys with chrome rims and green tints passing me, the neon palm tree signs over the bars below. I wasn't really seeing them.

Memory reached through my not-seeing and stole them all. While I was thinking about the past, the surface of the present disappeared into memory. The hot black sky, the Chevys, the road curving up over the buildings.

One day the surfaces taken by memory will be all I have to recognize myself by. The face I will have when I am gone.

THIRTEEN

26TH AND CALIFORNIA

I'll know me by the color. Drifting snow covered the short West Side blocks. It came halfway up the windows of the parked cars. They looked like the squinting eyes of white people. Clear irises. Day and night coming through them. Thirty days and nights coming down with the snow. I'm on my hands and knees in it, looking for a white bag of dope in front of two cops. In the white dust of the world, like a myth. The people yelling:

I don't believe it! Hey, smart guy, get your ass back over here.

On my hands and knees right in front of the people. Looking through the snow for the dope I dropped when the "here come the people" cries rang out.

Can you believe this damn junkie, Carl? I'm sifting through the white dust. Chicago, December 2001. Drifting white dust piled up to the windows. And everything I wanted. Everything I could have wanted turned to dust. Because the dope had stopped working. The dope had begun to malfunction. I don't know when. Maybe a month before. Maybe a year. My mind wasn't right.

Consider what dope is. Information. Processed by the brain. Dope molecules carry information to brain receptors. Heroin isn't some simple poison like cyanide. It doesn't turn off your kidneys. It isn't some raw sense pleasure like sugar. It doesn't make your mouth happy. What makes you happy? Sun?

Sunlight on a day when you feel like good things will happen? The beach? Like a honeycomb full of the honey of beach memories. The street you used to live on? Shadowed by a memory so early it doesn't have any shapes. It sheds dark drops of light on you, on the present-tense sidewalk.

What makes you happy? Dope goes to the brain. The polymorphous brain. The brain is the multiform possibility of happiness. It has roots that reach through time and drink from everywhere. The poet Hafiz wrote in the fifteenth century that wine doesn't make us drunk. We make the wine drunk in us. The happiness is mine, the memories are real. Dope is a connection. From past to present. From over there to over here. The connection lights up as past happiness pours through it and bubbles up now. Heroin is an interface with the brain's infinite happiness. Heroin is a white screen. All of memory's wonderful shapes projected onto it.

Heroin molecules are delicate. Complex. Hundreds of thousands in a twenty-dollar vial. As they pass through the envelope of my blood and hit the white heat of the chemical brain fire, they crystallize into the basic forms of pleasure. The alphabet of happiness. The code of memory. Time, sensation, places, and faces processed through the dope code. "There" passes through dope to reach "here." "Then" passes through dope to reach "now." After a year or so my brain can't imagine how it ever got by without it. Its natural roots die and the dope system takes over. Chip's roof, Eva's eyes, Baltimore sunlight gets mixed with fields in Burma, planes landing in the desert, dealers' phone numbers, prices of vials. I'm woven in. Thought feeling and memory comes through on the dope signal.

So when dope stops working it is catastrophe. An invisible comet explodes in the atmosphere. A flash, and all the world's processors turn into ash. All the world's alphabets pulverized. The world covered with a thin layer of fine bone-white dust. With tiny mutilated bits and pieces of alphabets. Meaningless. For months after the catastrophe, the pulverized information snows down.

When dope stops working it isn't just a problem with the dope. The junkie brain doesn't think, *We'll just have to find other ways of being happy.* Dope isn't a kind of happiness for a junkie, one kind among many. It is the code that makes happiness possible. Impossible. Dope malfunction. Information decay. I walk out into the sunlight and the raw matter stretches forever. Meaningless.

I don't believe it! Hey, smart guy, get your ass right back over here.

The senseless world of terminal addiction. No taste left in food. No color left in color, no sound left in sound. No dope left in dope. This was not a feeling I had; it was my world. The real world. There were telephones and sidewalks in it. People. Family members. Long and short distances. Moving my fingers over the familiar shapes like a person newly blind.

"You could smile a little when you see us, Michael. It's been months."

"I'm sorry, Dad, I just feel a little . . . tired. I need to borrow your car for a minute."

I still knew enough to get more dope. It's not a feeling exactly. More like an instinct. A primitive sense about where feeling might be found. The way blind tadpoles burrow into moist sand. I burrowed like that into the white dust on the West Side of Chicago. They call dope bags "blows" there. They call cops people. I was sifting through the dust in the bags. Through the pulverized alphabet of feeling. Patiently trying to puzzle the broken letters into one real word. Sleep for instance. Ah. There. No. Not yet. Finally doing enough to reach the simple physical properties of dope. The toxicity level. The off switch. Little overdoses every night. Like using a cell phone as a hammer.

But sometimes, from a distance, that first white bliss still flamed in the white grains of a new bag. I rushed back to my car with the dope clenched in the sweat of my hand. I opened it to find that the first time had left its angel shape in the white dust. Like a snow angel. In my dreams a white phone was ringing.

I met Tiger two weeks before the bust, when I was trying to score down by the old Cabrini-Green projects. These were their last days. The buildings were half-deserted. Scheduled to be demolished for condos. The drug trade was dying in the emptying projects, but you could still catch a dealer here and there. The trade was different in Chicago. Not like free-market Baltimore, where anyone who could get fifty bucks together bought a few bags and stood out on the corner. In Baltimore you pull up and twelve different dealers run up pushing and shoving to serve you. Every one an independent operator.

In Chicago the gangs had the trade locked down. The gang lookouts, paranoid of my whiteness, turned me away from the gang superspots. So I had to catch the stray desperate independent dealers. They were hard to catch, running fast from the cops, the gangs, and the junkies they'd burned.

Tiger was watching me as I got burned by an independent I'd cornered in the park. The dealer split. I opened the bag and flicked my tongue at the tasteless baking soda.

"Hey man," he said as I walked away dropping the burn bag and biting my cheek. "Hey man, hey man, hey man."

"What?" I said turning.

"I seen you want some blows," he said.

It was late December. Four o'clock, when the white of the day stands out.

"No not blow, dope," I said exhausted.

"Yeah, blows," he said.

"No. Heroin. Not blows."

"Blows, man."

"Heroin yes, blow no."

"Yes heroin, yes blows," he said. "We call heroin blows."

"Oh," I said. "I've been out here all day not knowing what to say to people."

"We call cops people," Tiger said. "Come on I'll take you to the lady I shop with."

We got in my beat-up Pontiac and rolled up Roosevelt. Of course I had to buy Tiger one. I wasn't familiar with the Chicago trade. It was better to give Tiger ten bucks than risk getting burned again. Plus the people were everywhere. The heat made the lady he shopped with keep everything in her panties. Her shop was in her panties. *I like to shop with you,* I thought.

We fixed in the abandoned project apartment Tiger was squatting in. The first brief flash of dope light blew the dust off my senses. The light lasted for sixty seconds. I had just enough time to look around. I noticed Tiger was a middle-aged black man wearing a Bears coat and orange mittens. Then I had a couple more seconds to see what was happening to me and to panic a little. Then it was gone. The facts and the colors were still there but my interest was gone. The dope was barely working anymore.

"It ain't much," Tiger said.

"Yeah." I said. "I'm getting off it anyway."

"Oh, I hardly fuck with it," he sniffed. "So where you stay at?"

"I'm visiting my family," I said. "Right now I'm staying with my sister up on the North Side. Roscoe Village."

"Oh yeah," he said. "It's nice up there. I got a auntie who lives up near there. Up near the Cubs stadium."

"I live in Baltimore," I said. "I just came here to, you know. Baltimore is bad. Um. I think I need a little more if you don't mind."

"I'll join you," he said.

I couldn't help but notice the extremely miserly way he handled his drugs. I'd only bought him one ten-dollar bag. I got three for me. I did a whole one right off, and now I was going to hit another. He took out the bag I'd bought him, which I saw to my wonder was still almost full. He shook out a very few grains. If I were quicker, I thought, I could have counted them.

I'd heard of fiends like this before. But I'd never met one. It defied common sense. Dope costs money. I always thought that once my money ran totally dry I'd have to kick. That would be it. A solid bottom to the disease. But look at Tiger. Even being dead broke and homeless didn't get you off the hook. The disease could string you along on a few grains a day.

How little money could the disease survive on? Ten dollars a day? What about three dollars? Fifty cents? I watched Tiger shake out his few grains from the bag. He smiled over it with that nasty junkie look, seeing his first time glowing in the powder. It was worse than watching an old man look at porn. Much worse. There was barely enough dope there to see anything in. I could never get clean.

"I'm going to school," he said.

"Same with me," I said.

When I got back in my car the radio said it was eight degrees out. My fingers were slow. I got scared for a few seconds as the new dope fell through the brain slot and I saw I was kind of dying. But it was only for a few seconds. Then the dope light went out and I could see normally.

I could see death like I could see the color of my shoes. Like I could see the other side of the street. It wasn't weird or scary. The other side of the double yellow lines on the highway. It's like walking across a room. You get to your chair and you stop and sit down. But before you sit down, you think, *I can keep walking. Or I can stop. If I stop, I'm here. If I keep going, I'm over there. There's no big mystery.*

But it is often easier to compose your mind on the big questions—like death—than it is to successfully complete everyday tasks. My experience provides plentiful evidence of the truth of this statement. I had a little trouble when I got back to my sister's from Tiger's, for example. It was hard to find a parking space. I parked on the crowded part of the block, where I knew I shouldn't. Sure enough, when I got out my car was sticking out over the sign that says no parking. I'd learned to expect the worst from those signs.

I got down on my haunches and looked hard. Was I over the line or not? Expect the best, but plan for the worst. What would be the worst? If they came by and chopped the car off right at the line where the sign was, it'd still drive. Maybe. But better safe than sorry. I got back in the car and tried to back up some more. I tried to fit ten inches into two inches, so to speak. Like fitting a twenty-ounce Coke into an eight-ounce glass. You can almost do it, if you pour slow and careful. Very careful, very slow.

When I got back out of the car, things were in a bad way. I was bleeding a little bit. The car was still over the line. And I absolutely had to take my depression medication. I didn't mean maybe. Emergency! I'd forgotten to take it for maybe two days. I didn't know if I could park the car again without it. That depression medication was really helping me. I didn't even feel whatever had started me bleeding, for example. That was just one example. The medicine was called Zoloft. It was also helping me kick dope. I'd been taking it for two years. It wasn't the fastest-working drug in the world. Slow but steady. You don't know anything about science. I believed in it.

When you go for a couple days without Zoloft, it reminds you with a little "ping" in your head. It's not like dope withdrawal or anything. But it isn't pleasant. It's like someone tapping you lightly on the back of your head. You turn around too fast and you fall down. No one is there but the ghost of Zoloft.

I got up off the snow where I had fallen. I got back in the car. The place I'd parked it in was too small for it but it didn't seem to want to get out of it. Get out of it! When I got to the drugstore I saw I didn't have my prescription with me. Or they made me see, rather.

"As I said, sir, we simply cannot dispense this medicine without a prescription."

"The proof that I have a prescription for Zoloft," I said reasonably, "is that I need Zoloft. Zoloft is not a drug that gets you high. No one in their right mind would want Zoloft this bad if they hadn't been taking it for months and then suddenly ran out."

"But sir—"

"Look at me. No one in their right mind wants Zoloft this bad."

He looked at me. He said he would give me three pills and charge me by the pill. I started to pay him, but then he said they didn't take out-of-state checks. I said I would buy it with an in-state check if he would let me put some vitamins on it.

"What is your return policy?" I asked. "In Baltimore you just need a receipt and they give you back cash."

"Sir, this check . . . your total is $114.25. We have a limit of fifty dollars per check at this store."

"But you said I could get the Zoloft."

"The cost of the three Zoloft pills is $11.15. The remaining $104.10 comes from this, uh, L-Carnitine and—"

"Never mind," I said. "I just have to run out and check on my car. It's a new Mercedes. I don't think it's very safe in this bad neighborhood."

I thought that telling him I owned a Mercedes would be a good lesson to him. When I came back in I wasn't feeling very well. There was a different person at the counter.

"The pharmacy is closed," she said.

"What? I was just in here," I said.

"We close at nine o'clock, sir. It is now almost nine-thirty."

I looked hard into her eyes. She met my gaze without flinching. This particular employee, I thought, has nothing to hide.

"I was checking on my car," I said. I stopped.

"OK," I said. "The pharmacy is closed."

I was able to pay for some of the vitamins at the registers up front. The employee at the register did find an opportunity to humiliate me, however.

"Um, sir? I think you're forgetting something."

"Oh, of course. Right."

I picked up my keys off the floor and left. It was one of those things you think nothing of at the time.

When I got back to my sister's block, there was no more dope left. Impossible but true. I parked and started to look for the missing bag on the floor of my car, but so much garbage got into the street while I was looking I was afraid the people would come. *Hey, smart guy.* So I drove back to the pharmacy parking lot, which was the only place I knew for sure I could park without getting towed. And it was beginning to be the only place I could be sure of in other ways.

"Hi, Jenny, this is Mike."

"Oh, hey. Where the hell are you? Are you still staying here tonight?"

"Yes, but I got a little lost."

"Come on! I have to work tomorrow."

"Sorry Jen, I'll be right over. Do you know the pharmacy on . . ."

I put my hand over the pharmacy phone and asked the cashier where it was located. I asked her again to make sure I'd heard right. Then I really had to laugh.

"Jenny, I'm sorry, but ha ha ha. I'm right down the street!"

"Idiot," she said and hung up.

There was nothing to laugh about once I got back in the car. The block looked like a mouth with all its teeth knocked out. I parked almost all the way over the No Parking sign this time. If they chopped it off now, nothing would be left. Some paint chips.

Can you believe this damn junkie, Carl?

Didn't anyone remember anything good about me? Plan for the worst. You can't plan for the worst.

I don't believe it! Hey, smart guy, get your ass right back here. Think I wouldn't see you pick up that dope right in front of my face?

I grimly walked all the way around Jenny's block two-and-a-half times before I found her building. This looks like it. This looks like it. This looks like it. I was biting the inside of my cheek.

When I finally got inside, I looked back out at the street and saw why it had been so hard to find her place. Everything looked the same. Not literally the same, but brick or stone, gray or brown, a little taller or a little shorter. Right turn or left turn. West Side or North Side. The city was filled with differences that didn't make any difference.

I don't believe it. I went with my family to a hotel downtown. *Hey smart guy.* It was a Christmas tradition. *I don't believe it.* I went to the bathroom when we got there. *Hey smart guy.* At dinner I had something to drink. *I don't believe it.* "I think you've had enough." *Hey smart guy.* They don't want to be responsible for the drinks you had before you got there. *I don't believe it.* The off switch was two-and-a-half bags. *Hey smart guy.* Tiger called from a 7-11. I don't believe it. I called the valet from my room. *Hey smart guy.* "Tell Dad I'll be back in twenty." *I don't believe it.* Icy morning like a mouth full of broken teeth. *Hey smart guy.* "They getting everyone together in the building." *I don't believe it.* "The people are here." *Hey smart guy.* "I swear I didn't score yet; I was just—" *I don't believe it.* They let me go; I didn't have any more money. *Hey smart guy.* Bend over pretend to tie my shoe pick up the bag quick walk away. *I don't believe it. Hey smart guy! Get your ass right back here.* Handcuffs, back of the cop car.

I don't believe it. Thought you were slick. Hey smart guy. They had Tiger on the concrete. *I don't believe it.* "Felony possession, intent to." *Hey smart guy.* Heard about one who found part of a toothpaste box and read it for weeks waiting for trial. *I don't believe it.* The people took me to a room in the castle. *Hey smart guy.* Lieutenant Abelove told me I was safer from sleep than ever. *I don't believe it.* Shut up, shut up. *Hey smart guy.* "You going to be just fine, Mike; they gonna lock me up forever." *I don't believe it.* "They gonna lock me up forever! Oh God." *Hey smart guy.* "Oh God, I done spent half my life in jail. Oh God, my mamma ain't raise me. Oh God." The people shut Tiger up. *I don't believe it.* Kind of glad they did. *Hey smart guy.* When I heard them hitting him I grinned like a devil. *I don't believe it.* It was like a little piece of feeling got loose and I caught it between my teeth. *Hey smart guy.*

The people let me make a phone call. I didn't have my heart in it.

"Hey Dad. Yeah I'm a little locked up."

"A little," the cop said next to me. *Hey smart guy.*

"It's kind of a traffic thing. I might need to be bailed out. Bring, I don't know how much."

I was still hoping for an I-bond. Released on my own recognizance. I'd had those before. But I'd never been locked on a felony before. In the morning they took us from the cell at the station where we'd spent New Year's Eve to the city jail at 26th and California. It was 2002. I saw Tiger in the back of the paddy wagon. He was all beat up.

"Do you think I'll get an I-bond, Tiger? Do you think maybe I'll get an I-bond?"

Tiger was silent. Finally the cop shut me up.

The wagon stopped and they hustled us out. 26th and Cali. *I don't believe it.* They dumped a few more paddy wagons of junkies and dealers into the big holding cell while me and Tiger were getting our bearings. I had two cigarettes in my jacket and eight dollars in my shoe. Everyone was lighting up. I borrowed a light. Hooray cigarette. The nicotine rush gave me back everything the people had taken. And more. I felt like I had not yet begun to fight.

"Gimme your goddamn money."

This from a skinny twenty-year-old gangbanger.

"No," I said. "Fuck no."

"I'll see you tonight," he said.

"I'll see you never," I said. I hit the cigarette like Rocky.

Some of the gangbangers were selling clonidine. Two dollars a pill. Clonidine is a blood-pressure medicine they give you at detox centers to ease withdrawal pain. I bought one. I got one of the last ones. They sold out quick. Clonidine works by making you dizzy. As far as I can tell. I'm no doctor. I sat on the floor for a minute. A big cop came in.

"OK motherfuckers, listen up. Everyone get up against the wall. Everything except your wallet and clothes goes on the middle of the floor. Now. Drugs, cigarettes, lighters, knives, combs, pens, needles. Drugs. Anything you put on the floor now, we will not charge you with. But when you leave this room, we will search you. And if we catch you with anything, we will charge you with bringing contraband into a secure facility. That's going to be time on top of whatever you're getting for whatever got you here."

Eighty pockets emptied on the cold floor. "You got a needle in your pocket, junkie? If I prick my hand on a goddamn needle I'm going break your teeth out." *Hey smart guy.* "With this."

Random brutality is effective population control in conditions of chronic overcrowding. "The jail guards are the same kind of people you see working in the stores you like to go to," Dave said once. "They're the people you don't know. The people who work in the stores are so friendly. You might think all the people you don't know are friendly like that. But the people who work in the stores act friendly because the boss fires them when they don't. What are the people like now?"

"Get us out of here."

"There's a hundred of us in a cell made for ten."

"I can't breathe."

"I can't stand up."

"Get us out of here."

"I can't lie down."

"Motherfucker passed out standing."

"So damn tight packed up in here motherfuckers can't breathe."

"Motherfuckers can't fall down."

"Motherfuckers can't turn around."

"Get us out of here."

The brown-yellow-white squirming cell-shaped mass of us pushed tentacles out through the bars at a lady cop walking past.

"Hey, bitch, get us out of here, fucking bitch!"

"OK, who said that?"

The people came by with their face talk and their billy clubs.

"Who said that? Who said that?"

There was no "who" that said that. No one. But the people demanded a who. They wouldn't talk to a two-hundred-legged cell-shaped monster. They demanded to talk to one person. Responsibility. They were going to teach us to take responsibility. We were responsible for our humanity. They looked hard into the cell with their billy clubs next to their faces.

"Who said that?"

They were going to cut one human being out of the squirming animal mass. Just to prove there were real people in there. The lady cop came close and jabbed her billy club in at a heart and two lungs.

"That's the one."

"Get him out of there! Pull him out of there!"

The cops pulled him out like a tooth and got him by the bloody roots on the concrete floor outside the cell. They started to operate. They grunted with the work.

"Oh man, that's fucked up."

"They can't do that."

"Man, that ain't right."

"Where's the video camera?"

"Better not put him back in here."

"All that blood."

"I need my medication."

"Motherfucker next to me bleeding."

"What day is it?"

"Stop bleeding on me, motherfucker."

Hours passed. Blood dried. When was our bail hearing? How long could they just leave us in here? Wasn't there a law? They pulled a few of us out. A few more another time. No one knew where. Everyone was glad there were less of us. They took a quarter of us out in one lump once. The mass sagged and split. I fell out the middle. I was an independent operator again. My nerves stopped at the edge of my skin again. I walked over to the sink and threw up.

We could hear them getting called out for the bail hearing in the bullpen down the hall. At 26th and Cali, the bail judge comes to you. You see him face-to-face through the miracle of technology. Technology that matches faces to crimes, crimes to degrees, degrees to bail amounts. Technology that projects the judge's human face down into the hole where the bodies fuse. Where you forget that you did what you did. Maybe someone else did it. Well, you better remember. Get ready to sit down in a chair and face the video judge. Face him like the human being that you are. Sit down in the chair by yourself. No one's touching you. Be responsible. A guard reads your name off a list. Now look up. Look into the TV face of the video judge.

"Video judge, video judge."

Anxiety coiled through our cell. One guy whipped out a comb from God knows where and started carefully working his hair. He probably pulled it out of his ass. Where else could he have hidden it? The cops found a single thin cigarette I had tucked into the back of my left sock.

"Video judge, video judge."

It was my turn to face the video judge. The guard pulled me out of the cell and pushed me down the hall and sat me down in the folding chair. He pointed up at the video screen. The video judge was a cube of pink and black TV colors. They had taken my glasses. They said my glasses were a weapon. Video judge looked like an open TV wound. A man in the cheapest suit I ever saw came and stood next to me. He was my court-appointed lawyer for the bond hearing. I craned my neck up toward the screen. Help me, video judge. I tried to adjust my facial muscles to the appropriate position. Three seconds. The colors moved inside video judge and sounds came out.

"Bond, twenty thousand dollars."

The guard took me back to the cell.

I saw him first. He was snuffling something in his hand. He looked up like what. I moved over.

"You got some dope, man," I whispered. "What?"

"I seen you got some dope, man," I whispered.

He was a big Latino man, Latin King tats. His face was dead bone white.

"What'll you give me if I do?"

"I'll bail you out."

"What?"

"I got money. I got a lawyer coming by to bail me out tonight. I'll bail you, too."

He grabbed my wrist.

"Oh hey man, yeah man. Look. You gotta bail me out. My bail high. But I gotta ounce of pure at my apartment. Fat ounce of pure. More when I'm on the street. I give you my girl's number. You can have the ounce tonight. Uncut pure raw. More tomorrow. You gotta bail me out."

I grabbed his wrist.

"Oh yes, yes, yes I will. But I need the dope you have on you now."

He grabbed my shoulder. I grabbed his arm.

"Oh yeah, please, you got to—"

"Oh yes, now, I need it—"

"Ounce today, ounce tomorrow—"

"Dope now, bail now—"

"Now, tonight, today, tomorrow."

He slowly spelled out his name and his phone number and his girl's number and another number that was maybe his mom's or his Social Security number while I knelt snorting that half bag, nodding at him, smiling, watching for the guard.

My minimum habit was ten bags a day. Half a bag just gave the withdrawal chills the energy they needed to snap my spine in half.

"This . . . shit . . . don't . . . do . . . shit," I sneered into the Latin King's skull. "You think I'm bailing you out for half . . . a . . . bag . . . of . . . *bullshit*?"

He looked sick but he got up fast. Two hundred and fifty pounds. At least. Those gangbanger junkies weren't on the street long enough to lose all the muscle they got in prison.

"Are you crazy? I will kill you."

I moved quick to other side of the cell and put my hands in my pockets.

"Who you got in here, *cabrón*? Who you got in here, *maricón*? We'll see tonight! You better get bailed out, mother-fucker! I'll see you in the showers, *maricón*!"

I thought how I would break one of my own teeth out in the shower with my fist and walk up behind him and tap him on the shoulder and push it into his eye. "Already dead," a Zen master said when someone told him they were afraid of dying. "Already dead." Outside the bars the people were beating a junkie who had a needle in his pocket when they searched him. "Already dead." I told the man who was processing me that I was in the methadone program and to give me my methadone and he smiled at me like the Buddha and said no.

The gangbanger who'd demanded my money walked by nodding at me and punching his fist in his palm. The withdrawal chills took my legs. Blood filled my mouth from the cheek I'd been biting. And the tang of the Latin King's dope burned through the blood. Through the blood. The tang of dope burned a hole in my blood. It burned a hole at the back of my throat.

My endless dope body streamed out through the hole. Poured out into the alleys and corners and jungles. Into Chip's roof and Baltimore and Candy Land and Florida and Burma and Nancy's apartment and the Church Without Walls. Into Funboy's eyes and Henry's arm and Cash's helmet and the Center for Addiction Medicine and the sky above Mrs. Nichols's house. Cut me gangbanger! Cut me Latin King! Like cutting the string of a kite. "Already dead." Already elsewhere. Already everywhere. No way to stop it.

My body in the holding cell at 26th and California, January 2, 2002. A tiny dot in the vast memory network. The whiteness bled through the memory routes until the past and future were infected. Until the street/jail difference disappeared. Until the Dom/Henry difference disappeared. Until the life/death difference disappeared. Until the then/now difference disappeared. Until the Eva/Funboy difference went, the Chicago/Baltimore difference went, the red-top/white-top difference, the bail/no bail difference, the Michigan/Florida difference didn't make a difference. The memory disease bled through the borders. Until the incurable world shone white and solid as a ball of metal.

FOURTEEN

FORGETFULNESS

I didn't have to pull my tooth out in the shower. My father showed up with the bail and a breaking voice before lights out. Good-bye jail friends. The incurable world. That's gone too. Along with a half bottle of prescription cough syrup I stole from my mother's medicine cabinet the next day. It didn't do much. I don't miss it. A week later they asked me my name at the rehab intake desk and I stuttered on it.

"Don't you know who you are?" the secretary joked.

Who am I? Writing is an aid. I prop myself up on this cane of ink and paper. When I look down at my life, the sadness is a thousand miles wide. When I let the cane fall and drop back down, I see the sadness is one inch deep. A thousand miles wide and one inch deep.

An inch below the surface my life is still unexpected and confusing. Like the taste of metal. It's on everything. What is that taste? Is it like the taste of dope? The taste. It tastes like blood. Blood tastes kind of like metal, that's what it reminds me of. Sharp. And it doesn't taste like metal exactly; it tastes like blood. The taste makes it hungry. Not me. The taste makes someone else hungry—not me, I'll be OK but I don't exactly feel like eating—someone inhuman.

Skies and roads and buildings have that taste now. I taste it when I sit still long enough for the sadness to vanish. It takes about half a second. Then that taste. Metallic like fear and metallic like joy. Like blood or like metal. Who am I? I'm running out of examples.

I have a few left. Cat called me last week. I hadn't spoken to her for months, since before I came to Florida. That last conversation before I moved had been brief and unsettling.

"Hey, Cat, I was just calling to say hi," I said.

"Oh, hi Mike." Her voice had some far-off spaces in it. Like on vacation when you give some teenager your camera to take a picture of you and your girlfriend against the view. When you get it back, you see your two tiny heads perched frightened in the lower left corner of the endless sky.

"This is a difficult conversation for me," she concluded.

"Oh, well I can call back if—"

"I'm in love with someone," she said.

"Oh," I said. I felt vaguely crushed.

"You really don't know?"

"No," I said.

"You'll be so upset . . ." Her voice trailed off. It was the middle of the day. "Look, I can't have this conversation right now." She hung up.

It bothered me. I felt ashamed that it did. It wasn't as if we were together. She'd broken up with me definitively five years ago, when she learned of my arrest in Chicago. After I got clean and came back to Baltimore, we went out a few times, then stopped. I was alone for almost a year, then met someone, fell for her, moved in with her, and broke up with her just as Cat was returning from Italy, where she'd been for a year and a half. We went out for dinner and she wore a blouse made of old lace. It was translucent. She was more beautiful than ever. At my bare apartment, with the full moon coming through the cheap curtains, she whispered, "I want to make you happy." She unscrewed the part of me that juts into the world with the other solid objects and it came loose and fell off and there was nothing solid left.

In moments of passion people sometimes say that they "forget themselves." But this self-forgetting is notoriously unreliable. It's like your lover telling you she's forgotten all about what you said when you were angry. I wanted a more complete forgetting. I didn't want to forget myself; I wanted to be forgotten. Love was one way. I wanted to come, not in the way you forget yourself, but in the way someone who passes you in the street forgets you. Freedom. I knew I never gave Cat any freedom like that. I resented her sometimes.

When I moved to Michigan she flew out a few times to see me. The last time she stayed a week. It was a disaster. She said she'd been diagnosed with adult attention deficit disorder and was taking some pills that helped her focus. The pills focused Cat into a blinding light that burned holes in the little routines that kept my days together. She'd race in while I was getting dressed.

"What are you doing?" she demanded.

"Getting dressed," I said.

I couldn't seem to find my belt. She picked up a book lying on the dresser.

"What is this?"

I opened my mouth to tell her, but she'd already lost interest.

"I'm bored as hell," she said.

"Cat, have you seen my belt around?"

"I think I threw it out," she said absently. "I cleaned up a bit while you were in the shower. You keep a lot of senseless junk around this place, Mike. You take *forever* in the shower. It's wasteful. I can't sleep."

Cat had always been a very tidy person. The pills focused her into a Cat laser. I turned it off. We stopped talking for a while. I met someone else, and started dating her. We broke up a year later when I moved to Florida. Then, with her uncanny timing, Cat called. I called her back, and that's when she told me she'd fallen in love. She didn't say who.

"You really don't know?"

How would I know? She was still living in Baltimore. I didn't like any of her friends. She'd dated a couple famous people and a couple rich people; maybe it was in the news? I let it drop, though it stung. *Maybe this is finally the end,* I told myself.

Then she called last week. I saw the number on caller ID and hesitated. I was afraid she was going to tell me she was married. I took a breath and answered.

"I haven't heard from you in ages," I said cheerfully, biting down my anxiety. My cheerful voice. That voice is shallow, but it is unafraid. Keep it close. "It's been ages since we talked. I'm living in Florida now; it's beautiful here." I spoke cheerfully; I listened carefully.

"Yeah, I'm sorry I haven't called before," she said. "I've had a pretty awful summer." The careful one inside me smiled.

"Oh no," I said neutrally, thinking this means she's not married, thinking why do I care, "anything in particular?"

"Well," she said inhaling, "I . . . um . . . I was hospitalized. Twice."

"What?"

"Oh, um. It's still not very clear to me." Pause. "The first time they, ah, I, was upset. And the police took me to the hospital. They kept me there for ten days. I kept asking why. My mother had to come from Texas to get me out. Then I was going to drive home to Texas. But I had a panic attack while I was driving. In Virginia. They kept me for three days, I think, maybe a little more."

"My God, that's awful," I said.

"Diagnosis amphetamine psychosis, ha. It's like a poem. It was the mostest . . ."

"It was the pills you were taking. I knew it."

"Yeah . . . you were right. You're always right. And now I can't concentrate. The pills, I miss them. I can't concentrate. I need to go to concentration camp. The old Cat is gone. Dissolved."

"Don't say that. You sound better now. Like yourself. Those pills made you strung out." *Those fucking pills,* I thought. "Maybe you should sue the psychiatrist who prescribed that shit. These psychiatrists are criminals!"

"He tried to help me," she said gently. "You see, Mike, those pills were the last chance to fix me, and now they're broken . . ."

"Everything is going to be OK," I said. "Everything is going to be fine." I said it cheerfully. Dear reader, dear Cat, please don't smile! The cheerful voice is shallow, but it doesn't fear death. It isn't afraid of anything. And it has no memory.

When you suffer from the memory disease, you need a little forgetfulness. Just a little. Just a little bit more than will fit in your human life. If you suffer from the memory disease, you need a forgetting that starts right now, turns, heads back toward your birth, passes it, and keeps going. When I got out of jail on January 1, 2002, everything reminded me of heroin. Even my lawyer.

On the afternoon of January 5, 2002, my lawyer sat before me. He was wearing a tie and had a light heroin complexion. His office was on a high floor of a high office building that reminded me of getting high and being high. The lawyer was moving his lips for money. My father's money, not mine. I didn't have any. If I had, I would have been high.

The lawyer had gotten the initial hearing pushed back six weeks. As a condition of my bond, I was not supposed to leave the state. Or carry a weapon. And so on. I kind of wondered what it would be like if the lawyer would just move his lips in the dark, in the place where I wasn't. It wouldn't be bad, I thought, but it wouldn't be too great either. I listened while my father and the lawyer debated what was more dangerous, shipping me to a treatment center outside the state for a month, or leaving me here and risking my rearrest when I tried to cop. Which I admit had crossed my mind.

"Now Michael," the lawyer said, "I don't mean to suggest—and I certainly don't believe—that you were in Ogden Courts for the reasons the arresting officers attribute to you. But—and I'm absolutely not suggesting any guilt here—do you think you will find it difficult—perhaps for reasons I don't need to know—to stay away from that location? Will you find it difficult—for personal reasons, let us say—to refrain from visiting that or any other location that would give rise to the appearance—and appearances can be deceiving—of an intention such as that alleged in this report? The intention to buy, to use, or to sell narcotics?"

"I—"

"There's no way," said my father. So the lawyer agreed to my being sent to a facility to be treated for my propensity to give the appearance of buying, using, or selling narcotics.

After we'd seen the lawyer, my father dropped me off for a brief visit with my mother. She was upset. I also discovered she'd had pneumonia recently. I excused myself, went to her bathroom, and found and drank that half-full bottle of codeine cough syrup. I blamed her for everything.

"You have to think of your future," my mother said.

"I know, Mom," I replied. I burped red.

That night I drank a six-pack of beer and ate some Valium. I went out in the cold to smoke a cigarette. The outside was full of distances that didn't go anywhere. The black sky droned, like a phone off the hook. Everything is going to be fine.

On the airplane to the treatment center, there were tantalizing glimpses of high speeds and vast distances. The world seemed to have enough space in it to lose me. That was kind of reassuring. It didn't do anything material for me, but it was like a little promise. A little "everything is fine" message. But it was also kind of like an old spy movie when the spy holds the message up to a mirror and it says something quite different. I was frightened.

Once when I was little with a fever watching television in a hotel room while my parents were downstairs at a party, the television played an old spy movie. The bad spy, silver and black like a melted mirror, held up the two words of the secret message. I don't think I could read then. I may have been closer to death than my parents ever knew. *And now no one knows,* I thought. I looked out the plane at clouds like secret writing.

The treatment center bus picked me up at the airport on January 7. At the intake desk they asked me some questions, I told them some lies, then they put me in a hospital room and monitored my blood pressure. They drew blood and did tests. I stared at the walls. After three days it was the longest I'd gone without any drugs or alcohol in seven years. After four days it was the longest in nine years.

My memory annihilated the watery unreal days between me and the drugs. The color of the hospital reminded me of new dope. Outside the window I could see a pale winter light that reminded me of getting high in the winter.

They cut off the withdrawal medicine. They left my nerves exposed in the low-thread-count sheets. They gave me pamphlets and books to read. They showed me videos to educate me on the severity of my disease. Scientific videos. They showed me a video of a junkie watching a video of a junkie shooting dope. In the video, people in white coats compared the brain scan of the junkie shooting dope with the brain scan of the junkie watching. The brain scans looked the same.

"The question is not just 'why can't they stop once they start?'" the voiceover intoned. "The more difficult question is 'why do they always start again once they have stopped?'"

Sometimes the two secret words of the fever movie in my parents' hotel room became the two words of my name. And I met an English guy named Peter in the smoking lounge of the ward. He was the personal chef of a Mexican billionaire. He was a crackhead. I met an alcoholic car salesman named Rodney. I met a thick southern guy about my age named Al. He was a coke dealer who went from snorting to smoking. His drug-dealer bosses had sent him to the treatment center to get him back to snorting. When he smoked he made mistakes. We were all wearing baggy blue hospital clothes. You had to look at our faces to tell us apart. We looked at our shoes.

A week after I'd arrived, they finally moved me from the hospital ward to a unit in the regular part of the treatment center. The unit I was assigned to held about twenty guys. It was divided into a number of rooms, which held between two and four beds each, and a large central area with a television, a large poster of the Twelve Steps, and a coffee pot.

They sent one of the inmates, Marty, to come pick me up from the hospital ward and take me to my room. He was a senior patient. Most patients stayed at the treatment center for four weeks. I'd already been there for one week. The patients who had been there three weeks were the seniors. They walked and talked differently. You could easily pick one out in a crowd. The seniors were entrusted with picking up the newcomers from the hospital ward. It fostered a spirit of camaraderie and provided an opportunity for the newcomers and seniors to mingle.

"This is a great treatment center," Marty said. "Last month I was at one in Atlanta that really sucked. There was hardly any focus on the Third Step. That's the crucial step. I was here last year around this time. They do a wonderful job with the Third Step here. I don't know how great a job they do with the Second Step." He frowned. Then he smiled.

"Everything is going to be fine."

I had never seen the Twelve Steps before and when I saw the huge poster of them covering an entire wall on the unit I had a little panic attack.

"Does this mean I can't even have a drink again?" I whispered to Al, who came up to greet me as Marty walked off.

"Well," Al said, "they are sure going to tell you that."

I got a cup of coffee. It was lukewarm. I think boiling water was prohibited. Then a cute little guy in jeans ran up and told us to be ready for group in five minutes. Al told me he was a rising rodeo star addicted to ketamine. My confidence in the treatment center sank. I had taken ketamine by accident once. I was sure no one could be addicted to ketamine. It was like going into a hospital for brain surgery and learning that they also treated people for demonic possession.

"Group in the lounge! Group! Group in the lounge!"

The twenty of us assembled on the long couches. I felt uncomfortably sober. All these new people. I hadn't done the face-to-face thing raw in nine or ten years. I tried to look cool. How did you do that, anyway? I couldn't decide on the correct expression. Smile? ("Look at that happy-face motherfucker.") Frown? ("Somebody steal your teddy bear, faggot?") Look people in the eyes? ("What the fuck are you looking at?") Stare at the ground? ("Look at me when I'm talking to you, bitch!")

I decided my best bet was to look stoned. I let my mouth hang open and my eyes unfocus.

"You feeling all right, Mike?" Marty said, worried. He turned to whisper loudly to the fat man sitting next to him. I picked up a few words. "New guy . . . big problem . . . high . . . smuggle it in their assholes . . . look at him."

Marty's whispering was cut short when a sly-eyed man with a gray ponytail bounced in and stood in the center of the room.

"I'm Kirk, and I'm the head counselor on this unit, and I'm an addict."

"Hi, Kirk," everyone said.

"I'd like to ask those of you who are new to the unit to tell us who you are." Everyone looked at me.

"I'm Mike," I said. There was a long pause. Al nudged me and whispered, "Say you're an addict."

"I'm an addict!" I said.

"Hi, Mike," everyone said.

"Now," said Kirk, "I know a number of you are pretty new, so to get to know each other better I'm going to go around and ask each of you to tell us a little bit about what brought you here. You first, Mike."

"I'm Mike, and I'm an addict," said the other Mike. He was a bright, confident-looking man in his late thirties.

"What brought me here," he said, "was 9/11."

There were sighs and groans around the room. Marty had a look of anguish.

"Yeah, it hit me pretty hard." People were nodding and sighing. One thin pale inmate had his lips pressed tight together and his nails dug hard into his palms. Al looked like he was praying.

"I work in the financial district. I drove in late that morning. I was in the Holland Tunnel when it happened. I lost friends that morning. I had friends who worked in those towers. Fuck." His face twisted up. Someone gave him a Styrofoam cup of water. There was no glass on the unit. Broken glass cuts and kills. Mike continued.

"So I started to drink pretty heavy after that. One day, a week before Christmas, I came home and my wife and my family and six of my closest friends were waiting for me. My new secretary even. I've got two. An intervention." He sighed deeply. "So now I'm here. I've had a tough time. I feel like I'm at about 80 percent right now." He looked around the room. "I'm at 80 percent and I'm trying to get back up to 110 percent!" He slapped high-five with the guy sitting next to him and everyone clapped.

"OK," Kirk said. "How about you, Marty?"

"Well," said Marty, "9/11 hit me pretty hard too. I don't live in New York, but I identify. In some ways my problem is that I identify too strongly. I was the first one up on the unit that morning. I was at a treatment center on the West Coast. They let people sleep in until nine there. It was shameful. High relapse rate. I saw the planes hit live on CNN. It was awful. I said the Third Step prayer, but inside it didn't feel right. It's like my connection to my Higher Power just died. When I got out, it took just five days before I relapsed. That's the fastest ever."

"My name is Tony and I'm an addict," said the next guy, "I don't work in New York either but it's like after 9/11 I just wasn't the same person. Inside, I mean."

"I'm Al and I'm an addict. I'm here just simply 'cause I messed up and started smoking that damn 'caine but I want to say to Mike on 9/11: I feel you, bro."

"My name is Peter."

"Hi Peter."

"I think September 11 was an absolutely terrible thing," Peter said. "I'm not American; I'm British. I want you to know I sympathize. I was out of the country at the time. I'm a chef and I wish I had never heard that you could smoke cocaine. I didn't have any problem with snorting it." He shook his head sadly. "I was on a private yacht when it happened, cooking for my employer and his guests. I can tell you that Mick Jagger was among the guests. I can tell you that everyone felt absolutely terrible about September 11. It affected us all. I don't remember much about October."

While Peter was speaking, I wondered, for the first time, how 9/11 had affected me. It was such a huge event. Everyone agreed on that. How could it not have had an impact on me?

I was just as much a part of the world as anyone else, even if I felt pretty aloof sometimes. I breathed the same air as everyone else. Was I in denial about 9/11? I cast my mind back to that day four months earlier. Cat had woken me up. She'd been all excited.

"Something has finally happened!" she said. I dragged myself out of bed and over to the TV. As I watched the replay of the second plane hitting the tower my jaw dropped. I couldn't believe it.

"Finally," I said. "Finally something big has finally happened."

"They say more planes are coming," Cat told me. "They say Baltimore could be a target. Ohmigod look!" We stared fascinated at the TV. She turned the volume way up.

"And then," I told the group. "Then I realized that this was a special day. I'd been planning to quit dope that day. I'd even written myself a note. But when 9/11 happened I thought, 'Nothing matters now, the economy is probably fucked, no one will have to go to work again. I can get high today for sure.' And I did, and a few months later I got arrested, and now I'm here."

The guys around me sighed and nodded. It felt good to be in a place where people understood. I remembered telling Cash about how I felt that day and Cash saying he was going to call the FBI tip line and tell them I had expressed joy at 9/11. With friends like that . . .

"OK," said Kirk when the last of us had spoken, "9/11 was tough for many of us. Especially those who lost loved ones. No one wants to minimize that. But, as tough as it was, we are here in 2002 now, and whatever got you started using, or made you use more, the simple fact is that now you can't stop. You wouldn't be here if you could."

After group a number of us stood out in the cold smoking, gathered around the other Mike. He had emerged as a natural leader. I felt kind of good that we had the same name.

"I agree with everything Kirk said," Mike was saying, "I mean . . ."

"Yeah."

"Right on, Mike." We felt an unfocused positivity. I found myself smiling. Looking back it's hard for me to disentangle my feelings from the others'. Everyone was talking at once.

"Man, motherfuck dope."

"Never again!"

"I don't know what the hell I was thinking."

"I do, and it was stupid."

"One day at a time."

"Everything's gonna be fine."

"The First Step, man, the First Step."

"You use, you lose."

"A day without a buzz . . ."

"Is like a day that never wuzz."

"That ain't right, man!"

"Ha ha ha ha ha ha ha!"

"Just keep your eyes on the First Step."

"And your hands."

"And your mouth."

Addicts have thin boundaries. Or maybe we have elastic I's. Huddled together in the cold smoking, I caught some of Marty's feelings, and the other Mike caught some of mine. We were all mixed up together. It was kind of fun. I'd always secretly wanted to join the Army. Comrades, brothers. That night we all wobbled together on the rehab center patio, a single happy animal, starving hungry, horny, dying, smiling.

Togetherness therapy. For the next three weeks I went to group therapy sessions and smoked and ate four meals a day. We were all in it together. Together. With no drugs, the addicts huddled together and lost themselves in the crazy group animal. It cavorted around the lounge and the smoking patio and ate the hours until eventually we'd have to go to bed. Separately. I'd find myself lying in bed alone, zipped up in the tight envelope of my skin, and God only knows what I felt. Two weeks without drugs? Three? Some people never slept. Sneaked out at two a.m. to the lounge to talk to someone, anyone, everyone. You want to talk about food? Cars? Music? God? The talk went from your mouth into his ear out his mouth into your ear out your mouth into his ear—the talk went faster—you started remembering what his wife looks like and your loneliness woke up inside him and didn't know where it was and wandered around and got happy. Talk faster. Faster.

It went too fast. The counselors looked worried. Tensions began to infect our group therapy sessions. People started burning out. The rodeo boy announced that he wasn't an addict. "I never really liked ketamine." He felt he was being held at the facility against his will. This was bad for morale. We lost two patients who left when they realized no one was going to stop them. Rodeo boy stayed. Al asked him bluntly why he didn't just get the hell out if he wanted to so bad. Rodeo boy replied that he wanted to, but he just *felt* he couldn't leave. He blamed other people for that feeling. I also had some feelings I knew weren't mine. I nodded.

Over the course of several sessions, it slowly came out that Tony believed that he had killed someone and buried the body on a construction site in Indiana. Mike called Tony a show-off, and Tony responded by suggesting that the only friends of Mike's who had perished in 9/11 were imaginary friends, and Karl had to cut group short. That upset Marty.

Every couple days, senior patients would "graduate" and we'd have a little ceremony beating tom-toms and yelling and giving emotional speeches about the senior's triumph. Mike was particularly good at the speeches.

"You will definitely make it," he'd say, looking straight into the senior's eyes. "You will definitely make it out there."

A guy named Tom graduated at the beginning of my first week on the unit and was back at the end of my third week. He said his mistake was answering the phone without checking caller ID. A few senior patients didn't graduate at all. Mike said that the staff had identified some patients as benefitting from a more intensive and extensive treatment regime. Mike was not one of them. He was at 95 percent.

By now Marty was telling everyone that the treatment center was one of the two worst he had ever attended. You weren't supposed to use the Internet, but one of the patients somehow gained access to the counselors' computer and downloaded and printed and passed around an article from a website saying that treatment centers were completely ineffective and that every single addict sent there relapsed except the ones who suffered only from "addiction hypochondria." The counselors, all of whom were alumni of the center, presented themselves as evidence refuting these lies. Marty unexpectedly emerged as one of the article's chief opponents.

"That's crazy," he scoffed. "Of course treatment works."

There were two huge windows in the treatment center lounge. I stared out. A high, thin winter cloud was coming apart. Ten seconds. Twenty.

"Oh!"

"Freaking out a little, Mike?" Al sauntered in chuckling.

"No, uh, I was just zoning out a little . . . and . . . kind of surprised myself," I said, getting up and pacing around. I felt frightened and embarrassed.

Because staring at the sky my eyes had started to get dry. Then they dried completely out like bones. Like dice. And the looking that was in them wasn't mine and wasn't of the world and was some kind of bad luck. I'd blinked and freaked. Made a loud sound. There was a sharp taste of metal in my mouth.

Even the weather seemed to be coming apart. After I'd been at the center for about three weeks, there was a sudden thaw. The temperature, which had held steady in the twenties, rose suddenly through the thirties and forties. It stayed in the high forties for two days. Clear skies. The light looked more yellow than white. More butter than bone.

The next day the temperature rose right through the fifties and hit sixty-five, where it remained for the whole afternoon. A lot of snow melted, and in the middle of the large fields that surrounded the treatment center you could see the tallest of the brown grass blades poking through. People went outside to smoke without their coats. Tony—who may have been a murderer—even went outside without his shoes. The counselors looked worried, ready for anything. It was as if the day had come loose and dropped out of January, dropped out of the calendar.

The day it hit sixty-five, I sensed the weather before I woke. I slept very deeply now. My sleep was intricate, like a bookful of sentences written one over the other. The way to waking was slow. There were maybe three half or fake wakings before my eyes opened.

The morning of the thaw I first saw the new light on the false walls of a half waking. I emerged from sleep into a sunny castle room. The room was a kind of pre-waking, a dream extension, but I didn't know that. I felt awake. I was going to meet someone. Her white face flashed back between the black lines of the wall of sleep. I'd been talking with her. Maybe something more. Her prints covered the missing parts of my body. We had an appointment. A meeting on the farthest outskirts of the castle, out where its halls and fountains faded and I could see the hazy outlines of the furniture in my bedroom in the treatment center.

I walked through the castle with long dream steps that hung in the air for several seconds. The secret of flight was in the length of those steps. New, real sunlight spotted my clothes and my arms. It pooled and glittered in my palms. The secret of flight was in it. My half-waking thoughts got tangled. I should hurry. Lieutenant Abelove was right. The way out was obvious. I opened my eyes. The rich light lay over my bed and the treatment center carpet. June light in January. It took me a while to see it was real and I was awake. I got out of bed and put on my clothes.

We ate breakfast in the light. A few hours later, the warm day clouded over. From obvious to secret. After group and before lunch I had a smoke with Peter.

"I just get so afraid," I said, "that when I get out, well, and then, there's also the—"

"Just relax," Peter said. "Everything is going to be fine," he said cheerfully.

The weird weather made the day go slow. At lunch there were silent minutes between bites. After lunch there was more time. Some people were counting things, days left, for example, or the number of plastic spoons in the drawers. Normally the staff—hypersensitive to boredom prevention—kept the schedule tight and stopped loose time from piling up. But that day we stood around with extra time coming out of our ears.

I got bored. Restless. Sitting around staring at the sky freaked me out, but sitting around bored, I couldn't keep my eyes off it. Marty and Al went to play pool in the rec center; I wanted to get some exercise in the open. I went outside and started walking, alone and without a coat, eyes rolling along the ground like dice. The air tasted like ashes. I walked until I couldn't see the treatment center. A huge crow flapped slowly by, maybe six feet above the ground. It startled me. The low clouds were in its feathers, and it flew soundlessly.

I found a small cast-iron chair abandoned out in the center of a field. It must have been covered by snow until the thaw. Now its old-fashioned metal curlicues were bare and warm. I sat down in it. I looked out at the low, heavy, warm sky, the masses of trees at the lake's edge, the wet edges of the lake ice.

I sat exposed there for a quarter hour, then walked back. My skin itched in the uncanny winter mugginess. My steps were slow to pull out of the wet snow. I felt like I'd forgotten something and walked back a little, then forgot and walked forward. The crow came back so I didn't have to remember it.

When I got to the unit I opened the journal the treatment center had given each of us and I wrote down what was inside me. It took me a long time. I would write a little. Then I'd wait and think and wonder. And then I'd write a little more. Each line had two words on it, two secret words. This is what I wrote:

IRON CHAIR.

CROW. HEAT.

WITCHES. MAGIC.

I read this today and wonder, why witches? Why magic? I don't know for sure, but I have an idea.

The only way to recover from the memory disease is to forget yourself. You see, I was in a memory trap. In order to get out I had to forget myself. In order to forget about myself, I had to be sure there was something outside to grab on to. But the memory disease had trapped all of my senses. I couldn't see outside. In order to get even a glimpse of what's outside, I had to forget myself completely.

You see? It goes in circles, it's impossible. How can I see what's outside if I have to turn away from what's inside to see it and I can't let myself turn away from the inside until I can see what's outside?

Witches. Magic. The little crackle of energy left around the chair and the crow came from the force with which the outside was thrown into me.

FIFTEEN

OUTSIDE

On the plane home from the treatment center it happened again. I woke up from a nap next to a cloud. Blinking in a blue space that wasn't inside me.

At the treatment center they'd talked a lot about a Higher Power who was supposed to suck me out of myself like a vacuum. But it looked to me like a pretty Low-Powered vacuum would do the trick. A nap, for instance. Maybe the point was not the Strength that broke me out of myself but the Weakness that kept me inside. Kept me barely. Who am I? *A person can be cured of anything,* I thought. I shivered.

When I got home, all everyone could say was how much better I looked. "Everyone" was my father, my mother, my stepmother, my sister, my brother, my half brother, my half sister, and Cash, who was living nearby. Well, my half sister didn't tell me how good I looked. She was six months old and couldn't really talk yet. My half brother Ryan was two. He took a little while to put his sense of my transformation into words.

"Ryan, don't you have something to say to your big brother?"

"I got candy today."

"Yes, but isn't there something else?"

"B . . . b . . . baseball card."

"Something about Michael?"

Silence. Loud whispers from Dad to Ryan.

"You look very better," Ryan said. Everyone smiled at me. I smiled back.

I'd returned to a world of children. Soft food. Small words said slowly. It had been agreed that I would stay in my father's basement until my legal problems had been sorted out and I got my bearings and could think about either writing my dissertation or getting a real job. I didn't have to make any decisions right away. Although I hadn't done any work in months, I was still on a dissertation fellowship. I was getting monthly checks, and didn't need to make an appearance on campus for another half year. Which was fortunate, because I wasn't supposed to leave the state.

I put my bags down in the small basement bedroom. The room was dense, with pink carpet, a couple hundred books in neat piles on the floor, and a small folding table holding my computer monitor and keyboard. A narrow crack under the door let in the ghost of children's voices from upstairs. A high thin window above the bed let in the day's ghost. It was there every day. At 5:00 p.m. I would watch it disappear on the far wall. It never woke me, but when I woke it was there. On overcast days it was less a presence than an absence. A rectangle lifted from the room's heavy gray. Over the six months I stayed in Chicago, I grew to think of that rectangle of light as a single friendly ghost—awake each morning, asleep each night. Good morning, ghost!

When you live underground, the light that comes through the only window is significant.

When I went aboveground myself, it was almost too much. In those early days I was still drunk on the feeling of freedom from withdrawal on the one hand, and from narcotic coma on the other. The air was too strong; the light was too strong. I've always loved what is too strong for me, but I can't take too much. For the first week I wore myself out with air and light and slept for twelve hours a day like a baby. After that I spent more time inside and underground. I spoke to no one but Cash and family, and mostly to the little kids.

Kids have always liked me, perhaps because I take a genuine interest in what interests them. I bet that dinosaur could kill that tank. What about an airplane? No, dinosaurs can't kill airplanes. Maybe a helicopter. It was healthy for me to be around them. Spiritual. In their world, death was something that could happen to you many times. Like tanks or dinosaurs. You could die a thousand times every second. The kids had positive attitudes. They didn't even smoke.

But sometimes seeing an unfocused stare in a child's eye, or hearing a fascinated childish inhalation, disturbed the oldest memories I had, which turned and touched others, which had words attached to them, and words are the halo of the white thing. I had to go to my room. I turned off my light so I wouldn't be disturbed and read self-help books by the light of the ghost's face. Every day a new one.

I ate tuna-fish sandwiches every morning at Panera. I didn't know about their high mercury content then, but I'm not sorry. I think mercury helps kill the memory disease. If I ever open a treatment center, it will serve tuna every day. On Tuesdays I would take Ryan to Chimpy's. This was a rundown, kid-themed restaurant with a pen filled with colored plastic balls and little mechanical animals that the kids could ride on. If you put in a quarter, the metal animals vibrated a little, or rose three inches into the air, or played dead. There was an alligator, a giraffe, a tiger, and a horse. They were all covered in dyed fur. Even the alligator.

"You know alligators don't have fur, Ryan," I told him. As an educated person, I felt responsible.

"Yes, they do," he said. He pointed to the alligator's dyed green fur.

"Yes, but that's not an alligator," I said.

"It looks like an alligator," he said.

"But it's not," I responded.

"Then what do you call it?" he asked.

"We should get going, Ryan," I said.

"What is it called?" he persisted.

"Well, we call it an alligator. But we don't believe it."

I tried to teach Cash some things, too.

"You know, Cash," I said one day when we were having coffee. "You should stop smoking pot."

"I don't have a problem with pot," he said.

"Then why don't you stop smoking it?"

"Later," he said.

"Now!" I said.

"Look, Mike." He sighed. "I know you've stopped using heroin, and you stopped using everything else because you think it'll put you back on dope, and I think that's great for you. You're doing a lot better. Just keep doing what they tell you; it's working for you. But stay away from me with that bullshit. My problem was with alcohol, and pot helps keep me sober."

"You know how insane that sounds, Cash? The fact is that—"

"Shove those treatment center facts, man. I've been sober and doing good for three years and you were strung out six weeks ago, so chill."

"What, so you think that recovery is just bullshit? That everyone relapses?" My voice went up an octave and I felt a little panicky.

"No, Mike. Everything is going to be just fine," Cash said cheerfully.

The fact was that Cash taught me a lot more than I could teach him. He taught me some good habits. My only habits were taking Ryan to Chimpy's and eating tuna fish every day at Panera. That left me with about eleven hours of blank air to process. It didn't bother me; I was collecting outside moments. Like the chair and crow at the treatment center, the cloud on the plane, a couple others. I tried to explain to Cash.

"Does that kind of thing happen every day?" he asked.

"Well, no, but it's like a promise of—"

"You need something that happens every day."

He was right. I needed something that happened every day. You don't forget yourself all at once, I reminded myself. The mercury in the tuna helps, but it's not enough. You must make forgetfulness into a habit. Like a waterwheel that continually pours forgetfulness over your life.

I set a few waterwheels going. I began to exercise. My father had a treadmill in the large open space in the basement outside my bedroom, and I started using it. I put on headphones and played trance music and ran and sweated and in the ghost light I imagined I was the president. I had never really gone in for regular exercise. It bored me to death, to be honest. The trance music made the running bearable, and imagining I was the president for some reason made the trance music seem less . . . feminine. If that's the right word. Sometimes I had to trick myself to get me under the waterwheels of my new habits.

My exercise habit was so successful I started some others. I started doing a little regular work on my dissertation. I got into the habit of going to NA meetings. I brushed my teeth regularly. I checked my email. I had tuna for lunch and something else for dinner and two snacks. Sometimes I had tuna for dinner, too. I got into the habit of watching a little TV before bed.

Habits are healthy. I never really had any before. Not any real ones. Sometimes people call drug dependency a habit, but this is misleading. That's really an antihabit. It isolates you from things, where a real habit marries you to things. If I am a body, a habit is like a room containing my body and a bunch of other things. Outside things. A treadmill, a TV, books, snow, dayghosts, relatives, dinosaurs, mercury, an alligator, a toothbrush, a car. The habit picks us up and whirls us together like a tornado. A cartoon tornado. It doesn't hurt.

Habits are like reunion parties for me and my favorite things that happen every day. Drunken reunion parties where people go home wearing pieces of other people's clothes. A bit of the treadmill, part of the dayghost, and a trance beat stuck to me as I took a shower and headed out to the NA meeting. After the meeting, a few new faces and some old NA phrases lined the tunnel of my driving habit, where stars, and trees, and a few houses and road signs circled around my bedtime television habit. When I came through the television, washed clean in the way the world looks—the television colors, the satellite weather—I was ready for bed. Sleep.

And in all my dreams the white thing posed in its own light. The first time, the white out. Like a pyramid, it rose anciently above the white sand. The clouds above Chip's roof circled on its limestone face. I knelt in the white dust and a voice whispered to me: *You are not your habits. You are not what you look like. You are not what you do. You are not what you think or feel or touch or forget. You are what you want.*

Those dreams—and I have them still, occasionally—cured me almost entirely of curiosity about myself. "You are what you want." Ugh. I woke up running from that voice. Who I am is not something I need to know. "You are what you want." Not that I'm satisfied with that answer, mind you. I'm not. But I know no way of answering that question that satisfies. The questioner is insatiable. A restless, reckless, endless desire drives the questioning. Who am I? Who am I? But who am I *really?* It's best just to forget it.

Of course sometimes, like the day of the chair and the crow, something will happen to stir it up. Ah, you say to yourself. Oh. That's odd. This crow is inside me? Who am I, anyway? Who am I *really?*

Just let it go. Soon, forgetting to ask the question becomes a habit. Take the average oldster, for example. The question could never occur to her. Her little dog could spontaneously combust, her car could turn into a bird. She'd wonder about the dog or the car, not about the self. And who could blame her? What cop, arriving on the scene to a pile of ash where the poodle used to be, would look at the nice old lady and say: "Who are you? No, not your name, I know that. I mean *who are you really?*"

The fact is, who I am, who anyone is, isn't a very important question. You can't possibly get a straight answer to it, for one thing. And if you do ("I'm half Irish, a quarter Scottish, and a quarter English"), you're really asking about something else. If you're satisfied with the answer, you're not asking the question right. Who am I? It isn't really a question. Questions have answers. Who am I? It's more like a religion. An old religion, left over from another time. A time when there was nothing to do, maybe.

And I'm interested doing, in action. I'm active. I could care less about the *who* of my existence. (Though it's not what I have, not what I lost, not what I look like, it's not what I want, it's not what I remember, it's not what I forget.) Who I am has little to do with addiction and recovery. Who I am isn't the first thing I need to know to get better, it's maybe the last thing. Who am I?

To be honest, it's this writing that brings it up. Here where there's nothing to hang on to, the question occurs. Who am I? Something from an old religion. And writing is an old technology. Writing is an aid to memory. An ancient technology for remembering. And it keeps remembering. It remembers in the dark. It works back to the moment of your birth and keeps going. It remembers the holy shapes of old religions in the story of your life, for example.

Who am I? The question keeps coming up in this writing. I want to stop it. I could stop it if I really wanted. Who am I? Like a fire, like this book is on fire. Who am I? The smoke curls around Eva's face, around the white tops, around Cash, Funboy, Baltimore, Chicago . . .

"You are what you want," dope whispered in my dreams. I ignored my dreams and cultivated habits. February turned into March. Huge open days, and when it snowed the snow was hard like sand. I'd stand outside my father's house smoking, licking tea from the little slit of a Starbucks cup top. Five or six grains of snow blew around on the concrete.

I went to court and met my lawyer outside the courtroom. He explained he'd gotten me enrolled in a program for people accused of drug felonies for the first time in the city of Chicago. It was called Drug Court for short. I had to go to a courthouse once a week for four hours for six weeks to listen to drug education lectures, and if I stayed in the state and didn't get arrested and passed regular urine tests, I wouldn't be convicted of the felony. The arrest would be expunged from my records. I could answer no to all the felony questions on employment forms. I thought it was ridiculous that simple possession should be a felony anyway, but I had to admit that, all in all, getting arrested seemed to be turning out for the best.

I got a sponsor in NA. His name was Ryan. He'd been clean for nine months, was a year older than me, and was a successful professional poker player.

"Stay clean, get money," he told me. "Stay clean, get money."

After a few months his rising card career carried him out West, where I hear he's still clean and thriving. But before he left he gave me some good advice. When I got the heroin itch and just couldn't take it I'd call him and he'd pick up the phone and cut me off and say: "Don't pick it up, and it won't get in you."

That was his advice. Don't put the heroin in you, and the heroin won't get in you. The brilliance of this advice shines only for addicts. To a normal person, it's redundant. To an addict, it's revelation. Don't pick it up, and it won't get in you. Revelation. Because you walk around paranoid. You're sure that somehow the dope will just *get in you*. How? Who knows? It just gets in you. That's your whole experience. You write "Don't Do Dope!" notes and leave them around the apartment, and the next day, or later that same day, you're high, writing some new ones. You ask yourself how, and there's no answer. The dope just got in you.

For example, I remember the long narrow streets home from Dr. Hayes's detox in Baltimore. I'd have been clean for one day, driving my car home with some meds for the withdrawals. Dedicated to kicking. Convinced. The narrow road went straight. The sidewalks were deserted, but there was a flutter of movement. What? Nothing. But the dope was hiding behind the streetlights. It was hiding in the white sky. When I got to the end of the block, the right turn was missing. When I got a little further, I was high.

"If you don't pick it up, it won't get in youse," Ryan said with his hoarse Chicago whistle at the end of the *you*. "Before you get high, youse gotta get the money. Youse gotta get in your car. Youse gotta drive to the spot. Youse gotta give the dope-boy the money. Get home. Get the dope out. Get it in you.

"That's some steps to getting high. It don't just happen. Every one of them things is things you can not do, and if you don't do every one of them things, the dope can't get in you. You will never get high."

It sounded insane, but he was right. He was a successful poker player. The method involved giving certain areas of my life a kind of close focus. It involved knowing when to really pay attention. I'm driving in the car. OK, now close in. There's the entrance to the highway. If I get on it going south, it goes to the dope spot. If I get on it going north, it goes home. Since I want to go home, I make a right turn and accelerate up the ramp, and pretty soon I'm at home, sober.

Another example. I'm in the restaurant by myself. Here comes the waiter. Now is the time to pay attention. What I say next will determine what I will drink with my dinner. If I say "gin," the waiter will bring it. I will drink it. I'll get loose and get busy and get dope and I'll be fucked. So I pay attention. When the waiter asks the question, I say, "sparkling water." Then I relax, life goes into soft focus again, with bubbles.

Another example. I'm in the bathroom at a friend's. There's the medicine cabinet. This is not the time when I relax. This is not soft-focus time. This is the time when I concentrate, focus, and don't open the medicine cabinet door. The door doesn't open. I don't know what pills are in there. When I leave the bathroom I'm sober.

This wasn't the way it used to work. Every addict knows how dope just gets in you. Dope just arranges things so that your actions are like a ball rolling down a hill, and at the bottom of the hill you're high. But there's a trick. There's a secret. It seems that dope comes from everywhere and goes anywhere, that it's omnipresent, omnipotent, a white god. But it doesn't and it isn't. It just seems that way. It's like when you wake up and your room is full of music. It seems like it's coming from everywhere. Then you realize your window is open. When you shut it the music stops. It's like that with dope. It only seems to be everywhere. In reality, it hides in certain places, certain spots, and if you know where those spots are, you can shut the window before it gets in you.

One place dope hides is in the moment when the dope-boy asks you for your money. Another place it hides is in the turn that goes to the dope spot. Another place it hides is in Funboy. If you're alert, and you know about the places in the world where dope hides, you can stay not getting high. The trick has two parts. The first part is to be alert when you're passing the place where the dope is hiding. The second part is to not snatch the dope out of that place and do it. This two-part trick is called a "choice."

"If you don't pick it up, it won't get in you." That was the invention of choice for me. My life wasn't like a ball rolling down the hill into the dope-hole anymore. I don't want to over-emphasize the power of choice. It didn't exactly turn my life into an airplane either. It was more like a hollow ball with a little hole in it for a window and a tiny mouse inside. By leaning hard one way, the mouse can alter the direction of the roll. It's a very sleepy mouse, and it can't pay attention all the time. But it can learn to recognize a couple simple signs and when it sees them, to sit up and pay attention.

I don't want you to misunderstand me. The mouse isn't exactly Einstein. This is where Ryan and I parted ways. For example, one day I picked up a popular music magazine that featured a glowing review of a new CD by the guy Eva had been living with in New York since we broke up. I slowly ate my heart out as I read it. Where was the choice here? The mouse woke up and started leaning and leaning and then he fell asleep. I said nothing to anyone. Here was a whole other world. I didn't know what to say.

I secretly followed the music charts and was secretly glad when the album flopped. But now I knew. Outside the world where friendly people patted me on my head and said "you didn't get high" in happy surprised tones and fed me mercury-laced tuna was a world where hot girls kissed guys who rode foreign cars and made complicated choices with their heads while their hands moved faster. I was twenty-six. When you're twenty-six, you need more than a sense of humor and a choice.

My habit of fantasizing that I was the president when I ran on the treadmill took on a new urgency in the face of these revelations. I was the president. The president! The trance music got louder and I ran faster. Cash called and left a message while I was running. Cat left a message. My one-twentieth-finished dissertation blinked on the monitor in my bedroom. The dayghost rippled on the wall. It was raining outside. It was springtime.

On a chilly spring evening, I stood in front of my parents' living-room window and pressed my fingers to the glass. The sunset sky reminded me of Morocco. And when the colors hit my eyes they turned into Eva's smile, her smell, the color of her skin. That spring, everything I'd lost found me. Eva was just one example. A famous writer once asked why, when we fall asleep, do we wake up with our own thoughts, our own memories? Why ours instead of someone else's? But we do. And I'd been asleep for years.

When I went in from smoking I would stand at the big window in the living room for a few minutes. I'd watch the sunset before going down to my basement to watch the dayghost disappear. The sunset looked dark, almost purple. It was full of the wings of everything old coming back to me.

This book goes from Candy Land straight to Chip's roof. From when I was six to when I was twenty-one. But that's just the history of my dope body. And in that first post-heroin spring, my ageless dope body was gone. I'd traded it for a body that was like an empty hive. In the spring the missing swarms flew back through the sunset to fill it up again. Age five, age eight, age thirteen, age twenty.

"I'm part of you," each new memory said as it flew through my eyes.

"Me too."

"Remember me?"

Another memory. And another. Had I really lived so long?

"After a few months off dope, you'll feel like yourself again," the treatment center people had promised. Myself again. Age three, age nine, age seventeen. It was like inviting a few close friends for an intimate get-together and having five hundred people show up. I wanted to slip out the back.

Not that I missed the dope body. I was sick of having the kind of problems that demons have—sick to death—but the scale of the human problem was breathtaking. It took my breath away, standing in front of those colossal sunsets. Red and purple. The memory of bedtime when I was four coming back in that color. The memory of my first kiss coming back. The way my bedroom smelled when I was ten and I was sick.

Once the grip of the memory disease loosens, you are not free of the pain of memory. The pain and the memories just change. It's not the dope memory that annihilates time, the dope world where your first time getting high is always new, always fresh in the thousandth bag of dope, the ten-thousandth. That time-eating angel or devil slept. Spring brought back my human memory.

In a human's memory the years are clear to sight and closed to touch, like glass. The heroin memory says: You will never leave. The human memory says: You will never return. Human memory brings back what is lost along with its lostness. Its pastness.

An absolute distance shines in the beauty of human memories. The memory of me rowing my canoe with my friends, when I was eleven, in the Upper Peninsula of Michigan, with the . . . The glittering water. The water glitters supernaturally when the total distance hits it. When every second of every day of every year that has passed hits it all at once. It glitters. The eyes of my friends too. My eyes too. Never mind. I don't know where these tears come from.

My grade school afternoons burned without being consumed in the blue television light flickering on my father's basement walls. And the sudden chill at dusk reminded me of school play rehearsals. Once I had a red cape and a play sword; Elizabeth had a blue gown made of terrycloth . . .

Everything came back to me. The holy question "who am I" was hard to sustain. It was hard to pretend I was some great mystery when every puddle and every slant of light knew me.

"I know you," said the evening chill, "you were the pirate in the school play."

"I know you," said the sunset, "your bedtime was at eight."

"I know you," said the puddle. "When you were little I showed you a bit of the sky."

Now the sky the puddle showed me had something to show me. The reflected bit of sky showed me . . . me. I looked at the puddle and my heart sank, full of ten thousand days.

Who am I? I am a being who is alive, fills up with time, and must die. In this human world, who I am has a simple answer. A first name and a last name. A body and a brain. Nothing more to me than what is in the mind of anyone who sees me passing and calls out my name.

Pretending there's more to me than that is dangerous. Perhaps it conceals a secret longing for the dope body, the time-less body, the white eternity. Worse, this chasing after mystery is tasteless. It looks pretentious on a being who is born and then passes away. A being so full of dead time he sinks when every-thing else rises. When the heavenly days come—late April, early May—he fills up with memory and pastness and sinks away.

Catching all those human memories—in the sunsets, in the smell of cooking, in an old book I found under my bed—that was hard. And being back in human time, knowing that I would eventually die, that was hard too. But even worse was having to get a job.

What kind of job? By that spring, everyone agreed manual labor was the answer. Manual labor. It's not good for Michael to mope around the house. What's he doing all day? Fiddling with that dissertation? What's he calling it? "Freedom from You?" What does that even mean? Manual labor. What else was I qualified to do? Undergrad degree in Russian history, partly through a grad degree in English literature. Partly qualified to be a professor; fully qualified to be a manual laborer.

Manual labor. The tenth floor of an office building under construction. It was like heaven. A wide-open bright space with nowhere to hide. And why would you want to hide? This isn't a place for hiding. What are you doing hiding over there, Mike? Didn't I tell you to sweep out this room an hour ago?

I knew all about manual labor. I was something of a master, in fact. I could teach you how to pick this up and bring it over there and put it down. Now pick that up. I think actually I'd be good at it. But no one ever offered me a job teaching manual labor. The job they offered me involved doing manual labor.

The word *manual* comes from the Latin word for *hand*. That's misleading. Because you don't have to be too good with your hands. I once worked with a guy who had a hook for a hand. He'd been a machine operator, then he had an accident and lost his hand. Now he was a manual laborer. Just to put it in perspective for you. Just in case you know Latin and think manual labor involves some kind of close and careful work with your hands. It does not. It's the kind of job you can get when you lose your hands. You can push boxes with stumps.

My father came to me with the suggestion after I'd been hanging out in his basement not getting high for three months. It was hard to argue that I shouldn't have a job. He'd been paying for me, helping me, never complaining about all the horrendous stuff I'd put the whole family through for years, the legal fees, the "borrowed" credit cards, etc. He'd been amazing, warm, supportive, loving. He let me stay in his house, drive his car. He paid for my car insurance, gave me money for clothes, movies, cigarettes. He'd asked for nothing in return. So when he mildly suggested that I should get a job, I could hardly respond by arguing that I shouldn't. It was maybe easier to argue that I *couldn't*. But to build up my self-esteem I refrained from taking that line. At first. Eventually I did take the position that I was incapable of even manual labor—and I stood firm on it—but at first I simply suggested that maybe I could get some other kind of job.

Dad saw through this for what it was—a way to buy time. The fact is that I had tried to get a non-manual-labor job before, and the result of that experiment made it unlikely that I could repeat it. After I graduated college, and before I learned that Johns Hopkins was going to pay for me to go to grad school for six years, I had called a temp agency and gotten an office-type job. I was supposed to work there for at least a year, and to give a month's notice before I left. I was going to be taking over for the secretary of a small firm. This lady knew all the little ins and outs of the place, the kind of valuable, essential knowledge that isn't written down anywhere. It was in her head. She'd train me, put all that stuff into my head, then she'd retire. It was stuff like what to do with invoices and where certain forms were kept. But I can't really be more precise because two days into my training I got the letter from Hopkins and stopped listening. I was going to become a professor. I decided I'd go to Europe on vacation with Eva in a month to celebrate never having to get a real job again.

So there was no need to pay attention to the training, I just needed to earn a few weeks' worth of money and then I'd be out. After two weeks of training me, the old lady left. There was an office party. The boss even took a picture of her symbolically handing over her keys to me. It was sad and fun. She'd been there twenty years. I got into the spirit of it, told her I'd miss her. I signed her card, "I can never replace you."

The day after the party I came in and moved some papers around. I got seen walking purposefully around the office and talking seriously into the phone. All day long people passed by and dropped forms on my desk. I stuffed them in the drawers when no one was looking. I had no idea what to do with them. After four days the drawers of my desk were full. There wasn't room for one more form. I'd have to start throwing them right in the trash can as soon as I got them. There were about sixty unreturned voice mails on my machine. People were starting to look at me a little funny. It was time.

Late that night I called in and left a message saying I had diarrhea and wouldn't be able to come to work anymore. The next day I got a nice but puzzled voice mail from the boss of the firm. The day after that, nothing. The day after that I got a very angry message from the temp agency lady saying I'd never work for her company again. She said she was going to send a letter to her friends at the other temp agencies in town.

An evil deed never goes unpunished. So it was that five years later I found myself holding a broom on the tenth floor of a Chicago high-rise and longing for a cushy office job. The sounds and smells of construction rose around me. I pushed the broom a little ahead of me, then my arm got tired and I let it fall.

"Here, Mike, let me show you," the supervisor said. "Like this."

He took hold of the broom and began vigorously sweeping with short, quick strokes, raising a thick cloud of concrete dust. I watched with ill-concealed distaste. My way of sweeping came from an older, gentler place. It was environmentally friendly. Closer to the earth. My sweeping let things be as they are: the dust, the light, the air.

"See? You don't even hold the broom right," he said. "Hold it like this. Now. I want this room swept clean when I get back."

I took hold of the broom in a weak and hopeless way. I smeared it along the ground until he was out of sight. Then I lit a cigarette and walked over to the window. There was a section of drywall propped up against a girder on the far side of the room. I contemplated it. Then I went and hid behind it.

The minutes passed. Actually, the seconds passed. If you are immortal and you want to get a feeling for human time, pick up a broom and head for a construction site. Manual labor is like a laboratory for isolating the properties of human time. Its weight, for instance. Each instant falls like a concrete slab on the one before it. Its slowness. Like a mountain falling down. Like a very old dog walking. Its weight. Like breathing with a fifty-pound dumbbell on your chest. Its slowness. Like reading a book in an unknown language.

And it never stops. And everything it takes is gone forever. I was back in it. I was outside the timeless dope body. Getting outside that body was thrilling. But the thrill wears off. It's not like you can keep doing it. It doesn't take much getting outside before you find yourself in a place you can't get outside of. You're just outside.

I crawled out from behind the drywall and checked my watch. Three minutes had passed. Two-and-a-half hours till lunch. I picked up the broom and began smearing it along the concrete. I checked my watch. It was going to take a while to feel comfortable with this outside time. To learn the tricks. It would take some time to find time's weak spots. The holes and the tunnels. The skipped moments and the repeated moments.

And what if there weren't any? I tensed; the broom froze in my hand. Then I relaxed. Of course there were. If my adventures had taught me anything, it was that time isn't solid. It's full of holes.

Ten minutes later I dropped the broom and walked off the job.

SIXTEEN

ENDLESS

When I drove home after walking off the job site I was shaking. I can't take this, I told myself. I can't do anything. Even manual labor. The speedometer needle shook. The houses on the side of the road sucked into themselves, sucked into themselves, sucked into themselves. *Recovery,* I thought. *You can't get back what you never had.* I drove with both hands. Seventy miles an hour. The people didn't care.

When I parked and got out the world was still rippling with the insubstance of high speed. I wasn't thinking about getting high. But it was thinking of me. The world was painted on one side of a plastic sheet, and an enormous dope high was standing on the other side. It snapped its fingers against the plastic and the world rippled.

I parked the car, went in and walked quickly down the basement stairs, not stumbling, breathing through my mouth. Into my bedroom. Picked up the phone and dialed.

"Yeah, Dad, I couldn't really take it. Felt very anxious . . . Yes . . . No . . . No . . . Yes I'm fine."

He was worried. The house was empty. It was the middle of the day. I looked at the dayghost. A single bright eyeball, rolled all the way back in the wall's skull. *What a thing to have in my bedroom,* I thought. *Where I sleep,* I thought.

In my basement room, with the lights off, a corner of my desk glowed under the dayghost's white eye. I sweated. I saw everything clearly. When you're a person, everything reminds you of something else. When I panic, as I panicked realizing no I can't no I'm unable even to do the simplest job I'm not made for this world, unmade for this kind of world—when I panic the memory webs burn off the things. Every veil, every mood, every memory flashes and smokes off them. This desk is this desk. The wall looks like the wall. The dayghost is white; the carpet is pink.

My panicked eyes darted around the room. The things made me panic more. I panicked at the inhuman way things look when I'm panicked. They look different. The things look as they must look to themselves. When they're alone. The desk looks the way the wall sees it. The things outside of memory. They're scared. The wall is solid shock. The desk frozen in minus ten thousand degrees of panic. The chair panicked, freaking, bent over twisted and hiding in the shape of a chair. This world is not safe.

I tried pulling myself together but when I closed my eyes or when I opened them now in addition to my desk the dayghost the chair the carpet me and no memory there was one other thing in the room. A thing that wasn't there.

"Pull yourself together. This is just a panic attack; you've had them before," I told myself.

But dope was in the room for sure now. When I pulled myself together I pulled myself together around the ghost of a white vial of dope.

"Pull yourself together!"

It was like trying to breathe with a hole in your lungs.

"Relax!"

I was pacing. The room was too small to pace in. I didn't have any Valium. The room was too small to breathe in. It was sucked in and breathless. I grabbed the pillow off my bed and placed it on the ground. Then I sat cross-legged on it. Hands clasped at my navel, palms down, thumbs barely touching. Like the picture of the Buddha on my book about meditating.

I sat cross-legged on the cushion. I threw my panicked gaze on the carpet three feet in front of me. My look was as sharp as a piece of broken glass. Every knot in the carpet stood out in it, looking the way carpet-knots look to themselves. Alien, amnesiac knots of carpet. Unrelaxing vision.

I counted my breaths. Tried to breathe through my nose. Counted the exhalations. I knew from the meditation book exhalations are longer than inhalations when one is properly relaxed. I was improperly panicked. *Relapse,* I thought. One, I counted. Two, I counted. *Relapse, relapse.* Three, I counted. *Relapse, relapse, relapse.* Four, I counted. *Money,* I thought. Seven, I counted. *Homelessness. Friendlessness.*

Seven, I counted again. Eight. *These breaths are coming too fast,* I thought. I tried to breathe through my nose. Try to breathe through your nose when you're panting. Your head gets kind of sucked in on itself and you wheeze. Breathe. The white thing appeared on the carpet. A white vial towering over the carpet. Like a negative of the black monolith from *2001.* Blink. Pink carpet. *It is negative,* I thought. *Count your breaths, idiot,* I thought. One, I counted. Two, I counted.

This is terrible, I thought. Three, I counted. Every breath was like swallowing a huge pill with no water. A horse pill. One after the other after the other. Pills full of black space. Four. Five. Six. A big bottle, get them all down. Seven, I counted. I had to open my mouth wide to get it around the next one. Seven, I counted again. I tried to breathe through my nose.

Just before the thoughts stopped I felt unbearably constricted. Bursting full of the horse-pill breaths. A quarter hour of sitting on an uncomfortable cushion swallowing breaths and counting them with half-open eyes. I lost perspective.

Part of my face moved under my vision where the breaths came and went. I couldn't tell how big my face was. It might have been three inches wide. Or thirty feet. I might have been a man or a woman. I was breathing from everywhere like a sponge. I couldn't see enough to see. No space to see my seeing from. Just the tiny square of carpet before me. All I could hear was my breathing. My mind at six thousand revs per second.

Spinning in my body like a wheel in sand. Three, I counted. Four, I counted. Five. Six.

Then it stopped and the numbers went forward alone. Seven. Eight. Nine.

There was space inside the numbers. Pills with outer space inside and a little outer-space coating and I swallowed them easily. One. Two. Three. Four. There was space in the way the carpet looked. The way the carpet looked to the carpet. My gaze fell on the carpet. Inside my looking two knots of carpet looked at each other. There was plenty of space in the way they looked. Outer space. Endless space.

There was space in my thoughts too, which were now also floating in space.

What about my job? I thought.

Space between me and the thought, and space between me and the thinker of the thought. Space between me and the thinker of the thinker. Who am I?

Cash once told me I like meditating because it's like getting high. I got angry when he said it. Meditating is nothing like getting high, I told him. It takes effort, for one thing. When you're panicking, for example. It's often boring, for another. You have to force yourself to do it, most of the time. And it doesn't get you high.

But I was wrong and he was right. Meditating is like getting high. But not for the reason Cash thought. Not because meditation and heroin give me the same feeling in my head. But because they show me the same thing in the world. The thing I like to see. The hole. Dope and meditation are totally different, but they show me the same thing because it's there to be seen. Because the world really is the way I want it. This world really is the way I desperately long for it to be.

Time is as insubstantial as smoke.

Cash is as insubstantial as smoke. I spent a lot of time with him in those days. Dave called two weeks ago and told me Cash's back drinking Robitussin. I won't talk to him since he kind of threatened to shoot me in California, but like anyone

I'm curious about what he's discovering. I think it likely that no one in America has drunk as much Robitussin as he has. I know America is a big place.

"He calls it metaphilosophy," Dave said, speaking of Cash's robo-thinking. He then read me some of Cash's latest emails.

"Perspective is based on the number one. Logic is based on two, and communication and relationships within and between beings are based on three. This is also the solution to Clarke's solution in *Rendezvous with Rama . . .*"

". . . I also believe that everything was destined to work precisely the way it has by the prime mover. Using Wikipedia I can easily tie together all historical events, many of them religious, in order to show the progression . . ."

". . . Additionally, the unraveling all started with Zoroaster . . ."

"The degree of madness is impressive," Dave commented.

I asked him to keep forwarding them to me, and I'd reflect on the new one each morning at breakfast. A tone of sublime compassion inflected the final emails. The subject line of the very last one read "Who will laugh." Here is the full text:

"Who will laugh at kindness, love, and good sense?"

I won't. Ten years ago, in the months after I got out of rehab, I was a disciple of Cash's kindness, love, and good sense. Every day I went to an NA meeting and then drove over to Cash's apartment. We talked for hours. He'd quit drinking a couple years earlier and was glad to show me around his sober lifestyle.

We talked about proper eating habits, quitting smoking, exercise. Cash showed me how to do a concentration curl, and explained what tendonitis is. He explained why it's not good to exercise too much. He explained that good things are only good if they last. An exercise, for example, is good only if you can do it in such a way that you can keep doing it for the rest of your life. He demonstrated, curling the forty-five-pound dumbbell slowly up.

"Twelve reps," he said through gritted teeth. "Three sets. Three days a week."

He didn't tell me everything. I noticed that his shoes were always lined up in a peculiar way. The pairs of shoes made a kind of lightning-bolt shape. One time I accidently kicked a pair over on my way to the bathroom. He didn't say anything, but when I got out of the bathroom they were lined up again.

The spring turned into summer. Cash lived downtown, west of the Loop. There were people around during the day, but it got kind of deserted at night. It was an area in transition. The old projects had been torn down but the new condo buildings hadn't gone up yet. When we walked the streets near his apartment talking about exercise and movies, there were maybe four or five other people around. A pretty girl jogging, two homeless men, and us. Everyone smiled at each other.

Sometimes the sun would set when we were walking. Cash, two homeless men, me, a girl jogging. We all smiled at each other. I smiled at them like I knew what it was like, and they smiled back the same at me. It was the middle of the summer in an empty corner of the city. A place outside the world. In that place, where no one gets out, it was safe to change places with anyone.

For example, during the days Cash and I would sometimes play tennis. We'd shout little jokes back and forth as we played, and after a while we'd fall silent, leaping and lunging around the court. I'd pretend to be a famous tennis player, a genius who'd perfected a single shot. I'd give interviews in my head as I watched the ball come and go. Sometimes I'd also reflect on how kind I was—what a great tennis player, so kind to children, so fond of animals. Which was odd because kindness was never ordinarily a quality I'd dwell on in my fantasies about myself. That's when I knew my thoughts had gotten mixed up with Cash's. He lunged after the ball on the other side of the net.

Afterward we'd eat barbeque. Some days we'd eat Thai. One day Cash said it was a good thing that my parents were letting me stay at their house for the summer and that I didn't have to get a job for a while. He said he thought I'd commit suicide if I had to get a job.

I disagreed. I felt that now that I was clean I could handle anything. But I remembered how time felt on that job site. Job time. I remembered it in my bones. The reason I was going back to grad school was so that I wouldn't have to do manual labor, I told him. He said he thought that was a good idea. Even though he didn't like reading and writing so much—in fact he despised intellectuals as cowards—he thought on balance it was a good idea, and planned to apply to grad school himself in the fall.

We went to lots of movies. One was about a castle and a village troubled by dragon attacks. You see movies like that on the shelves at the video store and think they never came out in theaters. But they did, and we saw them. Another movie was about an executive who was dying. The final scene in the hospital was nearly whited out with bright light coming in from the windows. We left strangely exalted. Another movie was about code breakers in World War II. Another was about gangsters.

While we were waiting for the film about dragons to start I heard a wonderfully happy song. The singer's voice was heavily processed and there were only four words in it: "Since I Left You," over and over, beautifully. The thing I like best about songs is when the voice is electronically processed. A computer that makes the voice go much higher than is possible in life, for example. "Since I Left You." The voice stands on the human being as on a diving board. Just the tips of its toes, and it's gone . . .

I bought the CD and played "Since I Left You" when I exercised. I imagined it was about drugs. I imagined it was about Cat. About Eva. About Funboy. About Dom. I'd put on my headphones, put the CD on shuffle, and run on the treadmill just waiting for the one song. Sometimes it would come on around the three-mile mark, when the initial tiredness in my legs had burned off and my chest was burning and I'd smile with my face breaking. Every day I'd smile once like that. Those smiles would come into the world wet with the sweat on my face. New, enormous, shapeless. Going everywhere, like babies.

Afterward I'd walk outside on the grass talking with my sponsor on the phone maybe or talking with my little half brother. My first clean summer. It's strange; those days don't stick in memory very well. And all the days that come after hardly stick at all. The bits in this book that take place after I got clean—like the part about moving to Florida, for example—were written right after the event. Otherwise I'm not so sure I'd remember them. In the summer of 2002, the river of my memory was emptying into a delta. I walked around with it falling all around me, falling through the sunshine. When it got dark, Cash and I went for a walk or went to see movies.

Once he said it was too bad he was a convicted felon because it would be nice to own a gun. He felt bad because there were some things in life that weren't worth going through, and if you didn't have a gun you'd probably end up having to go through them. Like what, I asked him. Like diarrhea, he said. Like chronic, constant diarrhea. The kind where you have terrible cramps and moan out loud, the food-poisoning kind. It just wouldn't be worth it to him, he said. It was just plain old-fashioned good sense, he said, to have a gun.

I went back to court sometime in July and they had the papers verifying that I'd completed all the conditions for first-time drug offenders to get the felony expunged. They said I could legally say on job forms that I had never been convicted of a felony. What did I care, the last thing I wanted was a fucking job, I told Cash. Yeah but you can get a gun, he said. For the diarrhea. When the really bad diarrhea comes, a gun is the only toilet paper that works.

One day, just before it was time for me to go back to Baltimore and grad school, Cash and I decided to drive through the suburbs where we'd grown up. It was forty minutes by car from Cash's apartment in the city. North of Chicago. West of the fashionable North Shore. East of the cornfields. South of the dead shapes of Kenosha. In the center of our first maps. Libertyville, Wauconda, Lake Zurich, Mundelein.

First we drove around the edges. The high school we'd gone to. The long straight roads where we had invented or discovered the idea of being high. The little stores with flat roofs that sold bottles of Coca-Cola.

Then we drove through the heart. In three slashes. The house off Route 12. The house off Route 176. And the forest preserve. And that was it. We left it there, bloodless, with nothing coming out of the holes we'd driven through it, and we left it lying there.

Maybe it wasn't a heart but an old, sprung trap. There's no way to pry it back open. The iron teeth, rusted with old blood, locked in a dead smile, harmless forever.

EPILOGUE

I've been clean for over a decade. The habits I formed in early recovery are like a machine. The machine's still running. I meditate, go to NA meetings, don't pick it up so it won't get in me, exercise. At night I make a list of stuff I have to do tomorrow. I don't think about the future.

Thanks to the machine, I've arrived at a good future without having to think about it. I live in a nice house in a nice suburb with my wife. My academic career has gone pretty well. I finished my dissertation in 2006, managed to get some good jobs in a famously crappy academic job market. Moved from Michigan to Florida. Now I'm at a great university in Ohio. I've published a couple academic books that have been well received. We have two nice dogs.

The machine's still running. It's no jet engine, but it works. The recovery engine: a makeshift contraption of group love, meditation, and common sense. Lashed together and set going. It works. From the outside it might look a little rusty, but once you strap your life to it, it'll pull you out of death and into good futures.

The problem is that not every addict can strap their life to it.

At first it seemed like every month I'd hear about another one of my old friends dying or getting locked up. Now most of them are gone. But I still get messages from the world of terminal addiction. I just heard Cash went away on a weapons charge. Last year a guy I used to go to NA meetings with committed suicide. The year before that a girl I knew in college overdosed. It's not unusual. The statistics are murky, but it's clear that many addicts never experience sustained recovery. The recovery machine works. But for one reason or another, many addicts can't seem to hook themselves up to it. It's easy to blame those who can't. To say that Cash, for example, is just too pigheaded. Or allergic to things spiritual. Or weak. Or lazy. But the truth is he isn't any of those things. At least not any more than I was. The truth is that no one really knows why our makeshift recovery machine works for some and doesn't work for others.

One day there will probably be a cure. We're still in the early days of addiction science. One day people might look back at us and wonder what the hell we were doing with our meetings and slogans. One day there could be a treatment that doesn't work for 10 percent of addicts or for 50 percent, but for everyone.

Maybe they'll even have a vaccine, like for polio. Maybe they'll be able to tell if you've got the gene that makes you susceptible to the lure of that never-fading first time. And if you do, they'll give you a nice shot of permanent forgetfulness when you're a baby. People of the future will never have to hit bottoms. They'll never have to kick in jail. Never have to lose their friends, their minds, their lives.

I hope we find a truly effective treatment soon. Thousands of smart people around the world are working on it. Dozens of research institutions, treatment facilities, government agencies. Progress comes slowly, incrementally. But there are hopeful signs.

In the meantime, we work with what we have. And I'm profoundly grateful for it. My daily life is good. I'm totally hooked into the recovery program. Most days I don't dwell on the problem. But when a kid I'm sponsoring relapses, when my niece just can't get clean, when I think about the faces that show up once to an NA meeting and never again, then I know that the cure that will replace our creaky recovery machine can't come soon enough.

But I have to admit there's something about the machine, something about the disease itself that I'll miss.

The addicts of the future, the addicts who have immediate 100 percent effective treatment, will be better off than we are. There's no doubt about it. But won't they lose something too? Along with all the gains, won't humanity lose something when the disease is eradicated? Don't get me wrong. I'm not a sadist. Of course I want a cure. But when they empty out the bathwater of addiction and recovery, there might be a little bit of baby that goes out too.

There's a story by Franz Kafka that captures what I'm trying to say. The story's about a prison. In the prison, they have a very old machine. It's a baroque, makeshift affair of needles, knives, and wires. When a convict is sentenced to death, they strap him to it. The machine very slowly carves the convict's sentence into his skin. It takes hours. It's agonizing. But at the very end, just before he dies, a look of total comprehension, total ecstasy, flashes across his face. To the prison guards, it looks as if the dying convict has been granted a glimpse of Eternal Truth.

The prison is in a distant, backward part of the country. One day an official arrives from the capital. He's educated in modern theories, a believer in scientific methods of rehabilitation. He's absolutely disgusted by the torture machine. It's barbaric! Inhumane! He orders it dismantled immediately. And of course, reading the story, we want the machine dismantled too. We're not sadists. Get rid of that medieval torture device!

But still, that look on the dying convict's face . . .

Perhaps one day, the book you've just read will tell the same kind of story as Kafka's tale. Addiction and recovery. A process where you have to hit a total bottom until you become willing to accept a spiritual therapy that works for only a fraction of us. In the future this might look like Kafka's machine: baroque, superstitious, makeshift, even barbaric. Right now this recovery machine is all we have—and it works. It saved my life. It saves lives every day. And it gave me something else. Like Kafka's convict, once my sentence had been carved into me, I received a glimpse of eternity.

But still we must hope that someday there will be a more effective, more efficient cure for addiction. The misery of the descent into addictive hell will be history. The slow, painstaking, creaky trip back up on the makeshift engine of recovery, that'll be history too. Tens of millions of lives will be saved. Billions of dollars.

And that glimpse of timelessness, that little chip of immortality that lies at the center of the disease and recovery—the endlessness of my first time, the endlessness I discovered meditating in my parents' basement—that'll be history too.

Something in a book. Something to wonder about.

McNally Editions reissues books that are not widely known but have stood the test of time, that remain as singular and engaging as when they were written. Available in the US wherever books are sold or by subscription from mcnallyeditions.com.

1. Han Suyin, *Winter Love*
2. Penelope Mortimer, *Daddy's Gone A-Hunting*
3. David Foster Wallace, *Something to Do with Paying Attention*
4. Kay Dick, *They*
5. Margaret Kennedy, *Troy Chimneys*
6. Roy Heath, *The Murderer*
7. Manuel Puig, *Betrayed by Rita Hayworth*
8. Maxine Clair, *Rattlebone*
9. Akhil Sharma, *An Obedient Father*
10. Gavin Lambert, *The Goodby People*
11. Wyatt Harlan, *Elbowing the Seducer*
12. Lion Feuchtwanger, *The Oppermanns*
13. Gary Indiana, *Rent Boy*
14. Alston Anderson, *Lover Man*
15. Michael Clune, *White Out*
16. Martha Dickinson Bianchi, *Emily Dickinson Face to Face*
17. Ursula Parrott, *Ex-Wife*
18. Margaret Kennedy, *The Feast*